UNDERSTANDING STONE TOOLS and ARCHAEOLOGICAL SITES

By
Brian P. Kooyman

University of New Mexico Press:
Albuquerque

2001 Second Printing.

University of Calgary Press
2500 University Drive N. W.,
Calgary, Alberta, Canada T2N 1N4

University of New Mexico Press
1720 Lomas N.E.
Albuquerque, New Mexico, USA, 87131-1591

Cataloguing in Publication Data

Kooyman, Brian P. (Brian Patrick), 1953-
Understanding stone tools and archaeological sites

University of Calgary Press: ISBN 1-55238-021-1 (Softcover edition)
ISBN 1-55238-035-1 (Hardcover edition)

University of New Mexico Press: ISBN 0-8263-2333-2 (Softcover edition)
ISBN 0-8263-2300-6 (Hardcover edition)

1. Stone implements. 2. Archaeology—Methodology. I. Title.
GN799.T6K66 2000 930'.1'028 C00-910155-1

We acknowledge the financial support of the Government of Canada through the Book Publishing Industry Development Program (BPDP) for our publishing activities.

Printed and bound in Canada by Houghton Boston Printers and Lithographers.
♾ This book is printed on acid-free paper.

Cover design by Doyle Buehler, Aces High.
Typesetting and page design by Cliff Kadatz.

Contents

Acknowledgments

An early draft of this book was used as a textbook for my Prehistoric Stone Technology class in 1997. The students in that class provided me with many comments on the merits and weak areas of that manuscript and their input has allowed me to enhance it considerably. Rejane Boudreau was particularly helpful in this regard. I appreciated Don Hanna's willingness to assist with, and appear in, Figures 15, 16, 17, 19, and 20. Most of the photographs in the book were taken by Gerry Newlands (Figures 1-5, 11, 14-21, 37, 38, 40-42, 45-47, 49-79, 94,95). His high standards and skill in highlighting the best in the specimens has made a significant contribution to the clarity and usefulness of the book (I am responsible for the other photographs). I was very fortunate to have Lu-Anne Da Costa as an illustrator. Her artistic talents, patience, and knowledge of lithic technology have made my crude initial sketches and comments come through better than I had imagined possible. Many colleagues have discussed lithic analysis with me over the years and I wish to thank them for the shared insights. Barney Reeves, Don Crabtree, and Marty Magne were particularly influential in sparking my enthusiasm at key times. A number of reviewers have commented on the text. Their suggestions have made me think about what I have said and justify my assertions. I have incorporated many of their ideas and these have greatly improved the book. I cannot overemphasize how much I have benefited from the encouragement, careful editing, and excellent layout assistance of the staff of the University of Calgary Press. Perhaps only those who have been involved in such a process can understand what a transformation this has wrought. Scott Raymond, my Department Head in Archaeology during the writing of the book, supported my efforts throughout and let me cut a few corners in other areas when I really needed the time. My family, Susan and Patrick, have been understanding when I had deadlines to meet and have given me the positive atmosphere I needed to keep on going. I hope that all of these individuals can see their hands in the work and know that I sincerely appreciate their efforts and support. Responsibility for the opinions and interpretations, of course, rests with the author.

CHAPTER 1

Introduction to Lithic Analysis

Throughout the archaeological record, in all areas of the world, the most frequent evidence of past human activity that we have is stone tools. Even though stone tools were replaced in much of the world by metal tools in most recent history, this process was not as rapid or complete as we often assume (Rosen 1996, 1997). Given the ubiquitous distribution of these remains, an understanding of the information they can provide us about human culture is one of the most important areas of training an archaeologist can have. The intention of this book is to provide the basis of that understanding.

This book is written for anyone interested in archaeology and human culture as reflected in stone (lithic) tools. Wherever one encounters lithic remains, be they in a museum or in a farmer's field, the full significance of their story cannot be seen without understanding the meaning of their form and variation. Small chips of stone may be fragments of broken tools or debris from the process of manufacturing stone tools. In the latter case, a closer examination of the pieces can reveal whether they are from the earliest stages of tool shaping, or from the final finishing stages. This more detailed information, in conjunction with the determined functions of the tools themselves, can provide insight into the role that the archaeological site played in the life of the people who once lived there. The distributions and concentrations of these remains across the breadth of the site can tell us about where people ate, where they slept, and where they cooked their food. In short, these fragments of stone are truly an open book waiting to be read. But like any book, the message cannot be understood until we learn to read. I hope that the following chapters will provide the fundamentals of the ability to read.

Reconstructing past culture through stone tools takes many routes. The techniques used to manufacture lithic tools developed over many thousands of years in many parts of the world. Deducing how the manufacturing occurred, tracing its regional and temporal development, and then tracing its global spread, outlines human technological development and patterns of ancient contact and migration. Many different lithic materials were used to manufacture tools and each held both possibilities and limits for producing tools to accomplish particular tasks. Identifying the various lithic types allows us to see the interplay of these variables of task and suitability. As well, this study permits us to see the development of new, and modification of old, manufacturing techniques as people of past cultures coped with the problems and challenges they faced. In many cases suitable raw material was not available locally and people had to acquire it from more distant locations. By studying details of composition for the lithic types used, we can uniquely characterize each local source of material and so trace where exotic lithic material came from. Not only is this interesting on its own, but it also provides insight into past patterns of trade and contact. These patterns of contact may have been based on preexisting social relations, such as alliances or kin ties, but also may have been the basis on which new social ties were forged. Either way, the study of these contacts through lithic source typing provides important insights into ancient social relations, past patterns of mobility, and group territory size.

When we look at the manufacturing process in greater detail, isolating the many steps in the process, we can begin to see how our human ancestors managed the task of lithic tool manufacture in a schedule of all of the other activities that they had to accomplish from day to day and during the course of a year. Different aspects of lithic tool manufacturing and maintenance were characteristically undertaken in different types of sites; hence stages in the manufacturing process can often be related to different settlement locales. Early manufacturing stages, such as roughing out the initial tool form, were usually done in proximity to the quarry location. Tool resharpening usually occurred where the finished tool was used, and extensive repair and re-working often occurred in habitation sites where much time was available to complete such labor intensive tasks. Detailed examination of both the tools produced and the debitage (debris) left as waste can allow modern flintknappers to reproduce the individual steps in the procedure by which past flintknappers produced tools. This can allow us to gain some understanding of the actual decision-making process of these artisans. The form of tools provides us with clues about how these tools were used. Tools often retain wear traces and residues on their edges from those tasks. Together, these types of evidence can lead us to an appreciation of the tasks undertaken at a site and how these tasks were combined and segregated at the site. Through the comparison of tasks at different sites, we can reconstruct what people were doing and how they organized those activities through space and over time. Combining all of these inferences, the study of lithic tools can allow us to reconstruct much about past human lifeways, on both large and small scales.

The objective of any study of archaeological remains is to reconstruct and understand past human culture. We want to understand what environment past people lived in and how they exploited and adapted to the possibilities and limits of that environment. It offered them both possibilities and limits. Human culture is, in part, the human response to those challenges. A significant aspect of the interaction of humans and their environment can be seen through their technology. Human culture is much more however, and ultimately what is most challenging for archaeology is reconstructing the social aspects of human culture: interpersonal relations and structures as seen in kinship, community structure and interaction; political structure; the economy; ethnicity; and interrelationships with other social groups as manifest through social contacts, such as economic trade and social exchanges. A study of lithic tools and manufacturing debitage can provide insight into all of these aspects of culture.

Drawing inferences about culture from lithic tools logically begins with an understanding of lithic tool manufacturing technology. The technology used to produce these tools is a very important aspect of human technology and a key aspect of how people exploited and adapted to their environment. It is also a product of the social structure and interactions of the people that developed the technology. Therefore, even this fundamental level of manufacturing technology has the potential to shed light on many aspects of culture. The place to begin is with the raw material that the tools were made from. How was it shaped into tools of a desired form? How can the traces of that shaping left on the tools be used by us hundreds or thousands of years later, to reconstruct how that shaping was done? Understanding the physics of fracturing of various types of stone can allow us to understand why certain manufacturing techniques were chosen over others and to determine which features left on lithic tools are a result of human choices and which are due to the fracturing properties of the lithic material itself. By looking at the properties of lithic materials we can understand why people chose particular materials for particular types of tools. These reasons could include both functional aspects of the material, such as edge sharpness or durability, but also aesthetic aspects such as color and smoothness of surface finish. A thorough understanding of chemical variation of materials can allow us to characterize source localities individually so that we can see where in the environment people obtained their material. The distance material was transported can provide insight into sizes of territory, patterns of trade, and wider aspects of social relations between ethnic and other social groups. By examining the details of how manufacturing was undertaken and, where appropriate, how production was divided or amalgamated into stages, we can see how the manufacturing of lithic tools was scheduled among the many tasks people had to accomplish on a regular basis, and we can see how different settlements were linked in the production process. This information contributes to our understanding of how the archaeological sites in a region are similar and how they are different, and how the use of these sites varied over a region and through time. By understanding the technology through replication studies of modern flintknappers, we can see how stone workers achieved the final products and how they solved the particular problems that arose in each individual tool manufacturing event. In fact, we can see this creative process not only at the general level of a culture's technological repertoire, but also down to the level of the skill of an individual flintknapper. The form of the tools gives us a clue to their function and use. This is rendered much more specific and often more reliable based on the study of the microscopic and chemical traces of worked materials preserved on a tool's edge. Varying traces of wear from different worked materials, in the form of striations, chipping, and polish, also provide clues to what each tool was used on. The form of tools often has only a very basic functional aspect and there is much elaboration of form that is due to cultural stylistic ideas, conventions, and popularity. These elaborations are often some of the best clues we have to cultural changes through time and across space. Finally, the use of all of these lines of evidence together allows us to draw broader implications as each illuminates a different aspect of culture, both material and social.

One aspect of these reconstructions of past patterns of lithic tool manufacturing and use, and hence also human culture, is that much of the information recovered from archaeological sites is derived from the context in which the material is found. The objects alone, such as tools, manufacturing debris, manufacturing tools, give only part of the picture. A tool in isolation from the other tools it was used with, and in isolation from the debitage from the resharpening and repair of it, cannot be fully understood. The activities undertaken at a site cannot be discerned without consideration of all the material left behind and information about what was found in proximity to what. For this reason, more information is lost about archaeological sites when material is picked up and removed from its context than can ever possibly be reconstructed from the few out of context items collected. Even in a plowed field where items have been somewhat displaced, the items left close to each other as the result of a particular task are still present in relative proximity to each other. If that spatial association is recorded and all material is collected, as is done in a professional archaeological excavation, even these disturbed materials can reveal a great deal. It cannot be overemphasized that collecting artifacts from archaeological sites is destructive of most of the information we are seeking to preserve, reconstruct, and appreciate. Items found can be examined where they are, and can then be left there where they were found, and one can still gain an understanding of what happened at a site. I hope that this will become increasingly clear as you read this book. Like wild flowers, archaeological remains can be studied and appreciated where they are found without having to remove them from the ground and destroy them for other visitors.

1.1 Early History of Lithic Studies

Until the end of the 18th century, whenever farmers found handaxes and similar stone tools in their fields in Europe, the scholars of the day alleged that the tools were thunderbolts or meteorites. The earliest example of someone actually stating that the pieces were stone tools was the writings of Michele Mercati in the 16th century (Fagan 1978:24). A French naturalist, Antoine de Jussien, wrote in 1725 that the "thunderbolts" (handaxes) were very similar to stone objects manufactured as weapons and tools by contemporary Aboriginals in Canada and the West Indies. Based on this similarity, he suggested that the European pieces were weapons and tools manufactured by early Europeans (Bordaz 1970:2). Later, the Englishman John Frere found a series of handaxes in gravel in 1797 (Daniel 1967:47). In a letter published in 1800 he claimed that these objects were weapons made by humans. Although this note caused little interest at the time, it was re-examined a half century later when Boucher de Perthes' discoveries at Abbeville were being championed, particularly by English geologists and archaeologists.

The next important event in stone tool analysis was the Danish shell midden excavations begun in 1806 under Nyerup (Harris 1968:146). C.J. Thomsen used this material to provide the first documentation of the Three Age System which conceived of European prehistory as undergoing a series of changes from an age characterized by the use of stone tools, to an age characterized by the use of bronze tools, and finally to an age characterized by use of iron tools. This system was also adopted in Sweden, particularly by Bruzelius (ca. 1816) and Sven Nilsson (ca.1838). Sven Nilsson was one of the fathers of archaeology, with his use of the Three Age System being particularly crucial. It is significant to note that as a child he chipped gun flints for his rifle and that he later noted that this helped him recognize humanly altered stone as tools (Johnson 1978).

During the 1850s and 1860s the English scientist Sir John Evans taught himself to flake stone. He also observed the workers who produced gun flints at the Brandon quarries in England. In 1868 he wrote that he did not accept that handaxes were indeed made by humans until he had proven it to himself by manufacturing them (Johnson 1978). In the 1870s monographs were produced on the Brandon gun flint workers. These studies, by Wyatt and Skertchly, suggested that the techniques employed in the quarries might hold the key to understanding prehistoric stone working (Johnson 1978). These works may be viewed as the start of scientific ethnoarchaeology in lithics, as opposed to "curiosity notes."

During these early years, papers on flintknapping were concerned with two problems. The first was the question of how prehistoric stone tools were made without metal tools. The second was the eolith question: were the pieces found in old gravels truly human-made tools, or were they simply naturally broken pieces of lithic material produced by geological processes (geo-facts)? By the 1880s it was clear that stone tools, such as hammers, were used to make the tools. But although many stone tools were and are universally accepted as having been produced by humans, in circumstances such as early occupation sites particularly in the New World (e.g., Calico Hills, Pikimachaj), the eolith controversy continues unresolved. In England in 1883, Putnam first discussed heat treatment. Also in 1883, another Englishman, Spurrell, examined workshop sites and tried to refit flakes and cores. By trying to reproduce the patterns he found, he began the first serious work on understanding how flakes are produced from prepared cores. In the Americas during these early years there was little concern with flintknapping *per se* since many people had seen First Nations people making stone tools; experts could provide no information not already known (Johnson 1978). What did occur, however, was a number of reports on how Native North American people still made stone tools, especially Native people from California; these included the detailed demonstrations by Ishi, the last member of a band of Yana people who lived and worked with Alfred Kroeber and Nels Nelson at the University of California's Museum of Anthropology in San Francisco from 1911–1916 (Whittaker 1994:56–57).

Although a few papers by Americans on First Nations flintknapping methods appeared in the late 1870s and 1880s, it was during the 1890s that a great number of such papers were published (Johnson 1978). Of particular importance at this time was the work of William Henry Holmes, who did much experimentation with manufacturing stages, among other aspects. He was very concerned with disproving any claims of early Paleolithic occupation in the New World. If more modern archaeologists had re-examined his research during the recent development of lithic analysis, they would have benefited greatly. Holmes' work discussed the many stages a tool goes through from preform to finished artifact, as well as the fact that many pieces found must be viewed as failures or rejects. He also noted that the trampling of such rejects and flakes on the workshop floor can give them the appearance of having been worked or used. It is interesting to note that another researcher, Mercer, experimenting at this time (1897), wrote that he had trouble producing argillite artifacts until he spoke with local curbstone cutters who dressed such stone with hammers.

The main work during the early years of the twentieth century was a continuation of the eolith debate (Johnson 1978). The research centered on experiments in natural and human flaking of stone and how to distinguish the results of these processes. Moir was the main proponent of eoliths as artifacts during this time while Warren was the main opposition to this idea. Both were British. Coutier produced a very detailed report on percussion and pressure flaking using various hammer materials (stone, wood, etc.) in 1929 in France. He discussed at least some of the features of flakes so produced. He also showed that heating flint to decrease its excess water content improved its flaking quality.

During the next ten years, a number of reports were produced on experimental flaking, including some more on the Brandon flint quarries. The latter included some corrections to earlier reports. In 1930 a film was made of the Brandon flintknappers. It is during this time that quite a number of reports came out on the specific lithic technologies of small regions. In 1936 Pei, a Chinese researcher working at Zhoukoudian with Breuil, produced an exhaustive study of geological forces fracturing stone and compared them to flintknappers. Johnson (1978:348) has characterized Pei's research as outstanding.

In 1941, Tindale and Noone produced the first record of contemporary Australian knapping (Johnson 1978). In 1940, Ellis produced a major work summarizing and evaluating all work on experimental and Aboriginal stone work to that time. This work was a very good synthesis.

François Bordes first began publishing experimental work in the late 1940s and Louis Leakey began publishing in the early 1950s. These two men were very accomplished flintknappers and were to be very influential in lithic studies, particularly Bordes. Bordes' seminal work began in 1955 with an article on the Levallois technique. In 1950, Blackwood published an ethnographic account of New Guinea flintknapping (Johnson 1978). Over a decade later, White obtained very similar results.

The 1960s saw the acceptance of flintknapping as a basic tool in lithic analysis. A major factor in this development was the work of Don Crabtree in the United States. Crabtree had become an accomplished stone worker by the time of his recognition. He was entirely self-taught; hence the insights he had acquired had been developed essentially in isolation from the flintknapping tradition that had been developing in Europe. In 1964, a conference was organized in Les Eyzies, France, where the three best flintknappers of the time (Crabtree, Bordes, and Jacques Tixier) worked together to exchange information (Johnson 1978). Fourteen nonknapping archaeologists were observers at the conference. During the following few years a number of films were made of Crabtree. As well, Crabtree wrote a number of articles in academic journals and in 1969 he started a summer lithic workshop. This workshop has since given hundreds of archaeologists an appreciation of, and often a skill in, flintknapping. Whittaker (1994:4), himself an accomplished flintknapper, has said that it was truly through the experimental work of Bordes in Europe and Crabtree in North America that flintknapping experimentation became an important part of archaeological research. Through the work of Crabtree in North America, and Bordes and Tixier in Europe, the study of lithic technology finally underwent a major new growth and advancement.

From this point on we enter what might be called the modern era of lithic analysis. I will touch on only a few points here.

The increased interest in replicating stone tools logically led in the early 1970s to an interest in the mechanical basis of stone fracture and the features associated with the debitage (flakes, etc. left behind)(e.g., Muto 1971b, Faulkner 1972, Speth 1972). Our understanding of these aspects of lithic materials has greatly improved over the years with the input of considerable knowledge from engineering studies (Lawn and Marshall 1979; Cotterell and Kamminga 1979; Le Moine 1991, 1994; Tsirk 1974, 1979). The development of microchipping usewear studies (see below) gave this area of study further impetus.

Another important event in lithic analysis at this time (in addition to the development of modern flintknapping) was the publication of the English translation of Russian Sergei Semenov's *Prehistoric Technology* (1964). This book was an extremely thorough analysis of traces of usewear on stone and bone tools, mainly based on the finding of striations on tool edges due to use. It was well documented by photographs, making the proof of the analysis claims very clear. The study was originally published in Russia in 1957, with the actual research having been begun in 1934. This book represents the genesis of modern usewear studies and ultimately gave rise to modern lithic usewear studies: the usewear microchipping of Tringham (Tringham et al. 1974) and later Odell (Odell and Odell-Vereecken 1980; Odell 1981), the usewear micropolish of Lawrence Keeley (1980) and others such as Patrick Vaughan (1981). More detailed studies of striations and striation morphology have also been initiated (e.g., Anderson 1980; Moss 1983; Mansur-Franchomme 1983, 1986).

Lewis and Sally Binford (1966, 1969) wrote a critique of François Bordes' interpretation (e.g., Bordes 1968, Bordes and de Sonneville-Bordes 1970) of variation in Mousterian age assemblages wherein he suggested that the variation was indicative of different time periods. They instead suggested that the variation was a result of the functional differences of these assemblages. This debate brought to the fore the entire question of whether formal types of stone tools were due to "style," random temporal change, functional differences, or some other factor or factors. This issue of the meaning of form remains a concern and has even led to the study of individual stone workers in prehistory (Gunn 1977).

Usewear studies brought new perspective to the discussion of form and function in stone tools, as has the study of protein and other residues left on used stone tool edges (e.g., Keeley 1980, Kooyman et al. 1992). Usewear research also prompted renewed interest in ethnoarchaeological studies in the few remaining regions of the world where stone tools were still made: New Guinea (e.g., Heider in 1967, White in 1967), Turkey (Bordaz 1969), Australia (e.g., Gould et al. 1971), Ethiopia (e.g., Gallagher 1977), and southern Mexico (Hayden 1987a; Kooyman 1980).

Many more avenues of research have been pursued in recent years. Studies of stone tool manufacture have led to models of tool production (e.g., Collins 1975, Bradley 1975). Chemical sourcing of stone, especially obsidian, has led to the tracing of trade routes, prehistoric economy, and colonizing migrations. Many of these studies are discussed elsewhere in this book, particularly in Chapter 10.

CHAPTER 2

Manufacturing Techniques and Brittle Material Fracture Mechanics

2.1 Introduction

The starting point for understanding what stone tools tell us about past cultures is an understanding of how stone is shaped to produce tools. Since we use the form of, and features on, tools to derive our inferences about culture, we need to appreciate how this form and these features arise. Some features are an inevitable byproduct of the manufacturing process, others are intentionally produced by the stone workers. The choice of a particular manufacturing technique results in both particular possibilities, and particular limits, on what can be accomplished. The features on tools provide information not only on the overall process, but often also on many intermediate steps along the route to the final product (a finished tool). Manufacturing any product also results in the production of waste or garbage. Some aspects of this debitage can be used to provide the basis for inferences about tool manufacturing processes and intentions. To interpret the patterns we see, we must understand their meaning. This chapter provides the baseline for that understanding.

2.2 Manufacturing Techniques

There are four basic techniques that can be used to shape stone into a desired form to make a tool (see Crabtree [1972:6–17] and Bordaz [1970:9–15] for further details on these techniques).

Figure 1: Flaked stone tool

1. Flaking: knocking small chips (flakes) of stone off the piece that is being shaped into a tool by hitting it with another object (e.g., another stone). After striking it enough times and knocking off enough flakes, the stone will be shaped into the desired form (Fig. 1). The resultant surface of the shaped piece is covered with the scars from these flake removals (negative flake scars). This technique results in fairly rapid shaping because a relatively large piece of stone is removed with each blow struck.

Figure 2: Pecked groove on stone maul

Figure 3: Ground stone knife

Figure 4: Polished stone axe

2. Pecking: essentially "battering" or "pulverizing" the stone with a hard object to remove portions of the piece surface until eventually the piece reaches the desired form (Fig. 2). The size of particles removed at each blow varies, but they are generally from powder to small grains in size. It is difficult to pulverize stone evenly in this manner, so the resulting surface is usually quite pitted.

3. Grinding/Abrading/Polishing: using an abrasive material to gradually grind or wear away the unwanted portions of the lithic piece (Fig. 3). Abrasives range from coarse-grained stones to fine abrasives, such as sand. This procedure is generally a slow process, usually removing only fine powder. Polishing (Fig. 4) is done with fine (small-sized) abrasives, such as fine sand, silt, and so on. An abraded surface will usually

Figure 5: Saw jade fragment

be covered with scratches (striations) from the working, but will be relatively smooth. Polishing leaves a very smooth, often lustrous surface. Polishing is sometimes considered to be a cosmetic or aesthetic feature having no functional value, and in many instances this could be the case. However, a very smooth surface does offer less resistance and a polished edge does penetrate more deeply into worked material (e.g., an axe into wood) (Bordaz 1970:99). A polished surface may also allow for a more complete, firmer contact in a handle (haft) and so a tool with a polished surface may stay more tightly in its socket. Conversely, the friction from a somewhat rough surface may lessen the degree to which a tool moves in its haft socket during use. Smooth surfaces are also less likely to damage hafting or lashing material, such as hide strips or twine. Finally, if a tool has sharp projecting ridges or edges, these relatively fragile areas may be broken off during use; therefore it is useful to remove them, in a controlled manner, such that loss of additional portions of the tool is minimized.

4. Sawing: employs sharp stone, abrasive stone, metal, etc., to cut off a large piece of stone to shape the piece (Fig. 5). This procedure is very rapid compared to having to grind or peck off a large segment, but it is also generally fairly hard work. It takes a long time to saw through stone although it depends on the hardness of the stone. (e.g., soapstone is a soft material that works relatively rapidly). Sawing can often only be used to give a general shape to a piece since it is really only feasible to saw off major portions. The piece obtained as a result of sawing is also quite angular, so further shaping is usually required. Such pieces are usually further modified by grinding and/or polishing.

The method, or combination of methods, that is used depends largely on the type of stone being worked. For example, not all lithic materials flake readily and those that do generally cannot be worked by pecking, since they shatter and flake rather than pulverize. The type of tool being manufactured also makes a difference. If a smooth final form is needed, grinding and polishing would be used. If tools are to be subject to much impacting (e.g., axes), a lithic material will be chosen that does not flake/shatter easily. Obviously such material also, then, cannot be manufactured by flaking. It is common to combine techniques to most efficiently arrive at the final product. For example, adzes (i.e., for adzing wood) were often roughly flaked into shape, since this was much faster than grinding, and then the flake scar edges were ground and polished away to give the adze its final, smooth form.

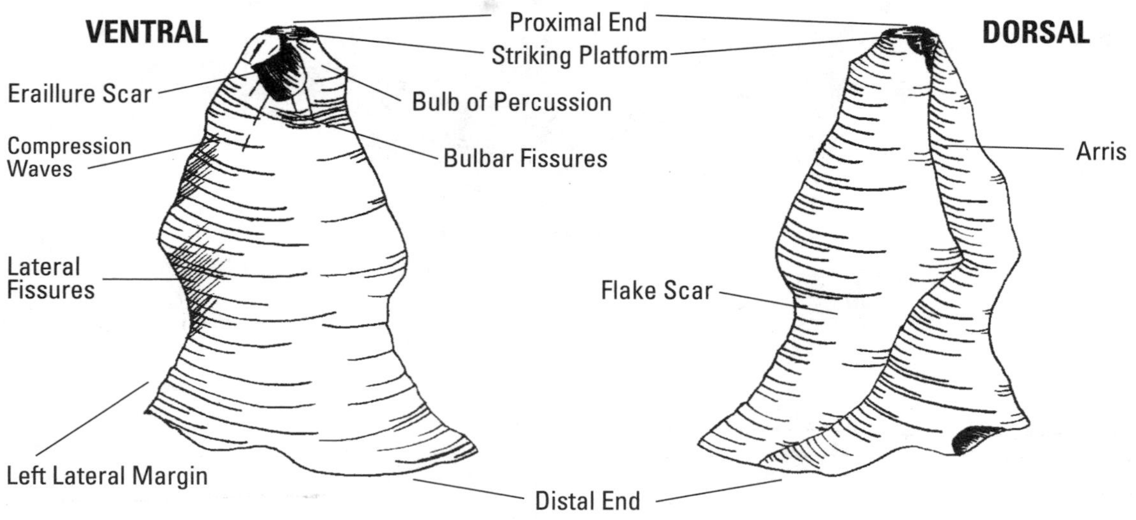

Figure 6: Flake features

2.2.1 Flaking

Before looking at the various methods used to produce stone tools by flaking, it is important to have some terms of reference for the description of flaking and the lithic features that result from it (see also Crabtree [1972] and Whittaker [1994:14–21]).

1. *Flake:* any small piece of lithic material broken off of a larger piece (the exception to this definition is shatter, see below). If the flake is quite elongate, at least two times as long as its width, and basically parallel-sided, it is called a blade. However, true blades are produced in a very particular manner, so not all elongate flakes are defined as true blades. If the piece in question is simply a fortuitous elongate flake (i.e., occurring by chance), it is often simply called a lamellar flake. This distinction can be difficult to make and some authors (e.g., Bordes 1988:16) do not use this term. (Note: Bladelet [Debénath and Dibble 1994:12] and microblade [Crabtree 1972:76] are terms, not identical, for small blades.) Flakes have a number of distinctive features that allow them to be distinguished from other lithic remains (see Fig. 6):

a. *striking platform:* area struck to cause flake removal. The striking platform is an entire surface of a core (see below), but a portion or remnant of the striking platform also remains on the detached flake. For this reason, a flake with this portion still present on it (i.e., the portion has not shattered or broken away on impact, etc.) may be referred to as a platform remnant bearing flake (PRB). Ring cracks and crushing may occur at the actual point of impact (see Fig. 7), where the detaching blow was struck and hence damage occurred due to the impact.

b) *proximal end:* the end of the flake where the flake detachment blow was struck

c) *distal end:* the end opposite to the proximal end; the end where the flake terminated or finally broke away from the core

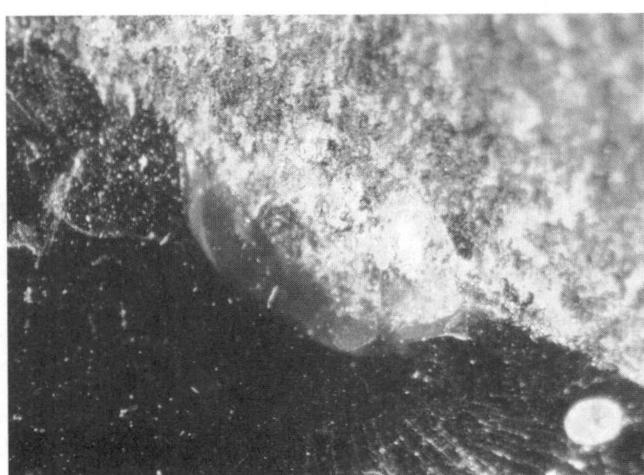

Figure 7: Impact point crushing and ring crack

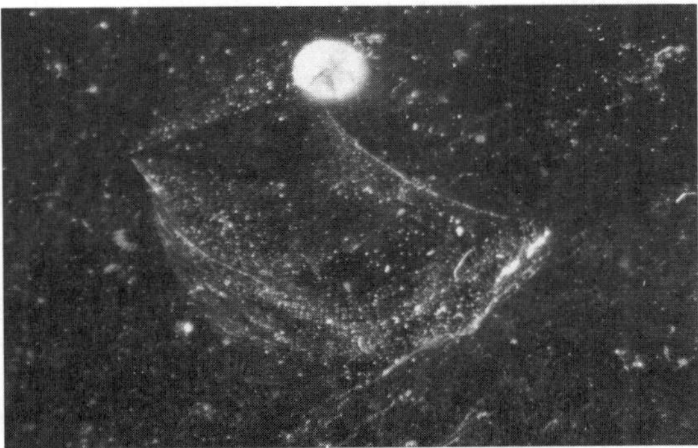

Figure 8: Eraillure scar

d) *ventral surface:* the new surface on the flake that was created when the fracture produced the flake. This surface was originally an inner portion of the core mass. The ventral surface tends to be relatively flat.

e) *dorsal surface:* the surface of the flake that was originally part of the outer surface of the core or tool the flake was detached from. This surface tends to have ridges and other, older flake scars on it.

f) *bulb of percussion:* a bulge (Fig. 6), generally cone-shaped, just distal to (below) the striking

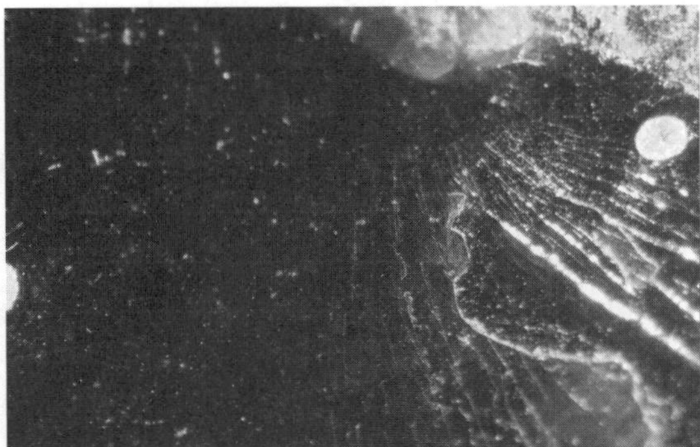

Figure 9: Bulbar fissures

platform on the ventral surface of the flake. It is a remnant feature of the way brittle materials fracture. It generally contracts toward the point of impact (where the blow was struck to remove the flake). This is also called the cone of force, a Hertzian cone, or sometimes just the bulb.

g) *bulbar scar or eraillure scar:* a small flake scar on the bulb of percussion that results from an extra small flake being detached when the main flake is detached (Fig. 8). This small flake is an eraillure.

h) *bulbar fissures:* very fine lines (crevices) present on the bulb of percussion that radiate out from the point of impact (Fig. 9).

i) *lateral fissures or hackles:* very fine ridges present at the lateral (outside) edges of a flake (Fig. 10). They are often oriented back toward the point of impact, more or less, but they are not always so oriented; often they are more oriented like the compression rings or waves (see below).

j) *compression rings/ribs/compression waves, conchoidal ripples:* these relatively prominent concentric ridges (Fig. 11) are another remnant of the fracture process. They radiate out from the impact area and are present on the ventral surface of the flake.

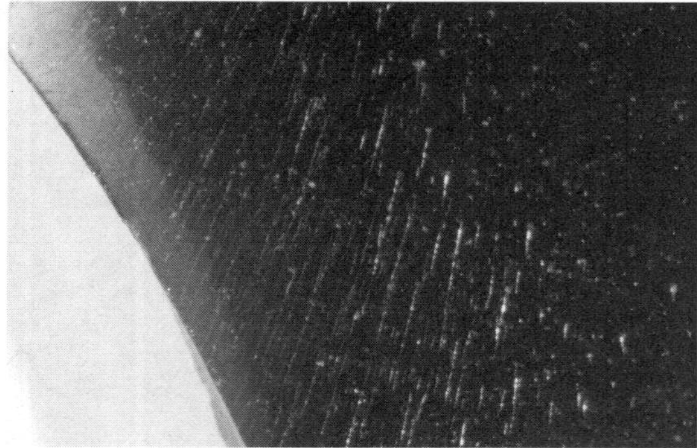

Figure 10: Lateral fissures

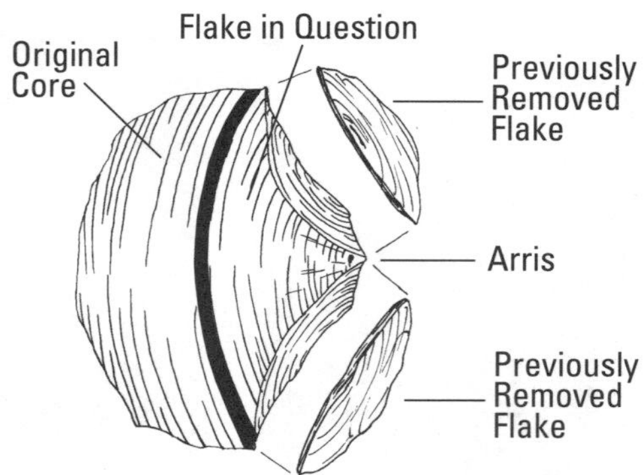

Figure 12: Arris formation on a flake

Figure 11: Compression rings

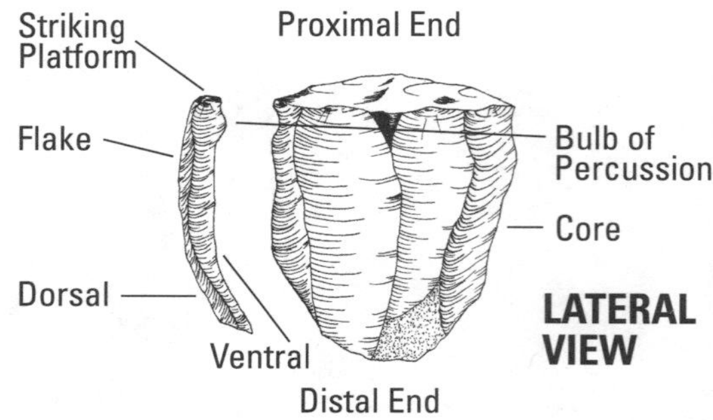

Figure 13: Flake removal from a core

k) *arris:* a ridge formed on the dorsal surface of a flake. The ridge is formed by the intersection of flake scars from previously removed flakes (two or more "negative flake scars") (Fig. 12). Although the definition of arris varies between researchers, it is often defined to specifically include only those ridges that extend more or less across the entire dorsal surface.

2. *Core:* any large piece of lithic material from which a flake or flakes have been removed (Fig. 13). Normally it is assumed that these flakes are used or shaped into tools, with the core not being used as any other type of tool. Sometimes cores also function as another type of tool such as a scraper.

3. *Shatter:* many of the small pieces or chips of lithic material detached during manufacturing are not flakes and lack all or most of the features of flakes described above. They tend to be rather angular, chunky or blocky pieces with no particular form (Fig. 14): they have no

Figure 14: Shatter

striking platform; they have no obvious dorsal and ventral surfaces; they basically lack all the ventral surface features such as bulbs, ripple marks, fissures, etc.; they generally lack mid-dorsal surface ridges (arris); and they have no obvious proximal or distal end. These rather amorphous pieces are termed shatter (the plural form is pieces of shatter, *not* shatters) (Bordes 1968:16; Debénath and Dibble 1994:11). The name is essentially a description of what they are: by and large, unintentional extra fragments of lithic material inadvertently detached at the same time flakes are detached. Shatter may be intentionally detached as well, or at least may be part of the success of the general purpose of a blow struck. Flakes themselves also frequently shatter on detachment, but these flake fragments can usually be separated from true shatter by their relative thinness and the remnants of various dorsal and ventral surface flake features.

4. *Debitage:* all discarded lithic debris from stone tool manufacturing. Debitage includes flakes, shatter, exhausted cores (i.e., used to the point where they can no longer be used to detach flakes) and broken core fragments. Wherever flakes are detached, various very small pieces of shatter down to the size of dust, and occasionally small flakes, are also removed. Anything less than 1 mm in size is referred to as *microdebitage* (Fladmark 1982).

5. *Fabricator:* any object used to modify a piece of stone by removing flakes (or grinding away materials, etc.).

6. *Objective piece:* any piece of stone worked on and modified. Objective pieces include cores, partially finished tools, and so on.

7. *Raw material:* the stone used to manufacture stone tools, before it has been modified from its natural form. Commonly, raw material comes in the form of pebbles, cobbles, and boulders, but it may also be quarried pieces of bedrock.

8. *Cortex:* archaeologists generally use this term to indicate an altered, weathered outer surface or "rind" on a fragment of lithic material. Technically, cortex is an altered outer surface that forms at the same time as the material in question and is a transitional zone between it and its parent material; altered surfaces due to mechanical or chemical weathering are weathering rinds or patinas (Luedtke 1992:107). Weathering rinds are produced by the rolling and abrasion of stone in rivers, glaciers, etc., or due to chemical alteration of the stone surface. Freshly quarried material, never exposed to weathering, may have a cortex but not a patina. Cortex and weathering rinds may be different from the rest of the rock in color, texture, hardness, and/or chemical composition. The term patina is often employed specifically to indicate a chemically altered stone surface (1992:108–109). These distinctions are often useful to make in studying the history of a material type or artifact, but the term cortex is commonly used for *any* outer, altered surface when discussing reduction stages (see Chapter 5).

2.2.2 Techniques to produce stone tools by flaking

The most basic technique that can be used is simply throwing one rock against another (Crabtree 1972:9–10). This is referred to as the *block-on-block* technique. The stone that the objective piece is thrown against is called the anvil. Rather than simply being thrown against the anvil, the objective piece may be swung against the anvil, being continually held in the hands throughout the swing (Debénath and Dibble 1994:22). It is unlikely that this technique has been generally important prehistorically. Most commonly, some tool was used to flake the lithic material (see Fig. 15 for examples). Percussion (see Whittaker [1994] Chapters 6 and 8, and Crabtree [1972:8–14]) refers to all the processes wherein the objective piece is worked by some type of hammer or percussor. The objective piece may be held in the hand during the working. This is known as freehand percussion. Alternatively, the objective piece may be cushioned somehow, as against the leg, or even rested on an anvil; it may also be held in a vise of some sort, or even between the knees or feet. The nature of the hammer itself is also important.

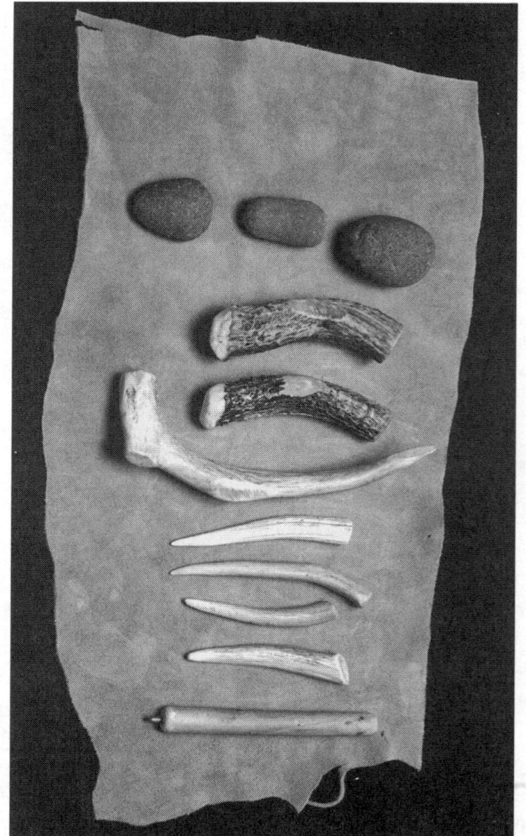

Figure 15: Examples of stone tools used in flaking lithic material: three hammerstones on top; below them, three antler soft hammer percussors (billets); below them, four antler flakers; on the bottom, a copper tipped flaker

1. *Direct hard hammer percussion:* direct refers to the fact that the hammer itself contacts the rock to cause flake removal (Fig. 16). Hard refers to the fact that the hammer is made of a hard, unyielding material, basically hard stone or metal. If stones are used (e.g., granite, basalt, flint), they are referred to as hammerstones. These hammers may be hafted to a handle to increase the force of the blow by increasing the arc it travels through before impacting the objective piece.

2. *Direct soft hammer percussion:* the difference here (Fig. 17) is that the hammer used is of a softer material that yields or deforms somewhat on impact, allowing the edge of the objective piece to sink into it slightly. These hammers are generally rather elongate pieces of antler, bone, or wood and are usually termed billets or batons. Some soft stones, such as sandstone, also fit into the soft hammer category.

3. *Bipolar technique:* in this technique the objective piece is rested on an anvil and then struck with a hammerstone. Depending on the force required to achieve fracture, the objective piece may be held on the anvil by hand. Alternatively, the anvil and/or objective piece may be buried

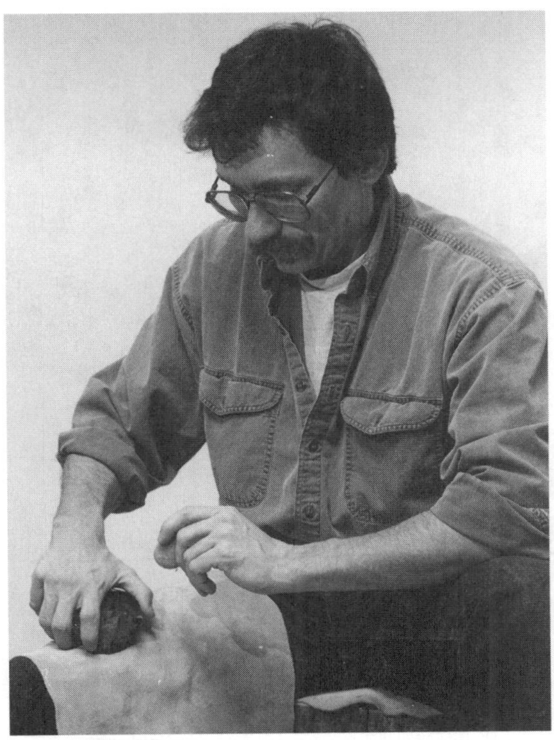

Figure 16: Direct hard hammer percussion

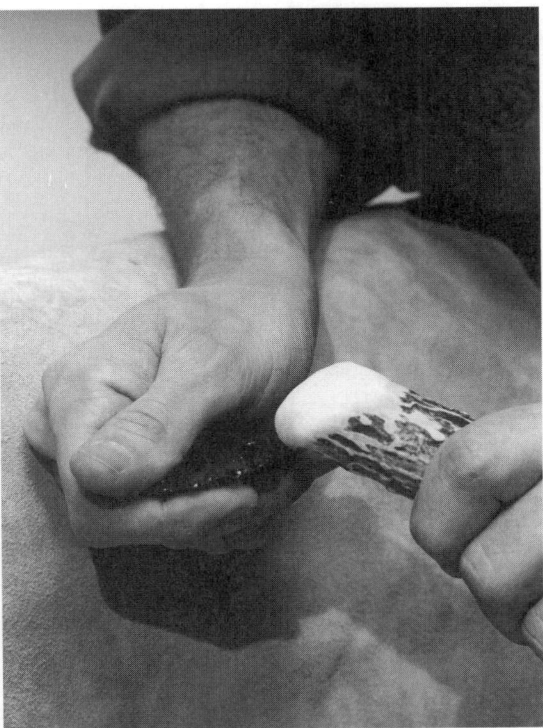

Figure 17: Direct soft hammer percussion

in sand. Such burial allows the worker to remove his or her hand from danger while at the same time ensuring that the anvil and objective piece do not slip away under the impact, dissipating the force of the blow uselessly. The hammer may be hand-held, hafted, or thrown. This technique may actually shatter the objective piece into a number of fragments, or it may simply split the objective piece in two. The anvil acts to "reflect" the force of the blow back into the objective piece and so there is a tendency to actually sheer the rock, leaving little or no bulb of percussion. Since the anvil also acts as a hammerstone, both ends of the flakes and core (or fragments thereof) produced can have striking platform features (e.g., crushing), as well as bulbs of percussion and ripple marks radiating out from the ends on the fractured surface (Fig. 18).

4. *Indirect percussion:* an intermediate tool, a punch, is used between the hammer and the objective piece (Fig. 19). One end of the punch is rested on the objective piece and its other end is then struck with the hammer, so that the hammer blow is applied indirectly to the objective piece.

All of these percussion techniques involve delivering a sudden, substantial force for a short time to cause the fracture. This procedure is called *dynamic loading. Static loading* occurs when a force is applied to the material and the force is gradually increased to the point where fracture occurs (by exceeding the "elastic limit" of the material). This process is what is used in pressure flaking.

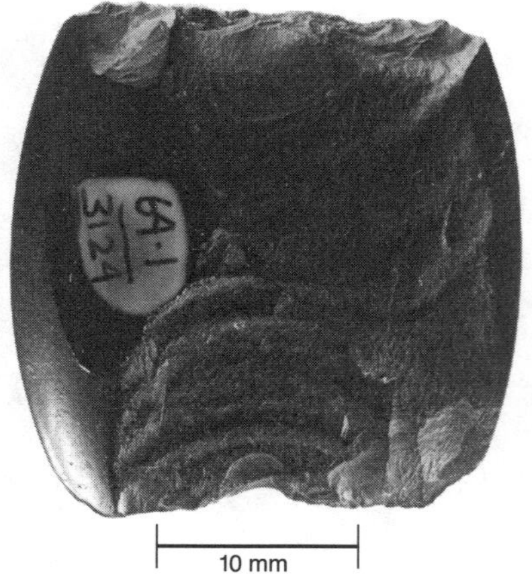

Figure 18: Bipolar percussion

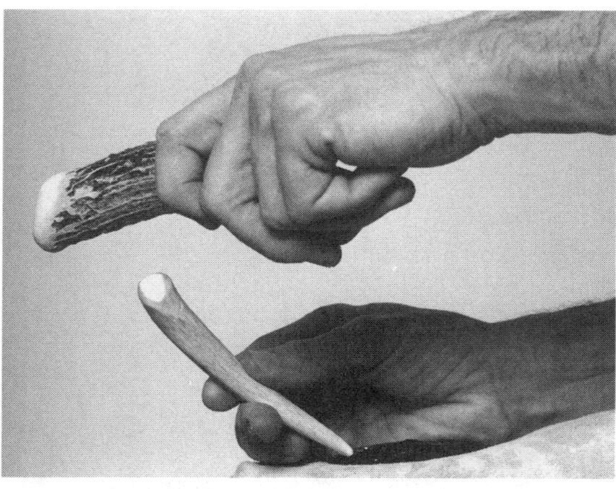

Figure 19: Indirect percussion

In *pressure flaking*, a pointed flaking tool (flaker) is rested on the edge of the objective piece and the pressure is gradually increased until the flake is "popped" off (Fig. 20). Flakers are usually made of bone, antler, or hardwood.

A variation on pressure flaking employs a chest crutch or a lever, both of which increase the amount of static load that can be exerted. The flaker is mounted in a long, T-shaped handle of the chest crutch. The top of the "T" is placed on the chest of the worker as he or she bends over. The flaker end is seated on the objective piece (held in some sort of vise). The entire weight of the body can be rested on the crutch to increase the load. If the flaker is put at the end of a lever, once again the amount of pressure can be increased.

2.2.3 Basic flake types

There are many ways in which flakes are categorized in archaeological analysis (e.g., Crabtree 1972). Flake types will be discussed in more detail later in the book, as will the meaning of flake features in terms of fracture mechanics, but for now only a basic categorization of flakes is needed. This categorization of flakes is based on the amount of cortex present on the dorsal surface and the form of the distal end or termination.

Flakes are fundamentally categorized based on the amount of dorsal cortex they have (left-hand side of flake in Fig. 21):

1. *Primary decortication flake:* the entire dorsal surface of the flake is cortex. Here, obviously, the flake has no dorsal surface flake scars. Decortication refers to the fact that the flake is removing part of the cortex from the objective piece when it is detached. Primary refers to the fact that no previous flakes have been removed from that area, so that the dorsal surface is entirely cortex covered. This situation suggests that the flake was probably removed very early in the process of working the objective piece, although this need not always be the case.

2. *Secondary decortication flake:* a flake that has some dorsal cortex (Fig. 21), but that also has a portion of the dorsal surface from which the cortex has been removed. These flakes, then, also have one or more flake scars present on the dorsal surface.

3. *Secondary flake:* any flake having no cortex on the dorsal surface. There are many

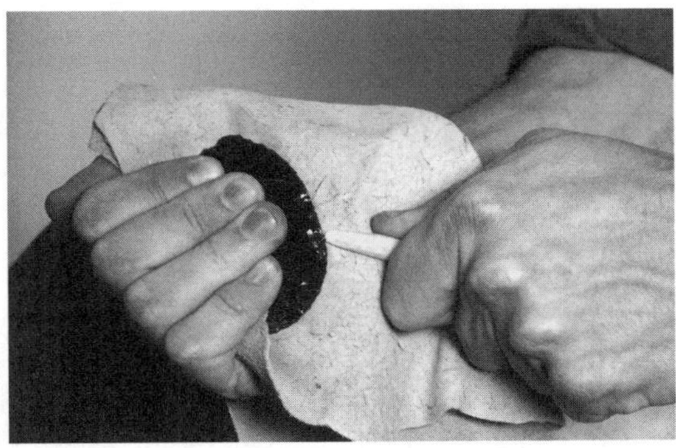

Figure 20: Pressure flaking

Figure 21: Secondary decortication flake

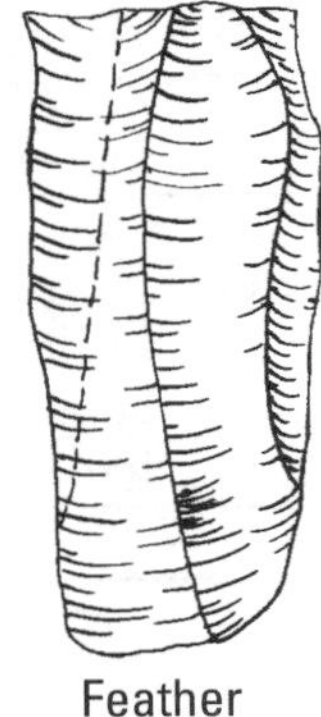

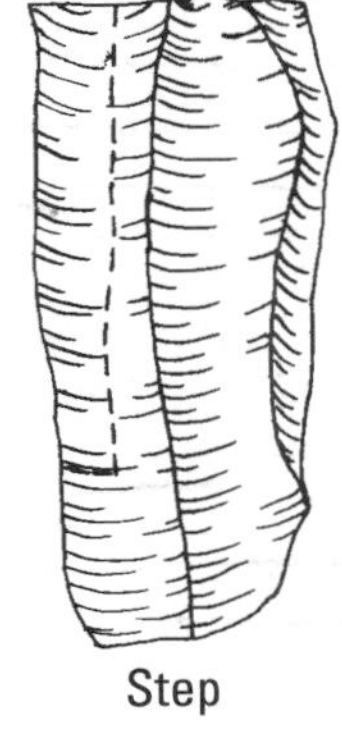

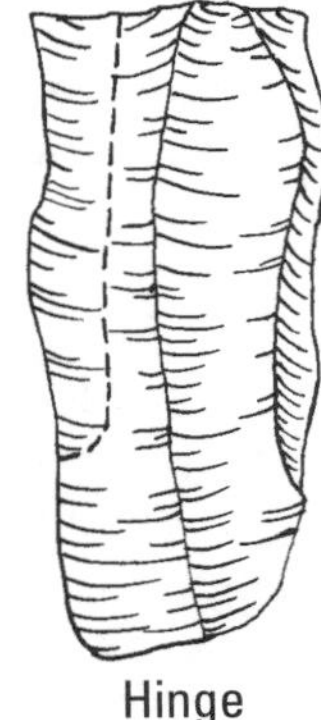

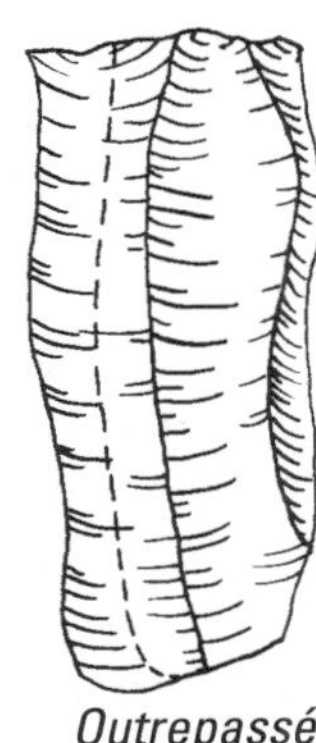

Figure 22: Flake termination types (flakes indicated by dotted lines)

subdivisions of this category. These variations will be discussed later in this book. If cortex is present on the striking platform only, most researchers still define the piece as a secondary flake.

Flakes are also categorized by the type of distal end termination they have (Fig. 22). The four main types are described here, but there are other types:

1. *Feather:* distally, the flake simply becomes gradually thinner and thinner until the distal end is reached and the thinning is reduced to nothing.

2. *Step:* the distal end terminates rather abruptly in a right angle fracture. This termination usually means that the flake broke (Whittaker 1994:17).

3. *Hinge:* the distal end of the flake terminates in a "roll" out to the core surface. Basically, the distal end is rounded. This type of flake is also called a dub flake.

4. *Outrepassé (overshoot):* the flake continues to the end of the core or tool and actually bends around the end to the opposite surface, in the process removing the end of the piece being worked (Whittaker 1994:19).

2.3 Fracture Mechanics

Fracture mechanics, also known as lithomechanics, is the study of the breakage of lithic materials that have been used to manufacture flaked stone tools.

Why does an archaeologist needs to know the physics of how and why lithic materials fracture? Does this knowledge tell the archaeologist anything about culture? Ancient stone workers did not understand the physics of material fracture, although they obviously understood how to use material properties to achieve their desired goals. Do we need to know anything besides the fact that hitting lithic material causes it to break?

We may not need to know every detail of the processes, but if we understand how the stone breaks we will also understand why earlier stone workers did things the way they did. We will understand what things were possible for them to do and what were not. Modern experimental flintknapping (stone working) can give many of these reasons and define many of the limits of the material, but any flintknapper or group of flintknappers have only their own, idiosyncratic experiences to draw on for these inferences. It is entirely possible that past people did things in ways that modern experimenters have not considered. Modern experiments can limit our view of prehistoric work if we assume that the methods we are aware of are the only ones possible. Archaeology has this problem in all areas of its study, where interpretations are based on analogies drawn from ethnographic people who lived in the last few hundred years. This problem has been referred to as the "tyranny of the ethnographic record"; the assumption that all past patterns of human behavior are to be seen in living populations in the modern world (Wobst 1978). Understanding how lithic materials break can suggest other interpretations for the patterns seen in archaeological remains. The understanding of the mechanics of fracture can also be used to define the limits beyond which human stone workers could not go.

Finally, in modern lithic studies we are turning more and more to analyzing the minute details of the features preserved on stone tools and lithic debitage. Every ridge and undulation on a flake or tool surface is being examined to interpret how the tools were made and who made them. In these circumstances of detailed analysis, archaeologists must know if these features are the result of the type of hammer used or because an anvil was used. Equally important, archaeologists need to know if the features formed because a flintknapper was left-handed or because the production of these features gave the resultant tools an aesthetically pleasing feature that all owners wanted on their projectile points or adzes. It is also important to know if a feature occurs only on a particular type of lithic material, such as obsidian. Lithomechanics may not be able to answer these questions directly, but what it can indicate is whether or not features are simply by-products of the fracturing process. If they are such by-products, fracture mechanics can also allow us to evaluate whether or not humans could manipulate the process to consciously obtain those features consistently. And if *that* is the case, that observation can tell us something of the basic procedures past stone workers would have undertaken to achieve that end. Having said all that, it must now be admitted that all the details have not yet been worked out and so what follows is a summary of the basic principles as we currently understand them.

2.3.1 *Fracture initiation and the Hertzian cone*

The lithic materials used to make flaked stone tools in the past are classified as brittle materials. In engineering, this refers to materials that fail (fracture) by well-defined crack growth. The following discussion of fracture mechanics is

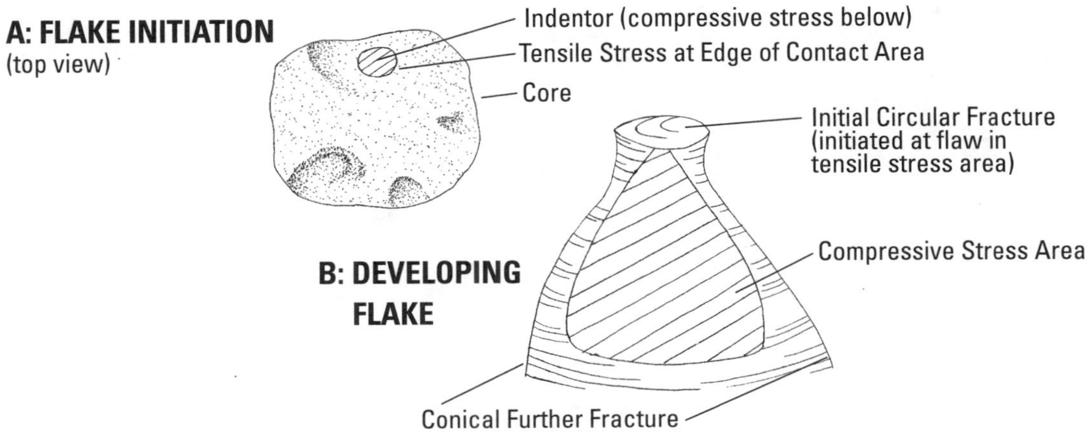

Figure 23: Flake initiation and development

taken in particular from two articles by Cotterell and Kamminga (1979, 1987) and one by Lawn and Marshall (1979).

When a solid is indented (impacted), a stress field is set up around the contact area. This stress field is simply the manner in which the stresses are distributed (i.e., the pressure exerted on the solid causes it to be stressed or strained). Fracture mechanics is the study of how a crack pattern evolves within the stress field (i.e., how the crack, or fracture, propagates or runs through the material) (Cotterell and Kamminga 1987:678).

When an indenter, such as a pressure flake or hammerstone, contacts a solid (e.g., core), there is an area of compressive stress directly below the indenter (Cotterell and Kamminga 1987:685; Lawn and Marshall 1979:68; Speth 1972). In a sense, the lithic material is being squashed together, although in fact it does not actually deform; a stress with that tendency is caused or formed. The compressive area is teardrop shaped (see Fig. 23). Also important is that strong tensile (pulling apart) stresses are set up at the immediate edge of the contact area. This situation is somewhat analogous to sitting in the middle of a bed; you compress the mattress below you and at the same time the spot you are sitting on pulls away from the edges of the mattress, setting up tension or strain in the mattress cloth. All of these stresses in solids are highly concentrated in the immediate indenter contact area and decrease rapidly as distance from the contact area increases. This pattern is the type of stress field set up around what are, in engineering terms, referred to as blunt indenters. These blunt indenters are the types probably usually involved in archaeological stone tool manufacturing (sharp indenters essentially pierce the solid on contact).

Brittle materials are weaker in tension than in compression. Due to this situation, failure or fracture in brittle materials almost always occurs where there is high tensile stress. In brittle materials, failure is generally initiated at existing microcracks or flaws in the material. These can be viewed as areas of weakness that are the first to break under stress. If glass lacked these flaws, for example, it would be one hundred times stronger. This theory of brittle material failure is called the Griffith Crack Theory (Cotterell and Kamminga 1987:678; Lawn and Marshall 1979:66). In homogeneous or isotopic materials, materials having no real variation in properties throughout the material but rather

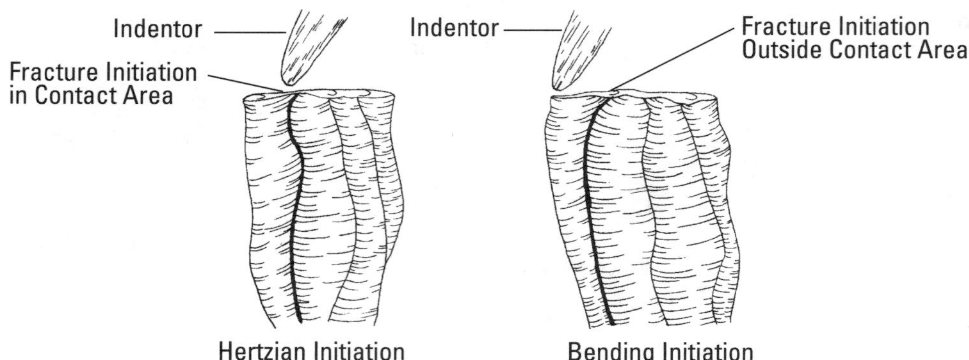

Figure 24: Fracture initiation types

having properties the same in all directions, such failure usually occurs at surface microcracks rather than at those deeper in the material. Fracture occurs at these surface cracks on the material since the stresses decrease rapidly with distance from the contact area and the contact area is at the surface. The indenter subjects the extant surface microcracks to increasing tensile forces. Once a critical value is reached in one of the surface flaws in the high tensile stress area *at the edge of the contact area,* a fracture is initiated (Fig. 24). The fracture then runs around the entire circumference of this high tensile stress area at the edge of the contact area, since there is more or less uniform stress at this distance from the contact area (Cotterell and Kamminga 1987:685, Lawn and Marshall 1979:68). Blunt indenters basically have circular contact areas, so the crack that forms is a circular crack. This crack is the so-called ring crack sometimes present on a flake striking platform at the impact location. This circumstance is also the reason why the top of the bulb of percussion (and the top of the Hertzian cone of which the bulb is part), is circular.

The crack also runs down into the solid, but does not penetrate very far. However, continued pressure is put on from the indenter and this causes the crack to penetrate deeper into the material (Cotterell and Kamminga 1987:685; Lawn and Marshall 1979:68). The fracture cannot propagate or run through areas of high compressive stress (it is hard to break things apart if something is pushing or compressing them together); hence the fracture front expands outward away from the teardrop-shaped compressive area below the indenter. This deflection of the fracture causes the fracture path to have a cone shape, the Hertzian cone (see Fig. 23).

In the case of a flake, the ventral surface exposes half of the Hertzian cone as the bulb of percussion. This feature arises because flake detachment almost never occurs with *only* a downward vector or angle to the force, but usually also with an outward bending component to it. This actually causes a compressive stress area on the "outside" edge of ring crack (Cotterell and Kamminga 1987:686–687) and so the fracture "flares" out around this to the surface (Fig. 25), producing only a half cone (and also producing the convex ventral edge of the striking platform).

After the fracture is initiated according to Hertzian mechanics, further propagation is very complex, particularly due to the influence of "free surfaces" (the edges of the lithic piece) (Cotterell and Kamminga 1979:104). This aspect of fracture has not been well studied.

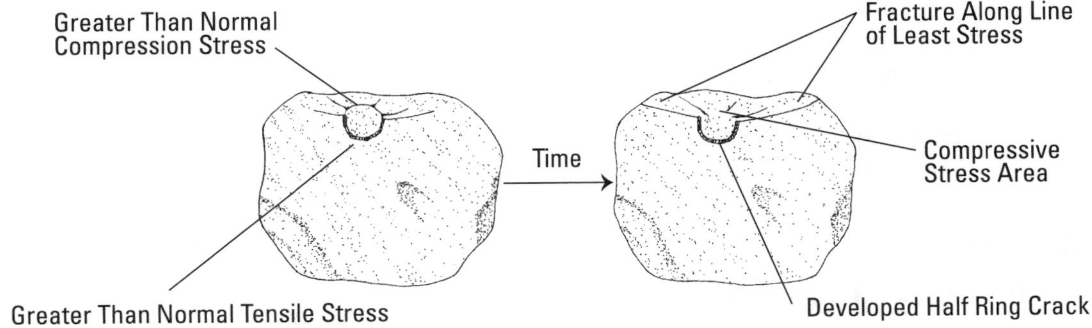

Figure 25: Fracture initiation when force has an outward component

In terms of the basic direction a fracture takes once it is initiated, if a stone worker's blow is directed basically into the stone (vertically) the compressive stress, which is the main stress, is parallel to the edge of the piece. The tensile stress, which is causing the fracture, is the secondary stress and works at right angles to the compressive stress. It would be very difficult to cause a fracture to run through the zone of major compressive stress. Since fractures follow the "path of least resistance," they parallel the objective piece surface and tend to be more or less straight.

The fracture tends to propagate outwards radially. However, when a stress wave in material intersects a free surface, the lateral direction of the fracture ends, so fracture occurs where the wave intersects the free surface. This factor explains why flakes removed from a featureless surface are wide and expanding, while those that have a dorsal arris are quite narrow. The featureless surface has no free surface for the fracture front to encounter and so the front expands all the way across the surface, whereas the arris provides free surfaces much closer to the location where the stress is initiated.

An example of another feature that can be explained by fracture mechanics is ripple marks (Cotterell and Kamminga 1990:147–149). Here the tensile stress wave causing fracture is intersected by another stress wave. This intersection of waves changes the stress field temporarily, and this temporarily changes the direction of the stress waves and hence the direction of the fracture. As the other stress wave passes beyond the fracture zone, the previous stress field is reestablished and the direction of the fracture returns to its previous line.

The fracturing outlined above is classic Hertzian initiation, where the crack that starts the flake occurs in the near area of the contact point. As the initiating force involved is directed more outwardly toward a core free surface, rather than vertically into the piece, there is an increasing tendency for the piece to be stressed in a levering manner. This levering causes more tensile stress to be built up at a distance from the contact area (see Fig. 24), where the levering or bending action occurs. Fracture in these cases occurs at a point further in from the edge of the piece, at a distance from the contact area. This type of fracture initiation is called a bending initiation (Cotterell and Kamminga 1987:689–691). Soft hammer percussion typically undergoes this type of fracture initiation. Hertzian fracture mechanics do not act in this type of initiation and no bulb of percussion results since there is no compressive stress field below the surface where the initiation actually occurs. Some of the other flake features, such as fissures, do still occur.

These are the basic principles of fracture mechanics. These principles provide an outline of how fracture occurs and an explanation for some of the main fracture-related features visible on flakes.

2.4 Analysis Implementation

Applying the information presented in this chapter to the interpretation of lithic tool remains is relatively straightforward. Initially, an examination of the debitage can give an obvious indication of whether flaking was used (i.e., the presence of flake debitage), as can a cursory examination of the lithic tools present to see if they have flake scars on some or all of their surfaces. Fragments of debitage from sawing may be identified by their straight edges where sawn and by possible striations or "scratches" on the sawn surface(s). Tools produced by sawing may also show such features. Other ground stone features, such as grinding striations, pecking impact indentations, and smooth shiny surfaces from polishing, can also be used to help separate the lithic material into these two broad categorizations: flaked stone and ground stone. This basic categorization is often the first stage in any lithic analysis. The next step in any analysis is usually to separate each of these categories into the different lithic types present. This separation, the subject of the next chapter, is important, among other reasons, because different lithic materials have different properties and so are worked differently and are used for different types of tools.

CHAPTER 3

General Lithic Types

3.1 Introduction

There were many types of lithic material available to people in the past for making tools. The choices made were based on what was locally available, what might feasibly be acquired via trade and contact with other people, the type of tools being manufactured, and how suitable each material type was for the tool in question. The lithic materials used demonstrate the many pragmatic and cultural choices made by people. As a result, identifying the material used provides insight into human culture and decision making. Accurate identification is also necessary so that comparisons can be made from one site to another. Such comparisons allow broader patterns of lithic material use and trade to be defined.

The raw materials used to manufacture lithic tools in the past are classified as either minerals or rocks by geologists. A mineral can be defined as a naturally occurring inorganic compound with a characteristic internal structure determined by a regular arrangement of the atoms and/or ions within it, with a chemical composition and physical properties that are either fixed or that vary within a definite range. A rock is generally defined as a naturally formed aggregate composed of grains of one or more minerals in varying proportions (although there are a few exceptions to this definition [Plummer and McGeary 1991:26]). Most rocks are composed of two or more minerals (Monroe and Wicander 1995:27), but mono-mineralic rocks such as dunite and pyroxenites (Bell and Wright 1985:110) do exist. All minerals, and so all rocks, are composed of elements, such as iron, silica, and sodium.

Rocks are formed through various geological processes and are subdivided into broad types based on their mode of formation:

1. *Igneous:* formed from molten material (magma).

2. *Sedimentary:* re-cemented particles of older rocks that have been broken down by weathering.

3. *Metamorphic:* rocks that are altered by temperature, pressure or chemical environment; can be formed from igneous, sedimentary or other metamorphic rocks.

The rock cycle (e.g., Plummer and McGeary 1991:44; Monroe and Wicander 1995:12-14) illustrates the relationships between the three basic types of rock. Magma is molten rock in the Earth's interior. Igneous rocks are formed when portions of that magma cool and crystallize into solid compounds. This cooling process is slow if the magma cools within Earth's crust, and the rocks formed are referred to as intrusive igneous rocks. If the magma reaches the surface of the Earth and cools, the cooling occurs much more rapidly, and the resulting rocks are referred to as extrusive igneous rocks.

Through various processes, igneous rocks become exposed to environmental agents and are subjected to weathering. Weathering results in the breakdown of portions of the igneous rocks and their transportation as small particles of sediment, which are subsequently deposited in places such as ocean bottoms and sand dunes. If this unconsolidated sediment is lithified (cemented or otherwise consolidated into a rock), sedimentary rocks result. Once formed, these sedimentary rocks may also be weathered and once again become sedimentary particles, contributing to the formation of more sedimentary rocks.

Once deposited, igneous and sedimentary rocks are subjected to other processes that expose them to heat and pressure. These processes include burial in sediments, contact with molten magma, and tectonic forces (occurring at tectonic plate boundaries). The heat and/or pressure cause alterations (recrystallization) in the rocks. This altered rock is called metamorphic rock. Metamorphic rocks can, in turn, be subjected to further metamorphosis to produce other metamorphic rocks. They can also be subjected to weathering and can be reduced to sediment, potentially contributing to sedimentary rock formation. All three rock types may be subjected to sufficiently high temperatures during metamorphosis that they are again liquefied, becoming magma and beginning the rock cycle again.

There are several thousand minerals on the earth (Plummer and McGeary 1991:34). These minerals have been divided into a number of groups, a simplified classification (Dolgoff 1996:152; Monroe and Wicander 1995:30) including

1. *Silicates:* based on the two most common elements in the Earth's crust, silicon and oxygen. Quartz, SiO_2, is a mineral in this group.

2. *Carbonates:* all including the carbonate ion, ($-CO_2$). Calcite, $CaCO_3$, is an example.

3. *Phosphates:* all including the phosphate ion ($-PO_4$). Apatite, $Ca_5(PO_4)3(OH,F,Cl)$, is an example.

4. *Sulfates:* all including the sulfate ion ($-SO_4$). Gypsum, $CaSO_4 \cdot 2H_2O$, is an example.

5. *Sulfides:* all having sulfur (S). Pyrite, FeS_2, is an example.

6. *Halides:* having one of the halogens (chlorine, fluorine, etc.) in the mineral. Halite (common salt), NaCl, is an example.

7. *Hydroxides:* having the hydroxyl ion (–OH). The pigment limonite, $Fe_2O_3 \cdot nH_2O$, is an example.

8. *Oxides:* all having oxygen (O) in the mineral. Hematite, Fe_2O_3, is an example.

9. *Native elements:* single pure elements without any other element in the mineral. These can be either metals (e.g., gold; Au) or non-metals (e.g., diamond; C).

Most common rocks are made of one group of minerals; the silicates. Silicate minerals comprise about 95% of the Earth's crust by weight (Monroe and Wicander 1995:31). Since this is also the mineral group that is important for stone tool manufacture, it is the only one that will be discussed here.

3.2 Silicate Minerals

The silicate minerals are subdivided into a number of groups. These groups are based on the elements present in the mineral and the molecular structures they form (Dolgoff 1996:152–158; Monroe and Wicander 1995:31–34; Plummer and McGeary 1991:30–35). A basic compositional division is often made into the ferromagnesian silicates, containing iron (Fe), magnesium (Mg), or both, and the nonferromagnesian silicates, which lack iron and magnesium. Finer divisions are made within each of these two large groups based on the specific minerals present. Common ferromagnesian silicates include olivine, the pyroxenes (including jadeite), the amphiboles (including hornblende), and biotite mica. Common nonferromagnesian silicates include quartz, potassium feldspars (including orthoclase), plagioclase feldspars, and muscovite mica.

The structures of the silicates are all based on the SiO_4 tetrahedron. The tetrahedron is a negatively charged ion and so does not exist on its own as a mineral. However, there are five manners in which tetrahedra combine to form stable minerals: as isolated tetrahedra (bonded to other minerals) (e.g., olivine, garnet), as single chains (e.g., pyroxene group), as double chains (e.g., amphibole group), as continuous sheets (e.g., the micas), or as three-dimensional frameworks (e.g., feldspars and quartz).

The elemental composition and tetrahedron structure are used to separate the silicates into groups. Some of the main groups commonly employed are

1. *Olivine:* isolated tetrahedra; ferromagnesian.

2. *Pyroxene group:* single chain; ferromagnesian.

3. *Amphibole group:* double chain; ferromagnesian.

4. *Biotite mica:* continuous sheet; ferromagnesian.

5. *Potassium feldspars:* framework; nonferromagnesian (K rich).

6. *Plagioclase feldspars:* framework; nonferromagnesian (Ca or Na rich).

7. *Silica (Quartz):* framework; nonferromagnesian (SiO_2).

8. *Muscovite mica:* continuous sheet; nonferromagnesian.

9. *Clay minerals:* continuous sheet; nonferromagnesian (complex Al silicate hydroxides).

The silicate minerals are archaeologically important in part because they combine to form many of the rocks that are used to make stone tools, particularly ground stone tools. These will be discussed in the section on rock classification. The only group within the silicate minerals that contains minerals that are themselves important for manufacturing stone tools is the silica (quartz) group. These minerals are some of the most important materials used for flaked stone tools and are discussed here.

Like quartz, the other minerals in the silica group have the basic 2:1 ratio of oxygen to silicon but they also have varying amounts of extracrystalline water. These silica minerals include chalcedony, chert, flint, jasper, and opal, among others. Small amounts of impurities, generally less than 10% of the crystalline material (Blatt et al. 1980:571), are usually present in these minerals. These impurities give the particular mineral other properties. For example, these impurities give quartz its various colors. Although most geologists refer to materials such as chert and chalcedony as minerals, their variable composition has led Luedtke to define them as rocks (1992:7).

The silica minerals (chert, chalcedony, etc.) are separated into four groups based on crystal size. This segregation based on size is arbitrary and in particular a chert may contain all size gradations from crystalline to amorphous (Blatt et al. 1980:571–572). In sedimentary (clastic) rocks it is not uncommon for quartz crystals formed in chert to resemble quartzite fragments, this similarity perhaps explaining the apparent finding of quartzite-like portions in some cherts such as occasional fragments of Swan River chert from Manitoba, Canada. Despite such problems, the following distinctions are frequently made:

1. *Crystalline:* the crystals are visible in hand specimen (e.g., quartz).

2. *Microcrystalline:* individual crystals can only be seen with a microscope (e.g., some quartz).

3. *Cryptocrystalline:* crystal structure can only be visualized by X-ray diffraction; based on direct observations and theoretical considerations, the minimum crystal size is probably about 0.2 nm (Blatt et al. 1980:571) (e.g., much chert, chalcedony, jasper, and flint).

4. Amorphous: lacking crystal structure (e.g., much chert, chalcedony, jasper, and flint; opal is pure amorphous silica).

The archaeologically important silica minerals are:

1. *Quartz:* this mineral has a vitreous luster (i.e., glass like) and lacks cleavage planes; although it is usually colorless or white, it may be of a variety of colors due to impurities; it is transparent to translucent and has a hardness approximately 7.0 on [Mohs'] scale of hardness (Bell and Wright 1985:60). When quartz is deposited as thin layers in other material it is termed vein quartz; in larger deposits it is termed crystalline or massive quartz.

2. *Chert/Flint:* there is some disagreement about whether these two mineral categories should be included together or if they should be separated (e.g., Crabtree 1967, Luedtke 1992:5-6). For the most part, flint is not a term North American geologists use. Luedtke (1992:5-6) suggests that all materials such as flint, agate, chalcedony, and jasper be seen as varieties of chert. She notes that most often flint is used to mean dark chert found as nodules in chalk deposits specifically, but that this segregation does not work well geologically outside of Britain. In her definition, chert is a general term for all sedimentary rocks composed of microcrystalline quartz. I advise using Luedtke's all-inclusive definition of chert to include chalcedony, jasper, flint, etc., but for many archaeological discussions these need to be separated from each other. When flint is distinguished from chert, it is segregated based on a darker color (black, dark brown, gray), the dark color being due to organic matter included in the chert (Blatt et al. 1980:571; Monroe and Wicander 1995:131). In this segregation, chert is generally defined as lighter in color and as showing a broader range of colors. There are exceptions to this rule. Chert accumulations are generally either as beds or as nodules in carbonate rocks (Blatt et al. 1980:575). Flint is often defined specifically as the nodular form, particularly when the nodules occur in chalks or marls. Conversely, chert is a term often reserved for massive deposits in beds or layers. This categorization seems to be the most common definition used to separate these materials, as used by Whittaker (1994:70) for example, when separation is deemed necessary. Chert may also form as nodules in other material (e.g., limestone). To confuse the issue of this distinction further, chert nodules in limestones may be so abundant that they coalesce in the plane of bedding, forming discrete layers (Blatt et al. 1980:575). Chert is about 99% silica and less than 1% extracrystalline water (Blatt et al. 1980:571); generally it has less water than chalcedony (see below); it has a luster that is usually dull to waxy; it is opaque, although it may transmit light on thin edges; it may be banded and may have inclusions (fossils or other); it has a [Mohs'] hardness of approximately 7.0. Chert forms in a number of ways. Many of these formation processes also apply to chalcedony:

(i) as a direct precipitate (from the sea), although many consider this to have been an uncommon event (Monroe and Wicander 1995:131). The evidence for this remains somewhat unclear, but a case has been made for the absence of any biological silica from diatoms, sponges, or radiolaria during the Precambrian, yet cherts from this period exist (Blatt et al. 1980:579) and are actually a much greater proportion of the strata (15%) than at any other time period. The initial chert would have been deposited as microspheres. Modern sea water is very undersaturated in silica (about 120 ppm) and hence is very unlikely to precipitate silica minerals. However, it has been suggested that in the absence of silica-consuming organisms, such as sponges and radiolaria, in Precambrian times the oceans were saturated with silica and that colloidal masses of silica would form. Such chert might theoretically also form as large beds. Direct precipitation from restricted marine and lake waters has been demonstrated. In circumstances where lakes are very alkaline (pH over 10), volcanic basin rocks and suspended silica containing sediment can have the silica eroded from them and taken into solution; silica concentrations as high as 2700 ppm have been reported and when runoff rapidly decreases the pH of the water, the water becomes supersaturated with silica and it is deposited as amorphous silica (in the circumstances studied in the United States and Africa, virtually none of the silica is of biological origin) (Blatt et al. 1980:581–582).

(ii) by replacement of a fossil or formation in a crack or fissure. Nodules in limestones often show banding suggestive of precipitation in cavities as amorphous silica gel (Blatt et al. 1980:576). "Ghosts" of biological silica components such as sponge spicules and radiolaria tests are common, and all stages in the replacement process are often abundant (Blatt et al. 1980:577–578). These observations are also relevant for the following point.

(iii) by re-solution, wherein silica is dissolved out of siliceous rocks and deposited separately, or is dissolved out of organic deposits (e.g., diatoms, sponge spicules, siliceous zooplankton, etc.) and redeposited. Sometimes nodules in limestones lack the internal structure described in (ii) above, and may contain microscopic carbonate inclusions that are interpreted as indications of replacement of the limestone by silica (Blatt et al. 1980:576). Sometimes nodules with an internal banded structure are referred to as geodes and are seen specifically as the result of silica being deposited in cavities as a result of percolation of groundwater; the structureless nodules are then specifically defined as nodules as opposed to geodes (Dolgoff 1996:230). Bedded cherts probably arose in one of two manners (Blatt et al. 1980:576–577). Some seem to have developed in deep sea floor sediments that are very fine and contained silica skeletons of radiolaria, etc.; the silica from these deposited skeletons was taken into solution and later deposited as chert beds. The other mechanism was probably similar to that described above for alkaline lakes.

(iv) in hydrothermal deposits (hot springs).

(v) as a result of contact metamorphism, wherein an igneous intrusion into a cherty limestone can cause melting of the silica in the limestone, which is subsequently redeposited.

3. *Chalcedony:* is a mineral made of quartz (SiO_2) and 1% to 9% water. In addition to the greater abundance of extracrystalline water, chalcedony differs from chert in having a distinctive radiating texture (Blatt et al. 1980:571). This radiating or fibrous structure can be seen in thin section analysis but is not discernible with the unaided eye or by X-ray diffraction (Luedtke 1992:6). Chalcedonies are usually light in color (colorless, milky, gray, white, light blue, light green, tan brown to darker brown) and are often banded. They may have inclusions such as dendrites (manganese growths). Chalcedonies usually have a waxy luster and are translucent (Crabtree 1967). Archaeologists tend to rely on translucentness to define chalcedony, but although most geologically defined chalcedonies (i.e., have a fibrous structure) are translucent, some translucent "chalcedonies" do not have the fibrous structure (Knife River flint is a good example of a non-fibrous rock that is translucent) (Luedtke 1992:6). Chalcedonies have a [Mohs'] scale hardness of approximately 6.5. Chalcedonies are commonly called agates (banded agate; moss agate, which has dendritic inclusions; etc.). Possession of a fibrous structure is the best criterion to use for defining a material as chalcedony, but in practical terms archaeologists are often forced to rely on the fact that a material is translucent to make

distinctions for individual pieces in an archaeological collection. Even cherts can be translucent on the edges, but, based on work by Ahler, Luedtke (1992:68) has suggested that cherts can be separated from chalcedonies based on the thinness of the material that will transmit light. When a piece is held 8 cm from the edge of the shade of a 75 watt light bulb, a very opaque chert will only transmit light where it is 0.5 mm thick or less, whereas chalcedonies and very translucent cherts will be translucent even at thicknesses of 20 mm or more.

4. *Jasper:* jaspers are a variety of chert and most archaeologists just refer to them as chert. Jaspers have a high percentage of added materials and these compounds give jasper its colors. Iron oxides are particularly important in the coloration, with the most common being deep, rich reds produced by hematite and the browns and yellows produced by limonite. Geologists often specifically refer to hematite cherts when they employ the term jasper (Blatt et al. 1980:571; Ehlers and Blatt 1980:502), but may also use it to include the brown jaspers (Monroe and Wicander 1995:131). Blue or black color is due to magnetite, another iron compound. Archaeologists usually use the term jasper for all red, brown, and yellow cherts, excluding the other colors of iron-rich cherts (Luedtke 1992:6). Jaspers are often banded and may have veins of chalcedony running through them. Jaspers have a dull luster and are entirely opaque. They have a Mohs hardness of about 7.0.

5. *Opal:* has a high water content (> 10 %), so is somewhat softer than chalcedony/chert and doesn't hold an edge as well. As previously noted, it is pure amorphous silica (Blatt et al. 1980:571–572). It is clear to white (although there are much more colored varieties, such as the "black" opal of Australia), translucent to transparent, and looks similar to chalcedony. It often replaces organic material in the fossilization process.

6. *Silicified woods:* wood fossilized by being replaced by opal or chalcedony, actually a fossil; also called opalized or petrified wood. The suitability of silicified wood for manufacturing stone tools varies depending on how much of the original wood structure has been replaced. In one sense, silicified wood is not a silica mineral, but it is a silica mineral that has replaced the original material. Its properties are not exactly like opal or chalcedony, since the residual wood structure affects how silicified wood fractures; silicified wood may step fracture at the growth rings, cell structure, knots, etc. However, it can often be used and split into "tabs" along the grain, much like cedar shingles.

3.3 Rocks

3.3.1 Igneous rock classification

The basic classification of igneous rocks is a combination of grain size (crystal size) and mineral content. Extrusive igneous rocks are those that cool above ground (i.e., in contact with the atmosphere, usually); they cool quickly and have small crystal sizes. Intrusive igneous rocks cool before they reach the surface; they cool more slowly and there is an opportunity for large crystals to form. The basic divisions of minerals that are important in defining rock type are the percentage of orthoclase feldspar (potassium feldspar), plagioclase feldspar (either or both, of sodium feldspar and calcium feldspar), quartz, and the ferromagnesian minerals (pyroxene, amphibole, biotite mica, olivine). All of these minerals are silicates containing both silicon and oxygen.

The classification of igneous rocks is illustrated in Fig. 26. The quartz and feldspar minerals are generally light-colored, whereas the ferromagnesian minerals are dark (generally green or black). As a result, the color of the rock varies depending on the percentage of these light and dark colored minerals, with minerals on the left of the chart being light-colored and

MINERALS \ GRAIN SIZE						PREHISTORIC USES
	Orthoclase	Abundant	None	None	None	
	Quartz	Abundant	None to almost none	None	None	
	Plagioclase	Abundant	Very abundant	Abundant	Moderate to none	
	Ferromagnesian	Little	Moderate	Abundant	Abundant to very abundant	
COARSE		Granite	Diorite	Gabbro	Peridotite	Ground tools/hammerstones
FINE		Rhyolite	Andesite	Basalt		Flaked tools (depends on silica content)
GLASSY		Obsidian				Flaked tools

Color lighter -- Darker (pink is orthoclase)

Figure 26: Classification of igneous rocks

those on the right being dark-colored. Rocks rich in ferromagnesian minerals are often referred to as mafic (e.g., basalt), whereas those rich in feldspars and quartz are referred to as felsic (e.g., granite); rocks rich in ferromagnesian minerals and lacking any feldspar or quartz are termed ultramafic (e.g., peridotite) and are found on the far right of the chart area (Best 1982:37). Felsic is also sometimes used to refer to light-colored igneous rocks specifically, and mafic to refer to dark-colored igneous rocks (Ehlers and Blatt 1980:41). The density of the rocks increases from the left to the right in the chart, from average densities of about 2.65 gm/cc on the left to about 3.3 gm/cc on the right (Dolgoff 1996:170). There are generally increasing amounts of iron, magnesium, and calcium in the minerals as one moves from left to right in the chart, and increasing amounts silica, potassium, sodium, and aluminum in the minerals as one moves from right to left. The silica content of igneous rocks is particularly significant in regards to their flaking quality and hence to their usefulness in manufacturing flaked stone tools. Ultramafic rocks are defined as those rocks containing less than 45% silica. Gabbro and basalt contain about 45–52% silica, andesite and diorite about 53–65% silica, and obsidian, rhyolite, and granite more than 65% silica (Monroe and Wicander 1995:54–56).

The chart reveals other relationships between igneous rocks. Magma that cools slowly allows the formation of larger crystals; hence the rapidity of cooling in formation is revealed by the transition from coarse-grained materials to fine and then glassy rock equivalents in each rock family (e.g., from coarse-grained granite to fine-grained rhyolite to glassy [amorphous] obsidian in the granite-rhyolite family). The rapid cooling needed to form obsidian and rhyolite means that they are usually extrusive igneous rocks, whereas granite is usually an intrusive igneous rock (Monroe and Wicander 1995:54). Rocks with mineral grains large enough to identify in hand specimen ("coarse" in the chart) are referred to as phaneritic, whereas those having grains too small to be so identified ("fine" in the chart) are termed aphanitic (Best 1982:36); in mixed grain size rocks a 50% division is used to define if the specimen in question is aphanitic or phaneritic. Rocks may have some amounts of glass visible in hand specimen, the result of very rapid cooling, and these are termed glassy. Obsidian is essentially a completely glassy rock and pumice is similar but filled with bubble-shaped vesicles that were produced by escaping gas (Monroe and Wicander 1995:58). Small holes in other rocks, such as dissolution cavities in sedimentary rocks, are termed vugs rather than vesicles; vesicles are typically conspicuously spherical in form (see Ehlers and Blatt 1980:34).

The chart also shows the progression in the temperature at which crystallization occurs. Magma contains a mixture of elements and as it cools not all minerals form crystals at the same temperature; hence not all rocks form at the same temperature. As magma cools, the first minerals to crystallize are the ones that form the minerals to the right in the chart, the ferromagnesian minerals: first olivine (producing peridotite, for example) at about 1,200° C, then pyroxene at about 1,050° C (producing basalt and gabbro), and later amphibole. Plagioclase feldspars are next to begin crystallizing; first the calcium-rich ones (rocks such as basalt) and later the sodium-rich ones (such as dacite), overlapping with the ferromagnesian minerals in crystallization temperature. Finally, potassium feldspars and quartz crystallize, this process being complete by the time the magma has cooled to a temperature of about 700° C. Rocks such as granite are the result (Dolgoff 1996:170–171). If, as minerals and rocks crystallize from magma, they are left behind a magma flow or precipitate out of the magma, the chemical composition of the magma is altered, and this explains how different igneous rocks are produced from the same lava flow. If these rocks remain in the magma, they often undergo further transformation as it cools and other minerals form. For example, olivine crystallizes at about 1,200° C, undergoes further reactions at 1,050° C and is converted to pyroxene (Dolgoff 1996:170–171). Not all magma masses have the same chemical composition, so the rocks produced from different magmas may also differ based on the composition of the original magma (Monroe and Wicander 1995:54).

There are other families of igneous rocks that are not shown on Fig. 26. Of some importance archaeologically is the syenite family, rocks found to the left of granite and rhyolite on the chart (Bell and Wright 1985:24–25, 84–87). These rocks contain primarily potassium feldspar, with some ferromagnesian minerals and sometimes a small amount of quartz. Trachyte and phonolite, both fine-grained members of this family, have been used in areas such as Polynesia (e.g., Kahn 1996). Often an intermediate family is segregated between the granite-rhyolite family and the diorite-andesite family: granodiorite (phaneritic) and dactite (aphanitic) (e.g., Dolgoff 1996:170). The characteristics of these rocks are intermediate between the other two rock families.

3.3.2 Separating igneous rocks in hand specimen

Granites are light-colored, coarse-grained rocks that consist primarily of quartz and either, or both, of potassium feldspar (orthoclase) and sodium feldspar (plagioclase) (Dolgoff 1996:169). Ferromagnesian minerals are absent or present in only small quantities, so the granites are generally light in color: mottled pink, white, and light gray, though dark gray, greenish, or pinkish gray when ferromagnesian minerals are more abundant (Monroe and Wicander 1995:56–57; Wahlstrom 1947:269). Biotite mica and hornblende are the usual ferromagnesian minerals present and muscovite mica (white) is also often a minor constituent of granite (Bell and Wright 1985:60; Wahlstrom 1947:269). The presence of quartz can be used to distinguish granite from diorite, which either lacks quartz or has it in very small quantities (Bell and Wright 1985:88). Rhyolite is the fine-grained (aphanitic), extrusive equivalent of granite (Monroe and Wicander 1995:57), but distinctively it often has phenocrysts of quartz or potassium feldspar as well. Some rhyolite has banding or layering caused by minor changes in mineral composition or gas vesicle concentration (Bell and Wright 1985:72). The pink color of some granite and rhyolite is due to potassium feldspar (orthoclase) (Bell and Wright 1985:60). Obsidian, pitchstone, and pumice are all glassy rocks chemically equivalent to granites and rhyolites (Bell and Wright 1985:76); in some cases these have been classified as glassy rhyolites (Wahlstrom 1947:282). Obsidian is a true amorphous glass, translucent, usually black, with a vitreous luster. Although black is the most common color for obsidian, its colors are quite variable: black, red, dark green, and even clear. Obsidian may have a variety of inclusions and may show flow banding. Pitchstone is similar to obsidian but has a duller luster and generally shows flow structures and more often has phenocrysts (Bell and Wright 1985:76). Pumice is filled with gas vesicles which gives it its distinctively light color and light weight (it will often float on water).

Similarly, andesite is the aphanitic equivalent of diorite (Dolgoff 1996:168). The main mineral in these rocks is plagioclase feldspar, which is white. Ferromagnesian minerals are more common than in granites and rhyolites. The abundant white plagioclase feldspar, in combination with the dark ferromagnesian minerals, gives the coarser-grained diorite its characteristic salt and pepper appearance (Monroe and Wicander 1995:55). Andesite is typically medium to dark gray in color (although there are many exceptions: andesite can be brown, red, green or even black, and diorite sometimes has a white, green, or brown shade to the gray) (Bell and Wright 1985:88, 92). Andesite often has small phenocrysts (Bell and Wright 1985:92) but lacks quartz phenocrysts. On this basis andesite can be distinguished from rhyolite, just as the absence of quartz can be used to distinguish diorite from granite.

Basalt is the fine-grained (aphanitic) equivalent of gabbro, but gabbro is an uncommon rock at Earth's surface in the continental crust (Monroe and Wicander 1995:55). Although plagioclase feldspar is a prominent constituent of these rocks, the abundance of ferromagnesian minerals (pyroxene and to a lesser extent olivine) makes these rocks very dark in color: basalt is dark brown, dark gray or black, and gabbro is similar, although its large crystals sometimes make other lighter colors prominent as well (Bell and Wright 1985:96–104). Basalt is the extrusive rock in this family, but within the intrusive rocks a distinction is often made between a deep intrusive, coarse-textured gabbro and a medium-textured diabase (Dolgoff 1996:168). Basalt can be dense or glassy relative to gabbro and is commonly vesicular. In some cases basalt may be confused with chert, but basalt is always very dark in color and often has phenocrysts which chert does not. Basalt is totally opaque and may have vesicles (chert may have vugs, but these tend to be more irregular to rectilinear in form; vesicles in basalt tend to be more spherical).

Volcanic ash is usually composed of glass shards, but may be composed of rock or mineral fragments. The glass shards are the result of the rapid production of gas bubbles in molten material and the shattering of the vesicles produced as a result of an eruption. This circumstance results in triangular glass shards that have the concave surfaces of the original vesicles (Ehlers and Blatt 1980:33–34). Consolidated layers of ash are called tuff, and because the particles are deposited in air or water, they often display size sorting horizontally or vertically. The deposited material is lithified by some type of cement, such as a carbonate or silica cement. Ignimbrite is a welded tuff and forms when the tuff/ash retains enough heat to weld the still plastic glass shards together (Ehlers and Blatt 1980:37). In these circumstances the weight of overlying material compacts the soft particles together and expels the trapped gas; intensely welded ignimbrite can look much like obsidian

(Best 1982:88–89). Ignimbrite, unlike obsidian, is completely opaque and generally has a dull luster rather than a glassy luster. A fractured surface of ignimbrite may have a noticeably rougher surface than does obsidian since the material fractures around the impurities it contains (Crabtree 1967), although it still has the marked conchoidal fracture of obsidian.

3.3.3 Sedimentary rock classification

Sedimentary rocks are classified mainly based on grain size and chemistry, but also to an extent based on the mode of deposition. One of the most commonly used grain size scales is the Wentworth scale, which classifies particles in the following manner:

Boulder > 256 mm
Cobble 64 – 256 mm
Pebble 4 – 64 mm
Granule 2 – 4 mm
Sand 1/16 – 2 mm
Silt 1/256 – 1/16 mm
Clay < 1/256 mm

A basic division in carbonate rocks employs a continuum between limestone, which is pure $CaCO_3$ (calcium carbonate), and dolomite, which is pure $CaMg(CO_3)_2$ (calcium magnesium carbonate). Dolomite contains at least 90% $CaMg(CO_3)_2$ while limestone has no more than 10% $CaMg(CO_3)_2$. Rocks containing between 10% and 50% $CaMg(CO_3)_2$ are termed dolomitic limestones and those containing 50% to 90% are termed calcareous dolomites (Bell and Wright 1985:138).

One manner of classifying sedimentary rocks employs grain size in conjunction with carbonate content. In this classification, given in Fig. 27, the term arenaceous means "sandy," argillaceous means "clayey," and carbonaceous means "having carbon".

A number of sedimentary rocks were used as raw material for stone tools, the suitability of the particular material depending on the silica content of the particles and the cement holding them together:

1. *Conglomerate:* conglomerates are lithified gravels with 25% or more of the particles being greater than 2 mm in diameter (i.e., at least 25% larger than sand-sized). The cements binding conglomerates can be of silica, carbonate, or limonite, but it is only silica cement conglomerate that can be used as raw material for flaked tools. Conglomerate can be distinguished from breccias because the latter have angular particles while conglomerate has rounded particles.

2. *Sandstone:* 50% or more of the particles in a sandstone are greater than 1/16 mm in diameter and less than 2 mm in diameter (i.e., they are sand-sized). Sandstones are classified into a number of types, particularly quartz sandstone, arkosic (feldspar) sandstone, and lithic sandstone (a mixture of various rock types). Cementing agents for sandstones include silica, carbonate, iron oxide, and clay. When broken, the fracture takes a path around the grains rather than through them (the latter case being the situation in quartzite).

3. *Greywacke:* greywackes are argillaceous sandstones (about 15% fine silt or finer) characterized by a high feldspar content (about 35%). Greywackes are usually gray-green to dark gray in color. The term has had many definitions since it was first introduced in the late eighteenth century, but it seems best to view it as applying to "dirty" sandstones, ones containing more fine "muds" than usual (Blatt et al. 1980:373–375). Greywacke is hard and difficult to flake, but it was sometimes used.

4. *Argillaceous (mud) rocks:* this rock group is characterized by having 75% or more of the

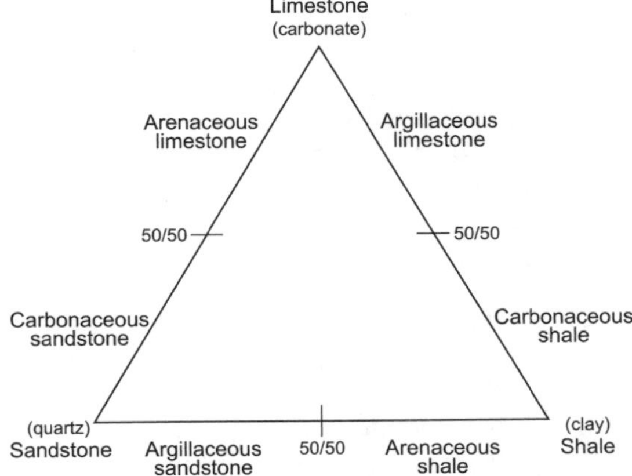

Figure 27: Sedimentary rock classification based on grain size and carbonate content

particles less than 1/16 mm in diameter (i.e., silt- and clay-sized particles). Siltstones (silt-sized particles) and mudstones (clay-sized particles) are massive and lack bedding planes. Conversely, shales have bedding planes. These rock types are generally too soft to be used in flaked stone tools. Catlinite is a red argillaceous rock, soft enough that it was often used for carving pipes and similar objects in the Great Lakes region of North America.

5. *Limestone and dolomite:* these rocks do flake but are generally too soft to hold an edge for very long and so were not usually used for flaked stone tools. Identifying whether a rock is limestone or dolomite can be done using the HCl test for $CaCO_3$: if dilute acid (10%) effervesces vigorously, the material is limestone; 10% HCl reacts only poorly with dolomite, but improves if the dolomite is powdered or if the acid strength is increased to 15%. Chert does not react. Dolomite may weather buff-colored (dull brownish yellow) because it often contains some iron, which oxidizes on weathering (Ehlers and Blatt 1980:423). Limestone weathers to a "dirty white." Limestone and dolomite are both soft rocks that typically show an interlocking crystal structure (although often too small to see in hand specimen), because calcite readily recrystallizes, and due to the presence of fossils. Dolomite generally shows crystallization, a rhombic form, whereas limestone may or may not show crystal structure (Bell and Wright 1985:52–53; Ehlers and Blatt 1980:430–431).

Although dolomite can form on its own, most apparently forms as a result of alteration of limestones (Blatt et al. 1980:512–515; Monroe and Wicander 1995:131). Limestone is generally a mixture of sand-sized carbonate particles and mud-sized (silt/clay) carbonate particles. The finer particles less than 5 nm(microns) in size, termed micritic, usually predominate (Blatt et al. 1980:460). Based on studies of modern sediment formation, these "carbonate mud" components begin as aragonite crystals, but in most limestones they have been altered to calcite crystals. Most limestones are formed of wave-broken fragments of aragonite skeletons of organisms that extract calcite from seawater, such as corals, shellfish, and algae (Monroe and Wicander 1995:131; Plummer and McGeary 1991:125). Fossils and various organic remains are commonly present in limestone. Limestone commonly undergoes dissolution leaving vugs of various sizes (Blatt et al. 1980:491), since calcite is readily dissolved in slightly acidic water (and also recrystallized) (Blatt et al. 1980:503; Monroe and Wicander 1995:131; Plummer and McGeary 1991:125). Silicification is also common in limestone, since the conditions favoring dissolution of calcite also favor the subsequent precipitation of silica (Blatt et al. 1980:503). Minerals such as chert are deposited as nodules and veins in vesicles and along joints that have been enlarged by dissolution (Blatt et al. 1980:491, 503; Ehlers and Blatt 1980:434). The usual source for the silica is dissolution of siliceous organic material, commonly sponge spicules, deposited into the same sediments as the calcite sediments (Ehlers and Blatt 1980:432–

434). The greater the degree of silicification, the better the limestone is for making stone tools (Crabtree 1967).

3.3.4 Metamorphic rocks

The most important metamorphic rocks for flaked stone tools are sedimentary rocks that have been altered metamorphically so that they are more flakeable; the metamorphosis either adds silica or makes the rock harder. Marble is a metamorphic rock that is often used, though for carving rather than flaked tools, produced from limestone or dolomite (Bell and Wright 1985:47; Ehlers and Blatt 1980:515–516). The most important metamorphic rocks used for flaked stone tools are:

1. *Argillite:* these rocks are weakly metamorphosed shales, siltstones and mudstones. Being composed of basically silt and clay-sized particles, they have a fine texture. High silica content (resulting from sources already described for sedimentary rocks) can make them flakeable, but more commonly they are used for ground stone tools. Unlike slate, they usually lack platy cleavage.

2. *Slate:* moderately metamorphosed rocks, more so than argillites. Slate has a platy cleavage and is mainly used for ground stone tools. If the metamorphism proceeds further, slate becomes phyllite and then finally schist (Ehlers and Blatt 1980:515–516) (see section below on gneiss). These highly metamorphosed rocks were used primarily as files or saws to work other materials. Phyllite is similar to slate in hand specimen but has a silky sheen on the cleavage surface and may reveal crystals (absent in slate). Crystals are clearly visible in hand specimen in schist and the rock can be split into flakes or slabs. Even higher grades of metamorphism result in a loss of schistosity and the development of textural banding, the production of a gneiss.

3. *Silicified siltstone/mudstone:* through metamorphism, silica is deposited into these rocks or replaces the original cement. Depending on the silica content, these rocks can flake very well. In hand specimen, the higher silica content can sometimes be seen in a "sparkle" to the rock when it is tilted to allow light to reflect from silica mineral surfaces.

4. *Quartzite:* quartzite is the most important metamorphic rock for flaked stone tools. Quartzite is sandstone altered such that when it is broken, the fracture does not break around the grains (as sandstone does), but rather the fracture passes through the grains (Best 1982:396). In some instances, rocks of this nature occur in unmetamorphosed circumstances and some geologists have referred to these sedimentary rocks as orthoquartzites; metamorphosed quartzites are termed metaquartzites in this scheme (Best 1982:396). Other geologists have noted that only quartz sandstones cemented with coarsely crystalline quartz or chert could break through the grains in this manner, however, and that the original definition of orthoquartzite referred only to sandstones with high quartz and chert content (a minimum of 75–90%) (Blatt et al. 1980:376). These workers favor retaining the term orthoquartzite for these sedimentary rocks having high silica content in the clasts without making any further restriction on the nature of the cement. Regardless, quartzites used for flaked lithic tools can be identified in hand specimen by their sugary to sparkling luster, this generally representing the fractured grain surfaces. Individual grains can often be seen in quartzites (with a microscope if not in hand specimen). Metaquartzites have undergone some recrystallization in the alteration process (Ehlers and Blatt 1980:516). For most purposes, quartzite, having finer grain size and a greater amount of silica cement to grain volume, is better for making flaked stone tools. There are many colors of quartzites.

5. *Gneiss:* a gneiss is any relatively coarse-grained metamorphic rock that shows banding (Bell and Wright 1985:45). Most premetamorphic structures like banding are destroyed during metamorphosis. Differential stresses are commonly produced during metamorphosis and, particularly when accompanied by formation of new minerals, these stresses result in the development of parallel structures (Ehlers and Blatt 1980:512). Gneissic texture is produced when the planar structures are due to textural differences in the minerals, such as granular versus prismatic, whereas schistosity is the result when the minerals are medium to coarse grained and platy (mica or chlorite, as in schist). Gneiss is often used as hammerstones, grindstones, and so on.

The material archaeologists often refer to as jade or greenstone is actually a number of different compounds variously identified as minerals or metamorphic rocks by geologists. "Jade" includes nephrite, jadeite, diopside, and aegirine, as well as varieties of these, such as bowenite and omphacite (Hammond et al. 1977:40–43; Bell and Wright 1985:154–160). Nephrite is an amphibole mineral, the others are pyroxene minerals. Both jadeite and diopside form as a result of metamorphosis of other minerals (Best 1982:371–374; Ehlers and Blatt 1980:618–624). Jade is a durable and very important lithic material that was commonly used for ground stone implements such as adzes, axes, and various ornaments.

3.4 Analysis Implementation

Researchers approach this step in analysis in many different manners, and many actually categorize the lithic materials types before they undertake the definition of whether tools are flaked stone or ground stone. In point of fact, it is usually most efficient to make both of these assessments at the same time and so segregate material into lots that are specifically categorized as flaked or ground with these divided into material types. In practice, most materials used for entirely flaked stone tools are rarely used for ground stone tools and so there is actually little overlap in this regard.

It is common to separate material into a number of initial categories that can be rapidly and easily segregated in hand specimen: sedimentary rocks, cherts, chalcedonies, obsidian, quartzites, and other metamorphic or igneous rocks. The basis for these categorizations are those outlined in this chapter, but usually it is texture/grain size, luster, translucence, and physical structure (e.g., layering) that are relied on for this initial segregation. It is also common to have an "unknown" category at this initial stage, for pieces that require closer examination to be categorized. Further divisions within these categories, and better definition of lithic types within the "unknown" category, usually require closer examination and often use of at least a low power microscope (about 40X). Finer divisions use many different features, of course. Even for those materials that cannot be more finely segregated, some basic divisions of color and grain size can be useful for looking at how different lithic materials are differently worked and used for different tasks. The finer categorization of lithic materials at this stage would also usually include separation of material types that can be identified to specific quarry sources. This process is the subject of the next chapter. Identification of lithic material from specific geographic locations allows us to trace patterns of trade, movement, and contact.

CHAPTER 4

Sourcing Lithic Materials

4.1 Introduction

Rocks and minerals characteristically vary in their structural and chemical composition from one area to another. These differences can be used to trace the origin of an artifact or the material used to make it. This knowledge in turn gives an indication of how trade networks and economic interaction occurred in the past.

Source determination can, in some cases, be done by examining macroscopic characteristics of the stone such as color, inclusions, and texture. More advanced chemical analysis techniques are usually required, however. Chemical sourcing has been particularly successful and widespread in examining obsidian use. In a restricted area, such as the Northwest Plains, it is possible to do some form of basic "sourcing" by classifying hand specimens. However, such sourcing can be quite difficult even in such a restricted area, so chemical sourcing is generally the only reliable method.

4.2 Sourcing by Non-Chemical Methods: Some Examples

It would not be possible to describe all the particular varieties of various lithic types that have been identified to specific sources, but some examples will indicate the types of criteria that have been used. For these examples I will turn to the northern Plains of Canada and the United States.

Probably the best known and most widely used lithic material from the northern Plains is Knife River flint (Clayton et al. 1970, Gregg 1987). This material has bedrock outcrops as veins and nodules in Dunn and Mercer counties in North Dakota. It is more widely distributed as a minor component of gravels in the Dakotas and into southern Canada. This material was used and traded as early as the Paleoindian period and was particularly widespread when used by Hopewellian people some 2,000 years ago. Since it is a chalcedony, it is translucent. It has a deep brown to honey-brown color. The brown may be swirled in appearance, looking almost mottled in these cases. It has white inclusions, commonly spherical in form. Its patina is white to a rather bluish white.

Another example is Swan River chert (Campling 1980). This material outcrops in the Swan River Valley in Manitoba, but is also found in limited quantities in gravel deposits where it was carried by the Laurentide ice sheet during the Pleistocene glaciations. These secondary deposits extend as far west as southeastern Alberta. Swan River chert is generally white to pink and from fine-grained to sufficiently coarse-grained to almost resemble a quartzite. When heat treated it acquires a pink to reddish-orange hue. A distinctive aspect of its coloring is a swirled, curdled-milk appearance.

A third example from this area is Top of the World chert, a fine-grained material outcropping in southeastern British Columbia. It varies from a gray translucent chalcedony to a gray chert and even to an opaque, blue-black chert. Gray colors and a waxy luster are typical. A key feature shared by all varieties is the presence of small black inclusions that can even be seen in the blue-black chert variety; these inclusions are fossilized sponge spicules.

4.3 Chemical Sourcing

A number of techniques are available to be used in looking at the actual chemical composition of a lithic material. Some of the most commonly and successfully employed techniques are:

1. *Thin section microscopy:* a technique that has been used for some 130 years for studying rock structure, minerals, and fossils. A sliver of rock is cut, usually using a diamond saw or thin wire saw, is polished smooth on one side, and then the polished side is mounted on a glass slide. The slice of rock is then ground to 30 nm thick on a grinding slab or wheel. Light will shine through a section of rock that is this thin and a polarizing microscope can be used to identify minerals (Hodges 1964:190–192). When polarized light is projected through mineral crystals, the light is refracted in a particular pattern based on the crystal structure of the mineral, in a manner similar to water droplets in the atmosphere refracting light to produce a rainbow. The resulting color patterns can be used to identify the minerals present in the rock. Many minerals can be identified in this manner. Various counting methods can be used to quantify the relative representation of the minerals present. Although minerals can be identified, specific elements (e.g., uranium, barium) cannot be identified. A major advantage of this analytical method is that gross aspects of the lithic material structure can be examined: fabric (particle orientation), crystal and grain morphology, cracking, texture, color, and so on. Many of these features can be useful in characterizing specific quarry sources. The basic problem that this method suffers from is that its ability to chemically characterize material is quite limited. It is also necessary to destroy part of a sample to undertake the analysis. This requirement can be at odds with the archaeological goal of artifact preservation.

2. *Heavy mineral analysis:* in this analytical technique, rock is crushed and either a heavy liquid or a magnetic separator is used to isolate certain of the rarer and more source-specific minerals (e.g., tourmaline, zircon, garnet). This type of analysis is limited, as is thin sectioning, as to which minerals can be identified. In addition, heavy mineral analysis does not have the advantage of being able to study rock structure. Quantification of the mineral composition can be difficult with this technique. The technique has the same disadvantages of thin section analysis: it is necessary to destroy part of the sample to undertake the analysis and only minerals can be identified, not elements.

3. *X-ray diffraction (XRD):* in this technique a small sample is bombarded with X-rays. The crystals in the sample deflect the X-rays (Hodges 1964:193). The altered pattern of the X-rays is recorded on photographic film, or a detector and chart recorder are used to count X-rays deflected at certain angles. The lines on a photograph or the peaks on the chart can be interpreted in relation to the structure of the mineral crystal that caused the deflection. The method can be quantitative (Cullity 1978:398–420). It mainly characterizes minerals. A portion of the sample is usually ground to a powder to homogenize the sample so that an atypical area is not tested. This situation means, of course, that a portion of the sample must be destroyed.

4. *Differential thermal analysis (DTA):* in this technique a powdered sample (0.1 gm) is heated under controlled conditions, and the amount of heat emitted or absorbed is measured. Various reactions occur in the sample due to its minerals undergoing physical changes and chemical reactions at various temperatures. These

reactions cause changes in energy emission. The emission pattern is typical of some minerals, but this technique is really more useful for clay mineral analysis. As with the other techniques discussed so far, a portion of the sample must be destroyed. The technique does not analyze elements, and it is not quantifiable.

5. *Electron microscopy:* electron microscopes are used mainly for studying morphology, texture, and other more general structural properties of lithic materials.

6. *Wet chemical techniques:* conventional chemistry can be used to identify certain compounds in lithic materials (Hodges 1964:192–193; Schüler 1971). These analyses are generally not as quantitatively accurate as may be required for sourcing studies. Conventional chemistry requires at least one gram of sample for analysis.

7. *Atomic absorption spectroscopy (AAS):* this technique is very useful and accurate and is commonly used. It is one of the best techniques to use for precisely determining the major, minor, and trace element composition of lithic materials. A sample in solution is sprayed into a flame and vaporized. Each element absorbs a particular wavelength of light. A monochromatic light of an appropriate wavelength for the element being analyzed is shone through the flame, and the amount of light absorbed is indicative of the concentration of that element in the sample. This is done separately for each of a number of elements, or a number of lamps are used simultaneously. The sample must be powdered and destroyed, but small samples (e.g., 0.2 gm) are often sufficient (Butler and Kokot 1971).

8. *Inductively coupled plasma emission spectrometry (ICPES):* this method is more rapid and produces less "noise" (interference) than does AAS, but it is a new technique that has not generally been available for use. Only a small sample (0.03 gm) is required. Argon gas is excited by radio waves to produce a plasma and the powdered sample solution is sprayed into the plasma. The sample atoms are then excited and emit light. This emitted light is measured and gives element types and concentration. This method is said to be more sensitive than AAS and XRF (X-ray fluorescence spectrometry, see below), but there are some compounds for which it cannot be used.

9. *X-ray fluorescence spectrometry (XRF):* this method is also called X-ray emission spectrography (Cullity 1978:423–441). A powdered sample is fused into a glass disc or pressed into a pellet and irradiated with X-rays or gamma rays. This causes the electrons to be excited and they emit secondary, or fluorescent X-rays. These fluorescent X-rays are characteristic of each element. The X-rays are then split into a spectrum (i.e., their various wavelengths) by an analyzer crystal; their energy is measured and a concentration can also be determined. This particular variation of the technique is called wavelength dispersive XRF (also called WDS) (Cullity 1978:421), and can only be used to analyze for one element at a time. Some ways of analyzing for more than one element at a time are also used, particularly energy dispersive XRF (or EDS). This latter method uses energy detectors rather than a crystal that splits the X-rays into wavelengths. It is somewhat less accurate (Blake 1990:30).

A major advantage of this technique is that it can be totally non-destructive, since the sample need not be powdered (but see Blake 1990:31). A very small area on a flat surface of a complete artifact can be bombarded. If the surface is not flat, the X-rays produced radiate out at various angles, and only a small amount reach the detector. Under these conditions concentrations cannot be calculated. Porous surfaces, such as obsidians with gas vesicles, suffer a similar problem. This problem can, of course, be overcome by powdering the sample. As well, if one assumes that all X-ray peaks are equally affected by the scattering of rays from an artifact surface, then the relative heights usually can be used to estimate concentrations and make it possible to source an artifact.

10. *Proton-excited XRF (or PIXE:* proton-induced X-ray emission): this technique uses protons (Fite et al. 1971:320) rather than X-rays to excite the sample electrons, but it is otherwise as XRF. The technique is more sensitive than XRF and may be used in a non-destructive fashion. The main disadvantage of the technique is that the equipment needed to produce protons is only available in a few research facilities. PIXE analysis only requires a few milligrams of material if a powder technique is used.

11. *Instrumental neutron activation analysis (INAA):* this method is often just called neutron activation analysis (NAA) (Dostal and Elson 1980:21-31; Fite et al. 1971:320–321). A small sample (< 0.1 gm) (e.g., Weigand et al. 1977:25) or a small artifact (making the method non-destructive in this latter case) is put in a nuclear reactor and bombarded with neutrons. Some elements undergo a nuclear reaction. As the radioactive isotopes decay they emit gamma rays. The gamma rays emitted are characteristic of each element and their intensity is indicative of concentration. This technique is very accurate and can be non-destructive (but see Weigand et al. 1977:26), but a nuclear reactor is required to produce the neutrons. This technique has been widely used and in particular has been useful in segregating cherts (e.g., Julig et al. 1989; Sheppard 1996).

12. *Electron microprobe analysis (EMPA):* this technique is used for element analysis, focusing on a mineral crystal or a similarly small single spot (Liebhafsky and Pfeiffer 1971:266–268). Several locations on a single piece may be analyzed. An electron beam is focused on the location and the electrons excite the elements in the mineral. X-rays are emitted as in XRF. Counting and quantification are the same as for XRF. A polished thin section is usually employed, but a complete artifact with a polished or flat surface can also be used (Hammond et al. 1977:41).

4.3.1 Main problems with chemical sourcing analysis

There are a number of issues in chemical sourcing which need to be noted:

1. The quarry sources must be systematically and thoroughly sampled to ensure that the total range in concentration of the various elements within the deposit is documented. Sedimentary rocks are particularly known for being highly, and often irregularly, variable. Due to the nature of the cooling process in igneous rocks, such as obsidian, there is a patterned variation in element concentration through many individual flows. Again, systematic sampling is a must if this variation is to be recorded. The detailed source sampling required has not been completed in many studies done in the past. The range in element concentrations assumed for each source based on such incomplete data may not reflect the actual range for certain sources. This means that some artifacts may be incorrectly ascribed to a particular source, or may be defined as unsourceable.

2. Each artifact is such a small sample of the original source that it may not reflect the element composition of the source very well. Under such circumstances an artifact may be misclassified. This situation can even be a problem for more generalized characteristics (e.g., material structure) used to source material, not just elemental composition (e.g., Hayden, Bakewell, and Gargett [1996:346–349]).

3. Concentrations and distributions of elements often overlap from one source to another. Separating each source from others can be difficult under these circumstances.

4. Unknown sources may exist. Such sources are often revealed in an analysis as a grouping of artifacts that fits none of the known sources, yet has a consistent concentration range for a series of elements.

Of the various chemical sourcing techniques outlined above, the ones that have been most used are neutron activation analysis, X-ray fluorescence spectrometry, and atomic absorption spectroscopy. Some examples of materials analyzed and the techniques used in their analyses are (methods in parentheses are ones not discussed above):

a. *obsidian:* just about every analysis technique has been tried on obsidian

b. *basalt:* neutron activation analysis

c. *marble:* (electron spin resonance), thin section analysis, (stable carbon isotope analysis)

d. *flint:* atomic absorption spectroscopy, thin section analysis, neutron activation analysis

e. *soapstone:* neutron activation analysis

f. *turquoise:* neutron activation analysis

g. *jade:* neutron activation analysis, thin section analysis

4.4 Analysis Implementation

The information obtained on quarry sources is central to reconstructing patterns of trade, seasonal movement, and contact with other people. These types of inferences are discussed and exemplified in Chapter 10. The basic data needed is the relative frequency of different material types (e.g., the percentage of total lithic material each known source represents by count or weight). General expectations are that the further a site is from a lithic quarry source, the less common that material will be in the site. In other words, people tend to use resources from local sources, when available, because it requires less effort. Where these expectations are not met we begin to see interesting aspects of human behavior. Closer sources may not have been within a group's usual territory; hence the source is not "socially" close. Strong representation of materials from distant sources may indicate social ties in that direction, these ties being of many types, but commonly were trading relationships or kin relationships. These distant sources may have been within a group's usual territory and more accessible than other sources despite their physical distance, or it may be that a particular material was preferred for reasons such as aesthetic appeal, spiritual significance, or because it worked better for particular tools and tasks.

To fully exploit the potential of this information, it is useful to further subdivide material types by form. This might include the percentage of each material type (finished tools, unfinished tools, flakes with cortex), each particular flake type or debitage category (see Chapter 5). The frequency of different sizes of pieces in each of these categories also gives much information. Different tool and debitage forms are produced at different junctures in the manufacturing process (the subject of the next chapter). Therefore, a frequency tabulation of the type and size of pieces in each lithic type gives a profile of lithic material use and associated human behavior. Normally distant lithic sources should be represented by mainly finished tools, and there should be little lithic debitage, because it is inefficient to transport lithic material from distant sources just to discard it. Distant lithic sources are rarely represented by large pieces, since it requires much energy or labor to bring large pieces of lithic material a great distance. Of course, in archaeological collections there are sites and particular lithic types that do go against these expected trends and they are especially revealing of the intricacies of human behavior. Simple frequency tabulations of lithic material types, and the specific form of the pieces in each material type, provide the basis for making such assessments.

CHAPTER 5

Lithic Reduction Strategies and Techniques

5.1 Introduction

Although this section will be basically about flaked stone tool manufacture, many of the general comments also apply to manufacturing ground stone tools. The study of lithic reduction essentially examines what happens to a piece of lithic material from the time it is obtained or quarried, through all the modifications it undergoes to become a tool, through the further modifications it may undergo as it is resharpened due to dulling or repaired due to breakage. This study includes everything that happens to the lithic piece, and its various portions and fragments, before it is ultimately discarded when it no longer has any function, or when it is lost. Obviously the actual quarrying process is the beginning of these events (see Ericson and Purdy [1984], Flenniken [1981], and Torrence [1986]).

There are a number of reasons why we try to reconstruct the entire process of manufacturing for the lithic tools we recover. The fundamental reason is that lithic tool manufacturing is a cultural process and cultural processes are the basis of archaeological study. By understanding the technology of lithic tool manufacture, we gain insight into the technological knowledge of a past people and how they used and combined those techniques to achieve their goals. We can see how skill and knowledge varied from one worker to another, and how individuals and cultures coped with problems as they arose. We gain an appreciation for the skill and traditional knowledge required to manufacture complex items, such as fluted Folsom points and Mayan eccentric flints. We can compare these reconstructions across larger geographic areas and through time to see how ideas originate and spread. We can use these patterns to study how different people achieve the same goals with radically different approaches, and we can illustrate the inventiveness of the human mind. To a limited extent we can actually integrate ourselves into the minds and ways of thinking of stone workers of the past. Not all archaeological sites in an area show all stages in the production of tools or particular tool types. By characterizing the manufacturing stages that occur in different sites, we begin to understand what type of site each is. In turn, we can link these spatially segregated manufacturing stages in differing sites to study the settlement pattern of a past people. This helps us understand how people utilize and adapt to their particular environment.

There are a number of different levels at which the lithic reduction process can be examined. In this section I will focus on three of these levels:

1. *Conceptualization of the overall process:* an overall production model or flow chart describing all the stages an artifact goes through to produce the end result (see Fig. 28 and Fig. 29).

2. *Analysis of specific stages:* based on what is actually done in each stage of the work, the products and debris from that stage will have particular features preserved on them. These features allow that production stage to be

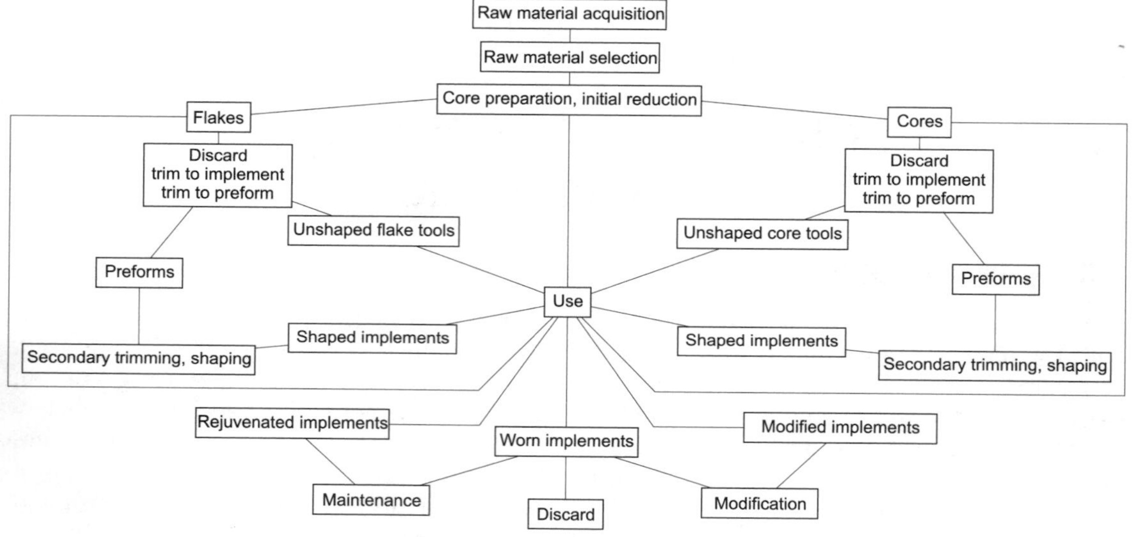

Figure 28: Reduction model example (adapted from Collins 1975)

defined or analytically isolated in any lithic assemblage.

3. *Manufacturing techniques:* based on the actual techniques used to achieve any particular end or ends in a reduction stage (e.g., what tool type was used to detach flakes), there will be features on the debitage end products that will allow definition of what manufacturing processes were used to shape the artifact into its desired form.

5.2 Conceptual Models

During the last 20 to 30 years, a common approach to lithic analysis has been to conceive of a series of definite stages a piece of lithic material must go through in its trajectory toward becoming a stone tool. In very general terms, an ancient stone worker first needed a piece of stone that was of an appropriate size and of sufficiently good quality that it could be worked into a tool. The flintknapper then had to work the piece to detach flakes until it was in roughly the form desired. In the final stage the worker then took a bit more care and carefully finished the tool, giving it the desired shape. Lithic reduction was viewed much like an assembly line, where the piece stayed in each stage for a defined period of time and had certain processes applied to it. This perspective leads to three basic definitions describing this continuum of events:

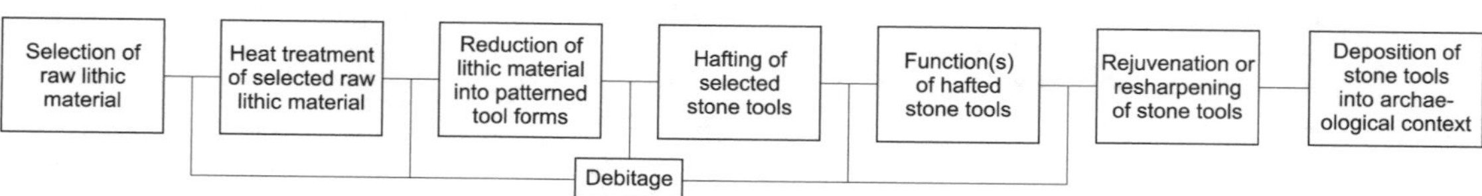

Figure 29: Reduction model example (adapted from Flenniken 1981)

1. *Blank:* a useable piece of lithic material of an appropriate size and quality to produce a desired artifact (Crabtree 1972; Debénath and Dibble 1994:10). It may be a totally unmodified piece (e.g., a river cobble); it may be a piece of quarried material that has had no other modification; or it may be a flake (or piece of shatter) that has been detached from a core. In the latter case the central point is that the piece has had no modification subsequent to its detachment.

2. *Preform:* a blank that has been further modified in some manner (Crabtree 1972). It is often possible to determine what type of artifact will ultimately be produced from the preform, depending on how far a piece was taken to get to the (usually culturally defined) preform stage. One of the problems with this division is that different researchers define blank and preform differently. Obviously, there is a production continuum involved and any point chosen as a boundary is arbitrary. Depending on the purpose of the analysis, it may be useful to define these forms differently. For example, it is common to define a preform as a piece that has been sufficiently altered so that the final form is obvious; a blank, then, would be any piece that had gone through the production sequence and modification to some stage *before* it was clear what the final form would be. I prefer not to use this latter definition because it can be very difficult to determine the intended use of the piece. If this subdivision is useful in analysis, the term "edged blank" (Whittaker 1994:201) is better to describe this stage.

3. *Finished product or tool:* Although this might seem simple to define, it can be difficult at times. For example, a preform for a handaxe might still serve perfectly well as a tool in its own right. It may be impossible to determine if the piece did or did not serve as a tool, or whether or not it was the end product. Similarly, it is generally felt that the final stage in manufacturing a projectile point was grinding the basal area where it is hafted to the shaft; this procedure prevents the point from cutting itself loose from the binding. But who is to say that such a procedure was always necessary, or whether or not edge grinding was completed several steps before the point itself was finished? A ground point might still be several stages before the finished tool stage.

Leaving these problems aside for the moment, these production stages and procedures are often put together into a general model (flow diagram) illustrating the complete production process (see Fig. 28 and Fig. 29). Although the use of such models can be abused, generally they do make a complex process comprehensible. However, the basic issue surrounding their use concerns how rigidly such models were adhered to in the real world and whether or not the production a stone tool is really more of a continuous process rather than a series of defined stages (e.g., Bradbury and Carr 1999). Particularly in Europe, in the use of the concept of *chaîne opératoire*, there is a strong suggestion that there are definite preconceived stages in the process and specific goals or end products for these stages (e.g., Debénath and Dibble 1994:22). More generally, it is agreed that a stone worker would have a mental template (an idea in mind of what he or she wished to make) (Rouse 1964). There is also general agreement that a flintknapper would have an idea in mind as to how to get from the unmodified piece of lithic material in hand to the finished product.

Some analysts feel that the mental template had to be rigidly adhered to and that only a small amount of variation was permissible. Certainly this was probably the case for some artifacts and is the kind of cultural norm that allows us to define artifact "types" from different time periods and cultures (e.g., specific projectile points, ceramic design). But others have argued that outside the realm of those highly specialized forms, the mental template was generalized, and quite a broad range of end products would have been acceptable. For example, a tool to cut meat can range from an unmodified but suitably shaped flake, to a highly worked knife of some description. The range of products the worker would be aiming for would *not* be this broad—it might simply be a range of edge retouched flake tools—but the extreme range gives an idea of the scope of what might be involved.

Along these same lines of thought, some researchers feel that there was a series of stages a piece had to go through to be considered a particular end product; such stages could not be ignored or substantially altered. Others argue that a stone worker had a number of avenues to potentially follow, all of which produced more or less the same or comparable results. Which of these particular pathways was chosen (and this is sometimes called pathway analysis) depended on a series of more immediate factors rather than a grand scheme devised at the onset. There are a series of feedback loops relating to various factors, such as raw material workability, flaws in the material, errors that occur, that are assessed after each blow or flake detachment (Young and Bonnichsen 1984). A particular pathway is eventually followed, not necessarily in a straight or direct route, to achieve the end product. These models are generally referred to as opportunistic or expedient. The argument would also theoretically extend to the suggestion that particular stages could be entirely abandoned, depending on the results of preceding work. There is also the question of whether the stone worker conceptualized lithic reduction in this fashion. From an archaeological analytical point of view, we can usually proceed without knowing the answer to this concern. Regardless of what the worker thought, we can arbitrarily divide up a sequence of events into analytically useful segments or stages. Although discussion has tended to cause a polarization of opinion, the idea that alternatives exist within each stage is actually a facet of the more rigid step-by-step models as well. Continuous and stage (*chaîne opératoire*) models of stone tool manufacture reflect different aspects of the same process.

The other main problem with these broad models is that for the most part they have been designed to characterize the production of complex tools, bifaces of one sort or another. A biface is a tool that has been extensively flaked over both of its major surfaces. Conversely, a uniface is a tool that has had all the flaking undertaken on one of the usually two major sides. Simple tools, such as edge modified flakes (tools with the bifacial or unifacial retouch confined to one or more edges), do not go through all the same stages. Basically, the finished form of such tools may be achieved by going through some aspects of only the early stages that would be definable for more extensively modified tool types. But even models such as Collins' that have been particularly criticized (e.g., Ingbar et al. 1989) for being rigid, step-by-step models, do account for the fact that, depending on the type of tool that is being produced, both primary and secondary trimming can be omitted.

A very important aspect of these models that must be considered is that they are largely based on our informed supposition, or in the better cases, with the added insight of replication experiments. The comment about use of largely informed supposition equally applies to the other aspects of lithic analysis, such as the features of lithic remains that relate to the types of techniques used and the stages an artifact went through during manufacture. We may not know all the procedures that were used in the past (Young and Bonnichsen 1984:135); in fact, we almost certainly do not know them all. If we do not conceive of these procedures, we do not structure our analyses to test for them. Many archaeologists construct their models and lithic analyses based on their own flintknapping experience. This is an excellent basis to start from, but it also has limits that must be recognized (e.g., Whittaker 1994:222–223, 234–237, 267). As Whittaker has said (1994:267), just because a modern flintknapper finds a procedure easy or efficient, there is not a guarantee that prehistoric flintknappers also felt this, or that they necessarily utilized the procedure; these are ideas to be tested. Even if a number of flintknappers pool their experience, they probably still do not know all possible approaches. Just as archaeologists have been concerned about the "tyranny of the ethnographic record" (Wobst 1978), the idea that all past human behavior must have been observed in historic period cultures, we must guard against allowing our modern experimental tool manufacturing to entirely govern our approaches to lithic analysis (see Thomas 1986). This archaeological problem is not unique to lithic analysis, of course. The principle of equifinality must also be considered here. Different combinations of factors can act in concert to produce the same end result. Given these circumstances, we may never know how some aspects of stone tool manufacture were accomplished. The basic approach to take in lithic analysis is to conceptualize the procedure in terms of a model, but at the same time be aware that the trajectory of the artifact through that sequence may change due to the results of any particular act in the production sequence (as Guy Muto [1971a] observed, in a sense the removal of each flake may be viewed as a stage in the reduction sequence). The work of Young and Bonnichsen (1984) shows very well how the flintknapper evaluates the results of each flake removal step to determine what the next step should be. It is also important to remember that stages for manufacturing simple and complex tools can vary considerably. Refitting manufacturing debris back together can also provide excellent insight into manufacturing processes, as Helen Leach (1984; Leach and Leach 1980) has shown (see Fig. 30).

Employing Collins' (1975) and Flenniken's (1981) models and augmenting them with others, particularly Magne's model (1985), the basic stages of lithic manufacture can be viewed in a systematic fashion. These stages are often termed reduction stages, since a larger piece of lithic material is shaped and *reduced* in size to produce a tool. In this view, a bifacial tool might go through the following stages:

1. The raw material is selected.

2. Blanks are produced.

3. A basic outline form is produced, essentially a shaping stage; much of this work may be confined to the edge of the tool (Collins' "primary trimming").

4. The tool is thinned and reduced in size to its basic form (a thinning/reduction stage) (this stage would probably also represent part of Collins' "primary trimming," but some of his "secondary trimming" as well).

5. The final form of the edge is modified as required (finishing stage) (part of "secondary trimming").

6. The tool is used.

7. A dulled tool may be resharpened (resharpening stage).

8. A broken tool may be repaired.

9. Discard.

Most of these stages and their division into steps in the reduction process require no explanation. Stages 3, 4, and 5, and the divisions between them, do require some justification however.

Whittaker (1994:202) described the first stage in biface production after selecting a blank as an edged blank, with the subsequent stage being a preform. The difference between the edged blank and preform stages was that the edged blank had flakes removed that were short and

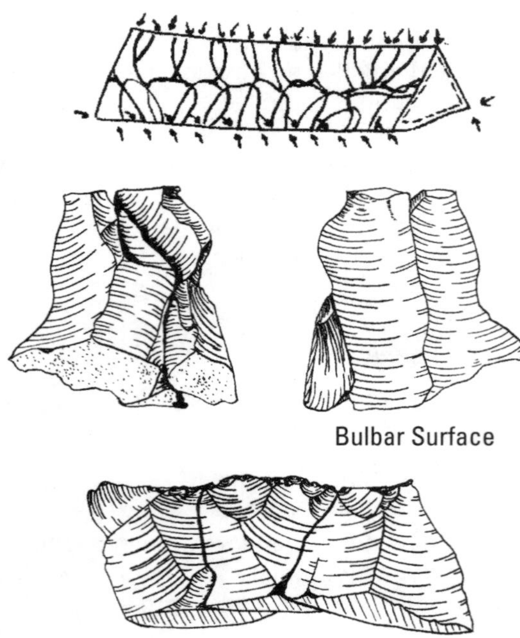

Figure 30: Refitting analysis used to examine manufacturing process (Leach and Leach 1980)

confined to the edges, whereas the preform stage employed flake removals that progressed well into the body of the tool (at least to the middle of the tool). His illustrations (1994:208–209) show that many of the flakes removed from the edged blank are very short and that all are confined to the objective piece edge. The edged blank stage Whittaker describes is what I have heard termed "shaping." Magne's student experiment instructions (1985:298) show marginal retouch to also be the initial stage in blank working in his approach to biface production. In the body of his study he mentions that his middle stage of reduction includes "...all the reduction events of marginal retouch tools, and the first half of the reduction events of all other tools..." (1985:106–107). He also states that marginal flakes and initial uniface and biface flaking involve edge straightening and mass reduction. Overall, then, Magne's research and approach to tool production includes a stage that encompasses a *shaping* of the blank outline. Bonnichsen also uses this approach: "...Bonnichsen removes excess material quickly, using pressure shaping flakes ..." (Young and Bonnichsen 1984:55) to prepare a flake blank edge for working. When Bonnichsen does this, he exerts pressure more or less straight down and so the flakes removed are short and create a bad angle that he then alters by removing a series of short, edge thinning flakes. Callahan also moves the edge in rapidly initially, using a shearing technique (Young and Bonnichsen 1984:81). This creates a broad edge because, again, the flakes do not progress far into the tool body. Callahan then thins the margins to reduce the edge angle for subsequent working. Young and Bonnichsen's monograph illustrates the nature of these flakes well (1984:183, 185, 191–194). The description of pressure shaping flakes for both Bonnichsen and Callahan shows that small flakes (1984:98) dominate this action. Based on these studies of flintknapping, then, there clearly is a shaping stage and this stage would be characterized by a short flake that is confined to the objective piece edge.

What I have defined as a finishing stage is also clear in studies of modern flintknappers. Whittaker notes (1994:203) that a biface can be finished in a number of ways, but that it is common to use careful soft hammer percussion or pressure flaking. He illustrates a biface that has been so treated (1994:211) and the key difference is the removal of a number of small flakes from the edge area. Such small flakes I call finishing flakes. A finishing stage is also defined for Callahan and Bonnichsen in the study by Young and Bonnichsen (1984:82). Magne also has a final stage in biface manufacture that entails straightening the edges and aligning and sharpening the biface point (1985:298). The finishing stage, then, seems common to a variety of flintknappers and seems a reasonable stage to define. The small finishing flakes would characterize the stage. The thinning and reduction stage would encompass the events between these two stages.

5.3 Reduction Stage Analysis

Before looking specifically at how reduction stages can be isolated in lithic assemblages, two specialized flake types need to be defined:

1. *Thinning flake:* a specialized category of secondary flake. It is specifically the flake type removed to thin and reduce one of the major sides of a biface or uniface. It is fairly thin, of generally moderate size ("moderate" depending in turn on the size of the tool being produced), and generally has moderate to complex patterns of previous flake scars on its dorsal surface.

2. *Bifacial reduction flakes:* thinning flakes that are specifically detached in biface thinning and reduction. These flakes are generally of moderate size and show fairly complex flake scarring on the dorsal surface and striking platform. The angle formed between the striking platform and flake dorsal surface (exterior platform angle) is quite acute—generally about 35° to 65°. The flake usually has a lip between the striking platform and the bulb (or initiation area for a bending flake) on the ventral aspect. Often these flakes tend to expand toward the distal end and tend to be rather curved (Whittaker 1994:185–187). The general order in which flakes are removed in lithic reduction to produce a bifacial tool is as follows:

1) decortication and generalized "secondary" flakes

2) shaping flakes

3) thinning/reduction flakes

4) bifacial reduction flakes

5) finishing flakes

6) resharpening flakes

The material presented in the next two sections is also summarized in Fig. 31.

5.3.1 Reduction stages

Some initial aspects of the tool manufacturing process have a significant impact on the subsequent debitage left in archaeological sites. The first important aspect is whether the piece of lithic material used as a starting point or blank in the production process is a flake (or a piece of shatter), or if it is a large piece of raw material, such as a river cobble or block of quarried stone. Obviously, however, even the production of a flake must begin with a larger piece of raw material as a core. The second important aspect is whether the stone tool being produced is simple or complex in terms of the modification required to manufacture it. There is considerable contrast between manufacturing tools that require modification and shaping of only the edges of the piece, and those requiring much more complex flaking and working over most of the tool surface, such as in the production of a uniface or biface.

Cortex (here used to denote *any* outer altered rock or mineral surface, as discussed in Chapter 2), the thin surface layer of altered material present on many lithic fragments, has long been used as a key indicator of stage in the reduction process. Generally, the presence of cortex is only characteristic of very early reduction stages, given that cortex represents the outer unmodified surface of a piece (Magne 1985). Mauldin and Amick (1989:70) found that essentially all cortex was removed from a core by half way through reduction events for that core. They also found that the percentage of cortex-covered debitage was very consistent from one core

EARLY	MIDDLE		LATE		
No usewear	No usewear	No usewear	No usewear	No usewear	Has usewear
Large, thick	Small	Most thin	Most thin	Small	
Cortex common	Short	Most elongate	Most elongate	Short	
	Rounded outline	Medium exterior platform angle	Acute exterior platform angle	May have acute exterior platform angle	
Little dorsal perimeter scarring		No lip	Lipped	May have lip	
	Little scarring	Medium scarring	Complex scarring	Complex scarring	
Cores Blanks Reduction debitage	Shaping	Thinning	Bifacial reduction flake	Finishing	Resharpening
0-1 platform scars	Two platform scars		Three or more platform scars		
0-1 shatter dorsal scars	Two shatter dorsal scars		Three or more shatter dorsal scars		

Figure 31: Characteristics of reduction stage debitage

reduction to another if the size of the flakes was also considered (1989:72–73) (i.e., if the cortex cover was compared within the same size debitage). The early stages of stone working will result in flakes characterized by cortex on the dorsal surface and these cortex-bearing flakes are very good indicators of the early stages of stone tool manufacturing. Shatter produced at this stage also typically has cortex on the "dorsal" surface, although the nature of shatter means that a true dorsal surface is difficult to define; the presence of cortex obviously indicates an original outer, (dorsal) surface. In contrast, then, secondary flakes (and shatter) lacking dorsal cortex are obviously good indicators of later stages in the manufacturing process.

There are other good indicators of the early or initial stages of stone tool manufacture. Anvils and hammerstones (especially large hammerstones), and other fabricators, are usually associated with these initial stages. Cores and core fragments are also good indicators of early stages, although obviously this depends on whether or not cores are used as the initial point of the reduction process. Large pieces of shatter also generally relate to these stages in the process, as do pieces of unaltered raw material (the stockpile from which worked stone was selected). It is worth noting here, however, that all stages in the reduction process are dominated by *small* debitage in terms of frequency (Mauldin and Amick 1989:78). However, if there is any large debitage, it is probably a result of an early reduction stage.

When a flake is removed from a piece of lithic material that is being worked, ridges are left on the surface of the worked piece where the flake-producing fracture intersects its surface (see Fig. 12 and also Fig. 32), the removal of the flake resulting in a negative impression (a flake scar) defined by the ridges. As additional flakes are removed from the piece, additional flake scars are produced. The scars may intersect, producing an even more complex pattern of ridges and scars. As a flake or a cobble (objective piece) is worked and flaked to produce a tool, more and more such flake scars are left on its surface. When a flake is removed later in the production sequence, it is almost certain to have more flake scars on its dorsal surface than would a flake

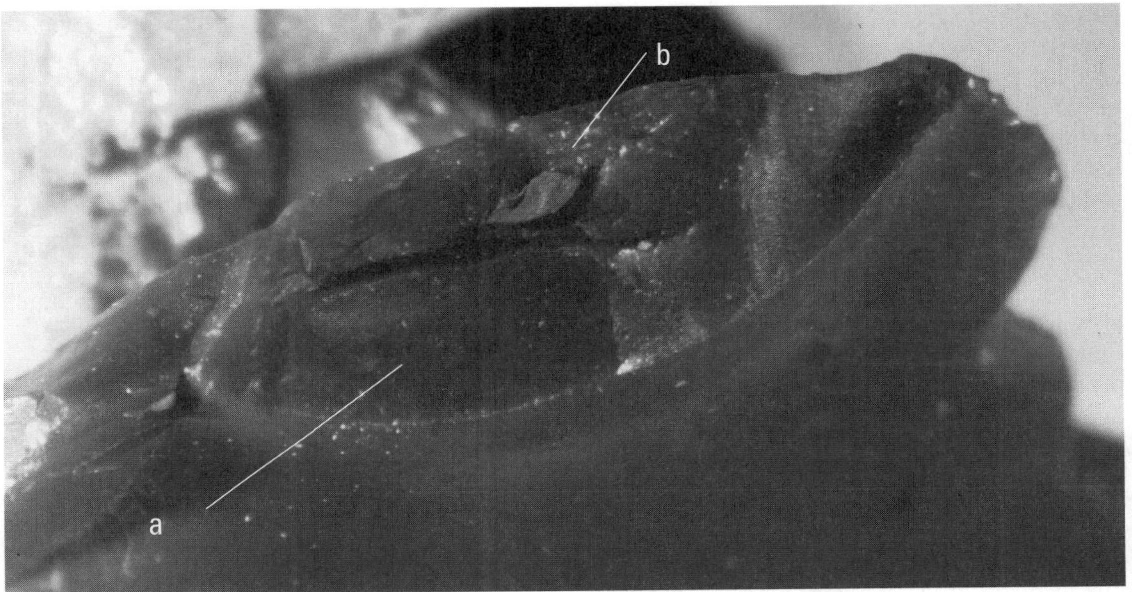

Figure 32: Flake scar formation on the striking platform ('a' indicates one of the striking platform flake scars and 'b' indicates an area of small step scars as a result of platform grinding. These latter small scars are not included in the platform scar count.)

from an earlier stage. Such flakes are removed from a scarred surface; hence their dorsal surfaces will be scarred. As with the amount of dorsal cortex cover, the complexity of the dorsal scarring on debitage flakes is a good indicator of the stage in the production sequence from which they are derived (Ingbar et al. 1989:124; Magne 1985:129). The same situation applies to shatter. Some studies have found that the density of scars per unit area is more closely associated with the stage than is the actual number of scars (e.g., Ingbar et al. 1989:124). This is because the number of scars preserved on a piece also depends on flake surface area (e.g., Mauldin and Amick 1989:73), with larger flakes logically also having more dorsal surface scars (though no more if surface area is also accounted for). Ingbar and colleagues (Ingbar et al.1989:126) derived equations to isolate core reduction from tool manufacture, finding the use of flake thickness, density of dorsal scar count, and flake surface area to provide good separation. In their studies, both Magne (1985:111–113) and Mauldin and Amick (1989:74) counted only scars greater than 5 mm in size.

In a similar fashion to the dorsal scarring of flakes, the number of flake scars on the striking platform of flakes increases as flakes are removed later in the manufacturing sequence (Magne 1985:129). Initially the striking platform is likely to be cortex or a portion of a single flake scar. But as the pattern of scarring on the tool becomes more criss-crossing and complex, so too will the pattern of scars on the location chosen for striking off flakes in the manufacturing process (Fig. 32). Particularly in the latter stages of tool production, striking platforms are specially prepared to assist in the removal of a particular type of flake to achieve a particular purpose. This preparation process also tends to produce more complex platform scarring patterns. For example, a small isolated platform may be prepared to concentrate and aim the force of a blow and hence the direction of removal and length and width of a flake. Due to the small size of flake striking platforms, all platform scars were counted in Magne's research (1985:113–114).

The degree of scarring on flakes is particularly important in differentiating the functions of small flake debitage and its position in the production sequence. Small flakes are generally detached from the immediate edge of tools and have three basic purposes:

1) shaping occurs in the early middle stage of the production sequence. Small flake removal is used to give the objective piece the basic outline form of the tool being produced. This process essentially entails chipping away irregularities, etc.

2) finishing occurs in the final stage of tool manufacture. Small flakes are detached to remove irregularities left from manufacturing to give the tool its final edge form (in the case of edge modified tools, this stage does not always exist; (1) above can be the working that produces the appropriately formed edge). (Note: finishing flakes have been referred to as sharpening flakes, but since they do not actually render the edge more sharp than an unmodified flake edge, the term finishing is more appropriate.)

3) resharpening occurs once a tool has been used and becomes dull. Small flakes may be removed to resharpen the edge.

Small flakes removed at the shaping stage will have few flake scars on the dorsal surface and on the striking platform. Those removed in the final finishing stage will have more scarring. Those removed in resharpening will also have scarring, but in addition these resharpening flakes should have a portion of a dull, rounded edge. This rounded edge is a remnant of the used tool edge, the portion removed in the resharpening process to give a fresh, sharp working edge.

Magne (1985) developed a model for assigning debitage to reduction stage categories based on experimental manufacturing of bifaces, primarily from basalt. His approach employed platform scar counts on flakes and dorsal scar counts on shatter in the following manner:

1) 0–1 scars = early stage (core reduction)

2) 2 scars = middle stage (shaping and early reduction)

3) 3 or more scars = late stage (finishing)

Although Magne did not specifically consider resharpening, resharpening flakes would generally fall into his late reduction stage. Odell's analysis supports Magne's data that 0–1 flake scars on the striking platform is an attribute largely associated with earlier reduction stages (Odell 1989:197).

In regards to segregating these various small flake types in analysis, it is worth noting that shaping flakes have few ridges, since they have few dorsal scars; hence the fracturing force is not concentrated by ridges. Instead, the force of the detaching blow expands outwards. Consequently, shaping flakes tend to be oval-shaped or distally expanded. Flakes removed to prepare a striking platform also tend to have this shape and to be even smaller. Although problems may arise in segregating these two flake types, other evidence for core reduction (discussed below) can be used to help address this issue.

Research has indicated that reduction stage and task is also reflected in the percentages of complete flakes, incomplete flakes, and shatter. Although not based on experimental data, Sullivan and Rozen (1985:762–763) suggested that intensive core reduction was characterized by a high percentage of shatter in the lithic remains (over 20% versus less than 10%) while unintensive core reduction was characterized by a high percentage of cores (some 15% versus less than 3%) and complete flakes (50% versus 20–30%). In this scenario, intensive core reduction presumably results in reduction of cores to unrecognizable fragments, although Henry's suggestion (1989:140) that still useable cores have facets similar in size to blanks seems a more objective criterion to use. Sullivan and Rozen also found that tool manufacture was characterized by a low frequency of cores (less than 1%) and a low frequency of complete flakes (some 20% versus about 30%). Baumler and Downum (1989:106) found core reduction to yield higher percentages of shatter compared to scraper manufacture (30–35% versus less than 10%), as well as lower percentages of complete flakes (less than 20% versus more than 30%). On the other hand, Mauldin and Amick's study (1989:83–84) shows that hammerstone type can also have a significant effect on the frequency of broken flakes. In their study, an antler billet produced about 15% complete flakes while other hammerstones yielded an average of about 60% complete flakes. Prentiss and Romanski (1989:94) found that trampling of a biface production assemblage increased the frequency of medial and distal flake fragments from about 30% of the flake assemblage to about 50%, and they suggested (1989:93) that less brittle lithic material should produce more complete flakes. Ingbar and colleagues (Ingbar et al. 1989:121–122) found that their data, as well as that of Prentiss and Romanski (1989), indicated that core reduction was characterized by fewer complete flakes than was biface production (35–60% for biface production, versus 15–35% for core reduction). Clearly, there are some inconsistencies in these studies. Given that Sullivan and Rozen did not do experimental work, their suggestions are most likely to be misleading.

Tools and broken tool fragments can also indicate which manufacturing process stages occurred at a site. If tools are made on large pieces of raw material rather than on flakes, the initial stages of manufacture are indicated by cobbles and similar large pieces, with only a few flakes removed in a patterned fashion. If tools are made on flakes, large flakes produced but rejected as blanks may indicate this early stage (here it is important to remember that flakes suitable as blanks will probably be further reduced and so will be absent from the assemblage [Magne 1985:98; Tomka 1989:139]). Tools rejected during the manufacturing process, and remaining unfinished, will indicate a particular intermediate reduction stage was undertaken since the piece in question was rejected at that stage. The final manufacturing stage is often indicated by grinding on some portion of a tool edge, this being related to hafting and the need to dull an edge so that the tool edge does not cut the binding (plant fiber, leather, and so on). A well-defined, regular outline may indicate this stage for tools that did not require final grinding.

5.3.2 Practical approaches to analysis

In determining whether flakes, or simply large pieces of raw material, were used as blanks for tool production, unfinished tools are the easiest materials to examine to make the assessment. If flakes were used, flake features will likely still be visible. Such features often include possession of obvious dorsal and ventral faces, a striking platform, compression rings and fissures, and a bulb of percussion. Such features may also be visible in finished tools. The presence of probable flake blanks and the presence or absence of cores and core fragments are other indicators.

Flake blanks are produced from cores by two basic methods: bipolar cores and platform cores. Bipolar cores are usually unmodified pebbles or cobbles that are placed on an anvil and then struck with a hammerstone. As an alternative to the hand-held method, the hammerstone may be thrown to impact the core if the anvil and core are first buried in sediment leaving only a small target platform exposed on the core. Previously modified pieces, such as other core fragments or large pieces of shatter, may also be reworked by bipolar percussion. Platform cores are cores from which flakes have been detached but which are not rested on an anvil in the detachment process.

Bipolar cores have a number of features that allow them to be recognized in an archaeological assemblage:

1) often small flakes have been removed from, and battering and/or small tabular scarring is present on, two opposite ends of the core (this *may* occur on only one end)

2) flakes have been removed from one or both faces, these flakes often extending the entire length of the core; the flake scars often leave no negative bulb of percussion, or possess a sheared bulb of percussion

3) the cores may be slightly convex in profile (as a result of having removal of less lithic material in the center of the core, where the flakes tend to become thinner)

4) the cores have no ventral flake scar, as opposed to bipolar flakes which do, since they were not originally flakes

5) the cores are sometimes rotated and have had flakes removed in the same fashion but at right angles to the initial series, as a result sometimes having two opposing platforms and/or areas of battering

6) the cores often have cortex on several aspects, showing the original piece was a pebble (if such artifacts have no bipolar fracturing features such as impact scars, they are often simply classified as split pebbles)

The fracturing process results in features on bipolar flakes that render them somewhat like bipolar cores, so it is appropriate to describe them as well. Bipolar flakes tend to have damage at opposing ends as does the sheared bulbar surface of bipolar cores. These features set them apart from other flake types. Bipolar flakes also often have patches of cortex in more than one location if the original pebble/cobble core was cortex-covered and if more than one set of flakes has been removed. They are quite thin and flat, more so than bipolar cores generally, and the central distinguishing feature of bipolar flakes compared to bipolar cores is that they do have a positive bulb of percussion, albeit usually very diffuse and sheared. The striking platforms of bipolar flakes tend to be small, and often essentially non-existent.

Platform cores are any larger stone fragments that have had a series of flakes removed from them in a non-bipolar manner. They may have a single platform from which the flakes were struck, or a number of different surfaces may have been used as platforms (these latter are then called multiplatform cores). Sometimes the placement of these multiple striking platforms seems unpatterned and the cores may be referred to as random cores; although such cores may represent rather unpatterned opportunistic use of the piece, this is not necessarily the case. The location of these removals is generally well planned. It has been suggested (Odell 1989:172, 194) that cores generally have strong, 90° platform/core face angles and so there is little need to grind their platforms to remove overhang, etc., when they are being prepared. For this reason, core reduction flakes are characterized by minimal dorsal perimeter scarring below the striking platform (see Fig. 33). In experimental testing, Odell found that all core reduction flakes had less than half the perimeter exhibiting such scarring. In contrast, later reduction stages generally showed dorsal scarring on about half or more of the perimeter (though

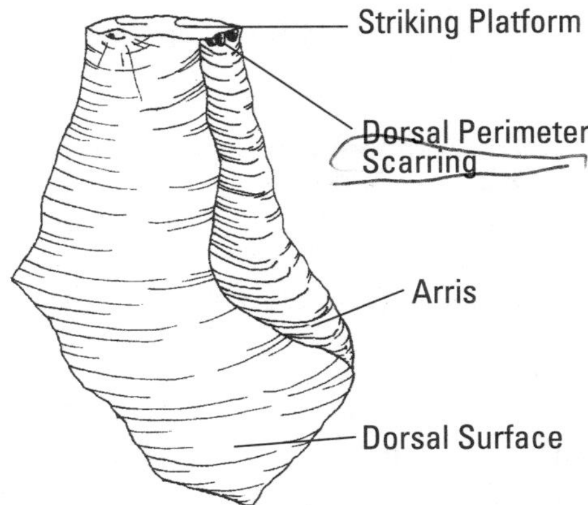

Figure 33: Dorsal perimeter scarring

not along the entire perimeter). As a result, flakes exhibiting minimal dorsal perimeter scarring, as well as cores themselves, can be used to infer the reduction of cores in an archaeological assemblage. Odell also found that bulbar scars (eraillure scars) were present on about 35–40% of core reduction flakes, versus being present on only 15–30% of the flakes from other types of reduction (1989:195). Odell also noted that the early stages in bifacial reduction showed less dorsal perimeter scarring than did later stages, as well as less platform modification (faceting, grinding, etc.) (1989:183, 197).

Examination of the finished tools from an assemblage gives a direct indication of whether the tools produced were edge modified only or if they were more extensively worked into unifaces or bifaces. It is common, particularly in the case of bifaces, for tools to be removed from the manufacturing (or use) site. In such circumstances, the only trace remaining will be the manufacturing debris left behind. As already discussed, a particular flake form, the bifacial reduction flake (BRF), is associated with the process of producing bifaces. The presence of this flake type can be used as an indicator of biface production whether or not any bifaces are present in the site remains (but as Ahler (1989:212) has noted, such "characteristic" flakes may be produced in small numbers in other reduction stages, so care in interpretation is needed).

A basic rule of debitage analysis is that in assigning a piece of debitage to a stage when there seems to be more than one possibility, assign it to the most advanced (latest) stage. For example, if a flake seems both a bifacial reduction flake (BRF) and a finishing flake, assign it to the finishing category. The reason for suggesting this approach is that each later stage builds from a piece of the preceding stage. Sometimes, even often, a piece does retain features of that preceding stage. In the finishing/BRF example, if an essentially completed biface is given the final finishing retouch on the edges, each of these flakes will have the form of a BRF (lipping, etc.) because it has been taken from a biface edge. The flake will, however, have been intended to be confined to the edge and so it will be unlike a true BRF, which would be more elongate so as to progress into the body of the tool. The flake in question will be short. Also remember that flake types are idealized types and so they might best be conceived of as following a normal distribution. Most flakes of a type will have the average form, but various individual circumstances will work together to produce a flake that is "atypical", on the tails of the normal distribution, such as a finishing flake that looks like a shaping flake.

In prioritizing flake features to define flake types in reduction analysis, a number of reasonable guidelines can be followed. The first guideline is that if the flake has rounding from use, particularly at the juncture between the striking platform and the dorsal surface of the flake, it is a resharpening flake *regardless of* its specific form. Obvious, well-developed rounding from use is often visible with a regular binocular microscope at about 30–40X magnification. The key point is obviously that the usewear identifies the flake as having come from a used tool edge and so, as a used tool, it has already gone through all the manufacturing stages it was "intended" to go through. Also remember that not all tools are formal bifaces. There are also edge modified flakes, utilized flakes, etc., which undergo little manufacturing modification prior to use. Despite being minimally altered, these specimens are completed tools and the flakes removed from them after use represent resharpening of a used tool.

With a little practice, the sharpness of the edge can be judged initially by feeling the juncture between the striking platform and the flake dorsal surface with the finger. Non-rounded edges "catch" the fingerprint ridges and often give the impression that the finger will be cut if it is pushed too hard onto the edge. If the edge feels more rounded, be certain that the piece does not have cortex or a secondary patina development that is giving this impression. Platform grinding "shatters" the juncture between the platform and dorsal surface; hence it is not rounded in the same way as rounding from use. A ground platform often feels sharp because the grinding has created a new (sharp) edge. Under the microscope most of the platform edge will look like shattered glass (Fig. 34) and usually will have only isolated patches of pebble-like textured rounding (Fig. 35). Many resharpening flakes do not evidence obvious rounding and low level magnification (30–40X) and macroscopic assessment will only identify the most blatant resharpening flakes. These flakes will probably be almost exclusively those from tools used on hard materials (e.g., wood or bone) or used to prepare hides.

Resharpening flakes will usually be relatively small, but big tools such as choppers and handaxes can also be resharpened and so care in using this assessment criterion is needed. Also, of course, resharpening flakes can be removed to change tool form or repair a tool. In a sense they may not be "resharpening" flakes, but regardless they are still late stage flakes removed from an already used edge.

Large, thick, usually irregularly shaped flakes are often produced, usually in the early stage of lithic reduction. These flakes cannot be classified as one of the more specialized flake types and are simply defined as primary decortication flakes, secondary decortication flakes, or secondary flakes. *Not all decortication flakes* are automatically grouped into this category and most secondary flakes can be more specifically classified as other flake types (e.g., sharpening, bifacial reduction, etc.). This group of flakes is generally associated with core preparation, are blanks from cores, may be due to other lithic block preparation, or may even be from early stages of "bulk reduction" (or occasional other random events). These flakes can be generally characterized as being at least 0.5 cm thick and at least 6–7 cm long, but of course there can be exceptions to these guidelines. These flakes are sometimes noticeably irregular in outline form and/or thickness. Large pieces of shatter also occur at this early stage in reduction, these generally being about 3 cm or more in size (although, again, this is only a general guideline, a 1 square cm piece of material is a pretty large piece of material to come from a more finished tool).

Shaping, finishing, and resharpening flakes are *usually* small. These flakes are all usually less than 2 cm in length.

Shaping flakes are both non-complexly scarred and short. It would be very rare for these to be at all elongate and they are likely to be approaching an overall oval to circular outline shape (due to an absence of flake scar ridges on the dorsal surface; hence an absence of flake elongation, as previously noted; see also Whittaker [1994:105–106]). Finishing and resharpening flakes are often more elongate. Platform scars should be 2 (less commonly 0–1, but 2 scars should be most common; initial outline shaping flakes on a flake blank will have 1 scar and initial outline shaping flakes on a split cobble will have 0 or 1, but rapidly the working

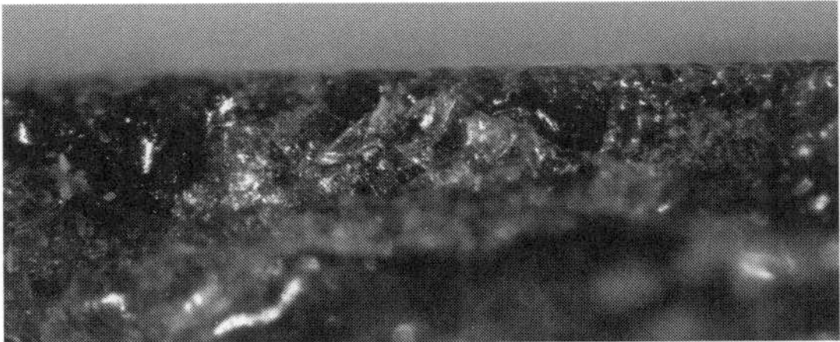

Figure 34: Ground striking platform shattered edge area

Figure 35: Ground striking platform rounded edge area

will begin to produce primarily flakes with two platform scars as the shaping progresses) (Magne 1985). I generally find dorsal scars to be up to about 4 to 6, though usually less (as already noted, scar *density* is probably the most appropriate measure of complexity to use for the highly variable surface area of flake dorsal surfaces). Overall flake form is the best criterion to use when in doubt. Shaping flakes *can* be more elongate, if the blank used is already quite thin, and so even early flakes can be made to progress well into the tool interior, or if the outline form of the blank is fairly acceptable right from the start. The former circumstance pertains especially if ridges can be progressively developed into the tool body by building in from a narrow end of the tool. However, most intentional shaping flakes should be of the normal, shorter form. Shaping flakes can be somewhat thicker than finishing flakes, but are often as thin. Where they are thicker, this is usually noticeable in the more proximal portion of the flake and less often in the more distal portion.

Finishing flakes are short, small, and complexly scarred (and lack usewear). They are thin, usually no more than 1–2 mm in thickness. If the flake in question has BRF features such as lipping, it is still a finishing flake if it is *short* since this shows it to be a flake intended for edge modification only. A BRF should be elongate to progress into the body of the tool on the assumption that these flakes are final overall modifying and form-smoothing removals. The "non-elongate" aspect is a key one to assess, rather than just relatively small overall size, since finishing flakes on a large biface (such as a handaxe) could be relatively large overall, though still not elongate. There is a problem with relying uncritically on the non-elongate aspect to distinguish between finishing flakes and BRF: small, elongate BRF could be used to modify an edge, and this might be especially desirable since flakes confined specifically to the edge may result in an edge that suddenly becomes substantially thicker. Such an edge becomes ineffective as a tool further into the tool interior and beyond the finishing flake scars. Finishing flakes generally have three or more scars on the striking platform. Although I am not aware of any specific experimental research looking at flake dorsal scarring complexity, my impression is that finishing flakes characteristically have at least 5 or 6 dorsal scars; I use this particularly when I am trying to determine if a flake is a finishing flake or a shaping flake. Finishing flakes from minimally retouched tools are most problematic to isolate, since they may lack complex scarring.

Bifacial reduction flakes are elongate, thin, often noticeably convex dorsally and concave ventrally, have lipping, and are complexly scarred. The lipping and elongation are the key traits. Possession of these two alone is a sufficient basis to assign a flake to this category, in my opinion, although I would be surprised if many BRF were not thin as well. If flakes have these features but lack lipping, they are from an earlier juncture in the reduction of the biface (when the edge angle, and so the exterior platform angle, was less acute and so bending initiations did not occur often; see below). These latter flakes are then thinning flakes. BRF are basically late stage thinning flakes. If the flakes have lipping but are short, they are finishing flakes.

Thinning flakes, then, are definitely elongate and thin and have complex scarring but lack lipping. The absence of lipping is, again, a result of the greater exterior platform angle of the piece at this juncture in the reduction process and the resultant absence of bending initiations. The earliest thinning flakes may lack the complex scarring and may be rather thicker, but they will always be elongate and there should not be many examples of this unusual thicker form in an assemblage. Thinning flakes and BRF will almost always be relatively thin as well: removing a long thick flake from a blank—which is by its nature quite small—would break most blanks/preforms. Thinning flakes may be somewhat thicker than BRF overall. Like BRF, thinning flakes tend to be concave ventrally and convex dorsally when the cross section of the flake is examined along a proximal to distal line. Like BRF, thinning flakes should be elongate so that the flake progresses well into the body of the tool being manufactured. Unlike BRF, based on Magne's analysis (1985) thinning flakes should usually have 2 platform scars whereas BRF should usually have 3 platform scars.

Earlier flakes are the result of core preparation and blank production, or of working a cobble/core block into the initial shape if not beginning from a flake blank. Thick, potentially quite large flakes should be the diagnostic results of this stage. Cortex is likely to be much more common in this stage, if the original raw material had cortex. Because blank production is a main feature of this stage, short flakes will not be the usual result and this should distinguish the core reduction stage from the shaping stage. An exception is production of a "core tool" from a large block of material or a weathered pebble/cobble. However, since this essentially begins from a shaping stage to form the piece into an appropriate outline, this reduction could be viewed as beginning at the shaping stage when "core tools" are produced. In this type of beginning, the initial shaping flakes may be considerably thicker and may have more cortex than is usually the case for shaping flakes.

Core preparation debitage may be, and often will be, much different. If cores are only minimally prepared, the flakes may largely lack dorsal perimeter scarring, although, certainly, well prepared cores (like blade cores) will have dorsal perimeter scarring. Generally the presence of cores, core fragments, and hammerstones should help in recognizing this stage. Large flakes removed to produce a single, relatively flat striking platform on the core may be present, as may specialized core preparation flakes such as crested blades (Bordes and Crabtree 1969; Whittaker 1994:232). Bipolar fragments (cores or flakes) may be present if cobbles or pebbles are split open and then worked as blanks. Particularly in this latter case, anvils may also be present.

5.3.3 *Determining platform boundaries and scar counts*

Defining the boundaries of a flake striking platform, and determining which scars to count on both platforms and dorsal surfaces, are skills that develop with increased experience. The following guidelines can be used to make these judgments.

When counting flake and shatter dorsal surface scars, based on the conventions already established (as previously discussed based on

Magne [1985:111–113] and Mauldin and Amick [1989:74]) only scars with a width of at least 5 mm are included. Normally scars located on an edge that seem to be from trampling, other damage, or occasional use, and "nibbling" scars along a dorsal ridge, are not counted since they do not come from the reduction process *per se*. Scars at the platform boundary of the dorsal surface are also not counted if it is probable that they are from edge grinding and other platform preparation, again based on the assumption that they are not particularly related to the reduction processes on the dorsal surface (see below also). Sometimes a large scar does originate at this boundary and it may be appropriate to include such a scar in the dorsal count. Dorsal surface modification does originate at tool edges, obviously, and care should be taken to include relevant scars originating in the platform area.

Platform boundaries can be difficult to identify. In problematic cases, following the curve of the platform ventral edge, where it meets the ventral surface of the flake, can be the easiest approach to use. The lateral margins of the platform are located where this ventral curve meets the flake dorsal surface (see right hand side of Fig. 32). Often the flake margins incline more steeply beyond this location as well, particularly in instances where the platform partially collapsed when the flake was detached. It is important *not* to include these inclined surfaces as "scars" in the platform scar count.

Normally all scars on a platform are included in the scar count. This is based on the fact that the platform represents such a small portion of the original tool surface that even small scars are likely to be simply small portions of much larger original scars. Although removing platform overhang generally detaches flakes from the dorsal surface (dorsal perimeter scarring) because the grinding is "downwards," both faceting and platform grinding may remove flakes from the striking platform surface since the direction of force is "along" the objective piece edge or "into" the body of the piece (Whittaker 1994:99–105). The flakes detached in overhang removal and platform grinding are usually small and are not part of the general reduction process that analysis seeks to measure in scar counts. Rather, they are the result of *one step* in the process, a step that happens to result in much local flaking. These scars are not producing a general change to the tool on a large scale; hence they do not provide information about generally how far along in the reduction process the piece has progressed. Therefore, these scars produced at the platform/dorsal surface interface on both surfaces of a flake should not be counted in either the platform or dorsal scar counts. Some of the scars at this interface, on resharpening flakes, may even represent usewear microchipping and so be entirely unrelated to the reduction process *per se*.

Faceting, the removal of flakes to shape the striking platform to assist in controlling flake removal, does produce scars that should be considered as part of the reduction process and so they should be included in the platform scar count. These individual removals represent modification of the surface of the objective piece specifically as part of reduction. They are each a single, planned, intentional removal for reduction of the piece to its final form. The problem that arises is that since they are initiated from the edge just as are the multiple small removals associated with platform grinding and overhang removal, it can be difficult to segregate these faceting scars from the others. Since flake platforms are so thin from the dorsal to ventral surface, usually less than 2–3 mm, and flakes intentionally removed with a flaking tool are unlikely to be any shorter than this, these purposeful faceting flakes should extend completely across the striking platform. Most of the scars associated with grinding and overhang removal will be shorter, confined to the dorsal margin of the striking platform. Most of the scars initiated from the dorsal margin of the striking platform that should be counted, then, are obviously of a larger size than those one does not wish to include.

Some of the scars originating from the striking platform dorsal surface edge may be more elongate than the obvious grinding/overhang flake scars, yet may not be long enough to have traversed the entire striking platform. It is often not obvious whether or not these scars should be included in the platform scar count, especially on large striking platforms. If one or two of these scars are obviously larger than the others are, I usually include them in the count. In terms of the similar scars on the dorsal surface of the flake (dorsal perimeter scarring), I only include them in the dorsal scar count if they extend considerably beyond the others and well onto the flake dorsal surface.

The ridges that separate scars, especially on striking platforms of flakes, can be difficult to see. Inclining the flake at different angles to the light can make the scars more obvious and easier to count as they reflect light at different angles. Sometimes the fingertip can be used to feel ridges that are difficult to see. The ridges can be particularly difficult to see on resharpening flakes, where abrasion has decreased their relief or has rounded them so that they merge into the general platform surface. Extra care must be taken in analyzing such specimens, as well as those that have developed a secondary patina in the sediments.

5.3.4 Mass analysis

An alternative approach to analyzing individual flakes and their attributes is a technique termed mass analysis. This technique has been primarily studied by Stan Ahler (e.g., Ahler 1989). It is based on the experimental research that has been conducted primarily with Crescent chert and Knife River flint (1989:204). In this technique, all material from an excavation is sieved through a series of progressively smaller screens and the number of pieces, the total weight, and the number of cortex-covered pieces (flakes, flake fragments, and shatter) are recorded for each screen size. The theoretical underpinning of the technique is based on two aspects of stone tool working: (1) stone working is a reductive process and, as the reduction process proceeds, the individual pieces produced generally become smaller on average; (2) if stone working is undertaken with a cortex-covered raw material, then as the reduction progresses there should be, on average, less and less cortex on the pieces produced later in the manufacturing sequence. Ahler conducted many experiments of various kinds of lithic reduction: reducing platform cores; reducing bipolar cores; biface edging (shaping); biface thinning; and production of simple retouched flakes (edge modified flakes). His experiments used both hard hammer and soft hammer percussion.

Ahler uses four screen sizes to sort his lithic debitage:

1) G1: 1 inch (25.4 mm)

2) G2: 1/2 inch (12.7 mm)

3) G3: 0.223 inch (5.66 mm)

4) G4: 0.1 inch (2.54 mm)

The main features of debitage patterning Ahler uses in reduction analysis are as follows:

1) ratio of count (frequency), G4/G1–3

2) percentage of material that is cortex-covered in G1–3 versus G4

3) mean flake weight (grams) of G1–3

4) percentage weight of each of the four size grades

The results basically show that core reduction gives larger flakes with more cortex and a lower

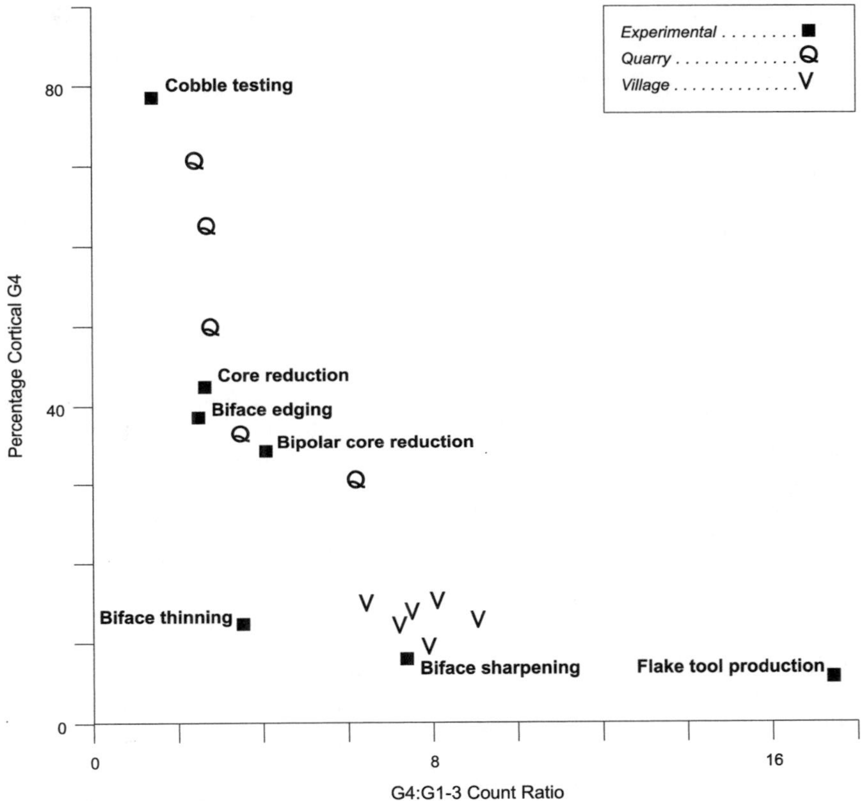

Figure 36: Manufacturing stages as reflected in mass analysis criteria

G4/G1–3 (small/large) ratio. Bifacial edging (shaping) is similar, but with much lower average flake weight in the G1–3 category. Bifacial thinning is characterized by low cortex percentage and a high ratio of small to large debitage (G4/G1–3). Bifacial shaping is difficult to isolate from platform core reduction. Ahler (1989:209) illustrates the patterns with a comparison of experimental data and archaeological data from sites where there is a good indication about the type of site involved (see Fig. 36).

The mass analysis approach faces a significant problem when analyzing mixed assemblages, although this statement also applies to a lesser degree when employing individual flake analysis. In a mixed assemblage with various reduction tasks and stages included, the diagnostic frequencies employed in mass analysis disappear as they are all mixed together. Individual flake analysis can look for particular flake types, such as bipolar, BRF, and thinning, to help define these stages, although simple presence of these types without considering their frequency (Ahler 1989:212) or other features, such as scarring complexity, can be misleading. As other research has shown, debitage size characteristics are complex in distribution and not all material has cortex. These features are central analytical underpinnings of mass analysis, so the fact that they vary is a drawback in the use of mass analysis. Also, to be more widely accepted, mass analysis researchers need to more systematically examine how different individual flintknappers affect the patterns (e.g., Ahler 1989:216–219) and how material type alters the patterns. As well, the technique ignores a great deal of relevant, useful information that other researchers have clearly shown provides a good understanding of the finer details of lithic tool manufacture, which the overview given by mass analysis cannot provide. A more practical problem is that many archaeological excavations do not use screen mesh sizes smaller than 1/4 inch (6 mm), so the G4 size class is often not recovered. This problem can be easily overcome with a sampling procedure for this smaller class of debitage. Mass analysis can provide a very good indication of the broad pattern of lithic reduction at a site, much as can Magne's (1985) system of using flake scarring complexity. However, as with that technique, it is best utilized in conjunction with individual flake type analysis to aid in assessing which stages are present in the mixed, composite assemblage. Individual flake analysis is also not without its problems, of course. As Ahler (1989:210–213) notes, the frequency of individual flake types must be considered in addition to simply their presence or absence, since not all flakes produced in a reduction stage will be only of the "diagnostic" type (and diagnostic types may be produced in small frequencies in other stages). In regards to these problematic areas for individual flake analysis, however, I would caution against relying too heavily on Ahler's data to measure the scale of the problem. His inclusion of inexperienced knappers may be somewhat misleading, as seen, for example, in how few bifacial reduction flakes his inexperienced knappers produced in biface thinning (Ahler 1989:218).

5.4 Ground Stone Tool Reduction Stage Analysis

As previously mentioned, much of the modeling of reduction stages used for flaked stone tools applies to the study of production of ground stone tools. Most analysis of production stages in ground stone tool manufacture has been of adze or celt manufacture (e.g., Cleghorn 1982; Leach and Leach 1980). Quarrying is much the same as for flaked tools, although obviously the lithic material acquired is often different.

The reduction process begins with either a flake or a fragment of raw material as a blank (e.g., Leach and Leach 1980:112). It is then common to produce the generalized form of the tool by a rapid reduction method (if the material employed will allow this rapid reduction), such as sawing or flaking. In adze manufacture this step is often referred to as producing a roughout. In many ways this roughout stage is equivalent of the initial shaping stage discussed for flake tool analysis. Discarded fragments of sawn raw material are good indicators of this stage. Kahn (1996:34–49) suggested that, based on a variety of adze manufacturing studies, flakes associated with the early stages of adze manufacture should be characterized by comparatively large size, greater amount of cortex, and fewer numbers of dorsal scars. Leach and Leach (1980:113) found that flakes from the initial stages of adze roughout had more dorsal cortex cover than did flakes from the final stages of adze roughout shaping. They were also more variable in shape and generally had only 0–1 platform scars. In particular, final roughout shaping flakes had a characteristic recurring shape and considerable dorsal perimeter scarring. Smith and Leach (1996:104) distinguish a shaping stage that produces the basic adze form by flaking, grinding, bruising, and/or sawing; the roughout stage would constitute the earlier portion of this shaping stage. Leach and Leach found that final stage trimming of quadrangular adzes gave large, thin flakes with exterior platform angles of near 90° (1980:116) and that triangular adze manufacture also resulted in the production of distinctive flake forms.

Williams ([1989], cited by Kahn [1996:37]) suggested that five stages could be defined in adze manufacture: production of a regularly shaped preform from a blank; reduction to a point where final grinding and polishing could be undertaken; grinding; polishing; and finally a resharpening and repair stage. Although Williams' study is specific to production of quadrangular adzes, it is significant that it demonstrated that flake debitage from the first reduction stage could be distinguished from the second based on the first having: fewer dorsal scars, more cortex, more acute exterior platform angles, wide flat striking platforms rather than chevron shaped platforms, and a flake form that was generally wide and thick with a marked distal curvature. Smith and Leach distinguished a finishing stage in adze manufacture, characterized by the use of techniques such as flaking, hammer-dressing, polishing, and/or grinding to give the adze its final form (1996:104). As with manufacturing stage analysis for flake tools, broken and rejected items can give excellent insight into these production processes (e.g., Leach and Leach 1980; Smith and Leach 1996).

Many of these aspects of staging in ground stone tool production are also reflected in the ethnoarchaeological study of Mayan mano (hand stone for grinding) and metate (slab base for grinding) manufacturing undertaken by Hayden (1987b). Metate blanks were split from large boulders or bedrock outcrops (Hayden 1987b:21–26). After this stage there were three more emically recognized stages in the reduction process (1987b:26–43): roughing out, done at the quarry where large flakes (generally 2–5 cm, but as much as 10–20 cm) were removed from the quarried blank to shape it into the basic form required and to remove excess weight, this roughout then being transported to the house-workshop for subsequent processing; a thinning stage which took the metate block to within a few millimeters of its final shape, done by removing smaller flakes (usually in the 1–3 cm size range); and a final thinning and smoothing stage, done by removing only very small flakes and pulverized grains of basalt from the nearly complete metate.

5.5 Heat Treatment of Lithic Material

There is good evidence of various kinds to show that prehistoric flintknappers heated various lithic materials to improve their flaking quality. This tactic did not work with all materials, but for many materials it dramatically improved flaking results. Crabtree noted (Crabtree and Butler 1964:1), for example, that heat treating flint could allow him to detach pressure flakes some four times longer than was possible prior to heat treatment. Heat treating apparently reduces tensile strength by about one-half (Olausson 1983:2). It has also been reported that heat treatment reduces the frequency of hinge terminations (Price et al. 1982:467) and step terminations (Olausson 1983:1; Purdy and Brooks 1971:323–4).

A common feature of heat treatment is that a material that previously had quite a dull luster develops a rather "greasy" luster (Crabtree and Butler 1964:1) or sometimes a somewhat vitreous luster (Purdy and Brooks 1971:322) (see Fig. 37). A change in texture also often results (Crabtree and Butler 1964:1; Purdy and Brooks 1971:323; Price et al. 1982:477), the heated piece having a much smoother texture. Whittaker (1994:73) refers to heat treated material as having an almost "soapy" feel and notes that the luster and texture differences are only visible on surfaces flaked after the heat treatment. A color change also frequently occurs, usually toward a pink or red shade (Crabtree and Butler 1964:1; Purdy and Brooks 1971:322). Crazing

Figure 37: Heat treated raw material: original rough, non-lustrous surface and smooth greasy luster surfaces created after flaking subsequent to heat treatment

may also occur (Crabtree and Butler 1964:2; Purdy and Brooks 1971:323; Price et al. 1982:467) and the material may actually fracture and/or explode. Obviously, these latter two results are generally not desirable.

When chert is heated, water in pores and cracks is lost at about 100–150° C and chemically bound water is lost at about 350–500° C. Between 100° C and 650° C impurities may oxidize (Luedtke 1992:101–102). Color changes resulting from heating are apparently due to changes in the oxidation state of small amounts of iron impurities in the lithic material (Purdy and Brooks 1971:323). In the case of Bald Eagle jasper from Pennsylvania, geothite decomposes to hematite, causing a yellow to red color change (Schindler et al. 1982):

$$2FeO\text{–}OH \longrightarrow Fe_2O_3 + H_2O \uparrow$$

At least in some cases this color change occurs before the other, useful, changes occur in the material. For example, in the study of Florida chert by Purdy and Brooks (1971), the color change occurred at about 240–260° C whereas the other changes the lithic material underwent occurred at about 350–400° C. The common change to a red or pink color is due to iron compounds oxidizing to hematite (Luedtke 1992:103). Patterson (1984) has noted that color changes also occur in materials that lack iron compounds and so the change in oxidation state of such compounds cannot be the only cause of color change, a point Schindler and colleagues (Schindler et al. 1984) accept as well.

The reasons for the changes in other properties are not known with certainty (Whittaker 1994:72), but some aspects of the change have been studied. Petrographic analysis and X-ray diffraction analysis suggest that there is no change in the SiO_2 (quartz) crystal structure (Purdy and Brooks 1971:323; Schindler et al. 1982). One change is that fractures apparently pass through these crystals in heated specimens, whereas they go around the crystals in unheated material. Purdy and Brooks suggested that impurities in the intercrystalline spaces melted, acted as fluxes, and fused thin surface portions of the SiO_2 crystals together so that they were more tightly bound. As a result of this situation, fractures went through the crystals rather than around them (Purdy and Brooks 1971:323; Olausson 1983:1). Most researchers agree with this theory (e.g., Patterson 1984), although some have suggested that the loss of intercrystallic water is also a factor (Price et al. 1982:468). The main problem with this suggestion is that even with fluxes, silica does not melt at the low temperatures used in heat treatment, so it would have to be the impurities themselves that are involved. Quartz (silica) does expand considerably during heating and contracts on cooling, so stress cracks might also be created which might aid in fracturing (Luedtke 1992:104).

However, not all research is in agreement with these findings. Domanski and Webb (1992:610–611) found conflicting results. Their work showed recrystallization *did* occur. They found that the heat treated material had smaller, more equal-sized crystals and that since the bonding between such crystals is lessened, fracture *around* them occurred more easily. Clearly, this is an area of lithic analysis research that requires further study.

A different explanation has been proposed for heat treatment changes in Bald Eagle jasper from Pennsylvania (Schindler et al. 1982). These authors have suggested that heating Bald Eagle jasper initiates a decomposition of one iron mineral to form another (geothite to hematite). This decomposition produces microcracks that then promote easier fracture (hematite is more dense than geothite by about 25%, but since there is no overall change in density for Bald Eagle jasper in this process, it is logical that there must be more space, which means more cracks). This situation is probably not a general mechanism (Patterson 1984; Schindler et al. 1984), since it seems incompatible with the smoother texture and loss of porosity most material shows after heat treatment. Also, not all materials have impurities that will decompose appropriately. Literal melting of SiO_2 grains is not likely to be the cause of the property changes, since unfluxed SiO_2 requires temperatures of about 1400–1700°C to cause melting (Purdy and Brooks 1971:323). In the case of Bald Eagle jasper, the more reflective luster after heating has been theorized to be due to more light reflected off the distinct facets of the hematite crystals.

The methods employed for heat treating lithic material vary, but basically the stone is usually slowly heated to about 300–450°C, after which it is slowly cooled (Crabtree and Butler 1964; Luedtke 1992:100–101; Whittaker 1994:72–74). Heating of cherts over 600°C causes a change in quartz crystal structure that results in strain and cracks in quartz crystals, making most cherts unusable (Luedtke 1992:101).

5.6 Analysis Implementation

Tabulations of the flake types and other features of manufacturing presented in this chapter are powerful implements for studying stone tool production. The frequencies of flake types, the number of scars on platforms and dorsal surfaces, manufacturing tools, and rejected and broken tool portions trace the importance of different steps in the reduction process. Integration of these frequencies with their distribution across lithic types reveals how different material types are differentially worked and provides particularly useful insight into acquisition of material types, the effects of distance on access to particular materials, and on trade and exchange. If a distant source is relatively well represented in the remains, direct access to that source may be indicated if early stage or large pieces are common. If most of that material is present as finished tools and resharpening flakes, trade is more likely to be the source of the material. A ritual or sacred value of the material is probable if it is used only for certain tools (such as ceremonial objects) or is found only in certain contexts in a site (such as burials). Material is probably of local origin if much early stage debitage is present and/or if large cores and blocks of raw material are present.

Normally one might also anticipate correlations between different variables: distant source material should be present only as small pieces *and* in late stage or finished tool form; local source material should have a greater percentage of early stage flake types *and*, in many cases, should be present as large pieces and maybe as cores or unmodified raw material. Any such expectations will be impacted by a suite of situational variables, such as time available at the quarries and the need to schedule other activities. The key to evaluating how these additional circumstances effect frequency of lithic materials and the form in which they are present, is to evaluate *within* a site assemblage. What is the frequency of each form (e.g., bifacial reduction flake) for a local lithic material as compared to a distant source lithic material? If the frequency of bifacial reduction flakes in the distant source material is not high, but rather is comparable to the frequency in a local source material, this suggests that early stage material is common; therefore minimally modified pieces of the distant source are being brought in. This may indicate a special significance for the material that justifies the extra effort, it may indicate unsuspected direct access, or it may include some other factor. Observation of this aspect of frequencies in other distant and local materials may isolate the specific cause or causes.

Basically, the approach is to tabulate the frequency data, define expectations based on purely "economic" behavior, and then evaluate the deviations from this optimal pattern to illuminate how social and situation circumstances alter human behavior from these expectations.

CHAPTER 6

Survey of Worldwide Lithic Technology

6.1 Introduction

This chapter will review the general development of lithic technology in the world and will also define many of the basic tool types used in discussing these technologies. Broadly speaking, the lithic traditions of the world are divided into five main stages and each of these will be discussed in turn. Many of the techniques developed in one period continued in use in subsequent periods or even from that initial period onwards. Even as early as the Lower Paleolithic, regional traditions often developed independently of the more general pattern at the time. This regional independence becomes particularly dramatic during the Neolithic, with people spread over most of the world by this time.

This chapter is in no way intended to be a comprehensive world prehistory, nor is it intended to be a thorough or exhaustive catalogue of technological developments in lithic tool manufacture. It would be a daunting, or even impossible, task to discuss all of these developments, and it would also be inappropriate in an introductory book such as this. The goal is to put some of the main innovations into chronological perspective. Wherever we study lithic technology, we are looking at a tradition reaching back over two million years. In human historical terms, most archaeologists work with material that is very recent in origin. This statement is particularly true for anyone working in the Americas. Study in any area of the world is enriched by an appreciation of the broader patterns of lithic technology development. This said, there are many innovations in the Americas and in the post-Mesolithic period in the Old World. These achievements are as remarkable as those of the earlier periods in human history and are as fascinating to study.

6.2 Lower Paleolithic

This period traces the development of lithic tool manufacture from its earliest beginnings some two million years ago to about 80,000 B.P. Earlier dates for the inception of stone tool manufacture are possible. For example, at Hadar in East Africa there are "apparently flaked" cobbles at 2.6 million B.P.

The Oldowan Industries typify the earliest stages of this time period, as seen at Olduvai Gorge in East Africa where they are dated ca. 1.9–1.8 million B.P. (Wymer 1982:67). These industries are generally initially dominated by "core tools," tools made from pebbles and cobbles directly, rather than being made from flake blanks (Gamble 1986:117). However, at Koobi Fora flake tools are more common but very few are retouched. In the early Oldowan industry, these core tools are primarily choppers—core tools that had a series of flakes removed along one area to form a single useable edge. Choppers generally have a moderately steep angle on the working edge, about 40–70°. Sometimes a distinction is made between choppers, where the edge retouch is unifacial, and chopping tools, where it is bifacial. It is usually assumed that these tools were used for a variety of functions, from butchering animals and breaking bones for

Figure 38: Acheulean handaxe

marrow to preparing vegetable foods (such as removing husks).

Flake tools, where the blank from which the tool is made is a flake rather than an unmodified pebble or cobble, are also present from the earliest times, mainly as scrapers. Scrapers are tools that have a used edge that had quite a steep angle, usually about 80–90°. Such an edge is very strong and so can be used in tasks requiring a great deal of pressure, such as scraping animal hides or scraping wood or bone. A naturally steep edge may be used unmodified, in such cases the only trace of use is the usewear that develops on the edge. When this damage takes the form of small flakes along an edge, it is referred to as microchipping usewear or use-retouch. If the edge must be modified to be used, modification of the edge area only is referred to as retouch. Retouch may be bifacial or unifacial, but it is usually unifacial on scrapers with the flake scars on the trailing edge (so that there is a smooth surface with no flake ridges contacting the worked material that might damage or scratch it). Although flake scrapers comprised only a minor component of the earliest Oldowan assemblages, by the end of the so-called Developed Oldowan about 700,000–600,000 B.P. (Wymer 1982:67) they were the main tool type (1982:69). In Europe a comparable industry is seen in the earliest tools from Britain, the Clactonian Industry. This material dates to about 245,000 B.P. (Gamble 1986:140).

The next main technological advance, still within the Lower Paleolithic, was the development of the handaxe (Fig. 38). It is entirely absent in Oldowan industries, although some are present in the Developed Oldowan (Wymer 1982:95). Some authors use the term biface to refer to all handaxes and then subdivide bifaces into various forms (Debénath and Dibble 1994:130), but the term handaxe is still very widely used. The step of flaking a pebble from two opposite edges to form a pointed implement is a logical progression from manufacturing a chopper, and some African sites (e.g., Olduvai Gorge) have such simple tools, often referred to as proto-bifaces. The handaxe is the first biface; it has all or most of its edges flaked well into the tool body on both faces. Usually the flaking covers all or most of both faces. Handaxes are usually pear-shaped, although they vary from almost circular to triangular. They are generally 10–15 cm long.

The earlier handaxes were apparently produced by direct, hard hammer percussion, although the developmental process to later forms is complex (Bordes 1968:51; Gamble 1986:144; Wymer 1982:103). This inference is based on the observation that the flake scars show deep bulbs of percussion, these typifying hard hammer percussion. The resultant tool edge is quite sinuous. Such a sinuous edge limits the tasks the handaxe could be used for (Bordaz 1970:21, 24–25). Furthermore, hard hammer flakes tend not to progress far into the interior of a tool, so that the resultant cross section is thick in the tool center and the tool is rather awkward to use. Later, in the Acheulean (after a site at St. Acheul, a suburb of Amiens in France), two technological advances occurred that allowed an improvement in these aspects of the handaxe:

(i) the advent of the prepared platform. The edge of the tool was flaked to give a striking surface that was roughly perpendicular to the face from which the flake was to be removed. This allowed a blow to be struck at a better angle so that the flake carried further over the face of the tool, resulting in a thinner cross section that was also more tapered from the edge to the center.

(ii) the flakes so removed during handaxe preparation were also much thinner at this later time, and often had long, parallel lateral margins (sides). This is probably due to the origin of the soft hammer percussion technique, using a baton or billet of antler, bone, or wood. It is particularly the diffuse bulb of percussion commonly associated with soft hammer percussion that is important in allowing greater control over the form of the tool edge. This is the origin of what have been defined above as thinning flakes and bifacial reduction flakes.

In Europe, the earlier handaxes produced entirely by hard hammer percussion are termed Abbevillian (after a site at the town of Abbeville in France). The later Acheulean handaxes appear to have been "roughed-out" (preform) by hard hammer and then finished by soft hammer; hence both flake scar types are seen on these specimens. (Bordes 1968:52; Wymer 1982:103). Having said this, Abbevillian handaxes continue in use into much later contexts (Bordes 1968:51; Debénath and Dibble 1994:150).

The earliest handaxes come from Olduvai Gorge (Tanzania) and Gadeb (Ethiopia) in East Africa, where they form a separate but contemporary tradition with the Developed Oldowan beginning about 1.3 or 1.4 million years ago (Wymer 1982:93, 103, 108). In Europe the precise date is less clear, but the early Abbevillian handaxes probably date to about 500,000 B.P. (Bordes 1968:54; Debénath and Dibble 1994:4). At Swanscomb in England the Acheulean handaxe industry dates to before 326,000 years ago (Gamble 1986:140; Wymer 1982:92).

The other typical tool of the Acheulean was a large cleaver (Bordaz 1970:27). It was of a similar size to the handaxe, but was made on a flake and had a wide straight working edge at right angles to the long axis of the tool (Debénath and Dibble 1994:130). It was made either as a core tool or on a large flake. Though common in Africa, cleavers are rare in Europe.

Flake tools also continue in use during the Acheulean and it is worth noting that many aspects of earlier industries continue in later periods. Choppers and simple flake scrapers, for example, continue in use into sites only a few hundred years old (and into the twentieth century in Australia, New Guinea, etc.).

During the more recent portion of the Acheulean, sometime shortly after 200,000 B.P. and the onset of the Riss glaciation but before 130,000 B.P., the Levallois technique was invented (Bordaz 1970:31; Bordes 1968:55–58; Champion et al. 1984:41–42) (Fig. 39). The earliest examples of this technique date to this time in several locations in Europe and Africa. The Levallois technique is the basis for the succeeding Middle Paleolithic stage, beginning about 80,000 B.P. At this earlier time period, however, its distribution is scattered (Champion et al. 1984:41). Included among the earliest sites is Ehringsdorf (Germany), with an absolute date of 225,000 +/-26,000 B.P. (Gamble 1986:140, 146, 150).

The essence of the Levallois technique is that the core from which the flake was removed had been specifically prepared to produce the flake shape desired (Bordaz 1970:31–32; Bordes 1988:26; Wymer 1982:116–117). Prior to this, although there might have been a pattern to flake

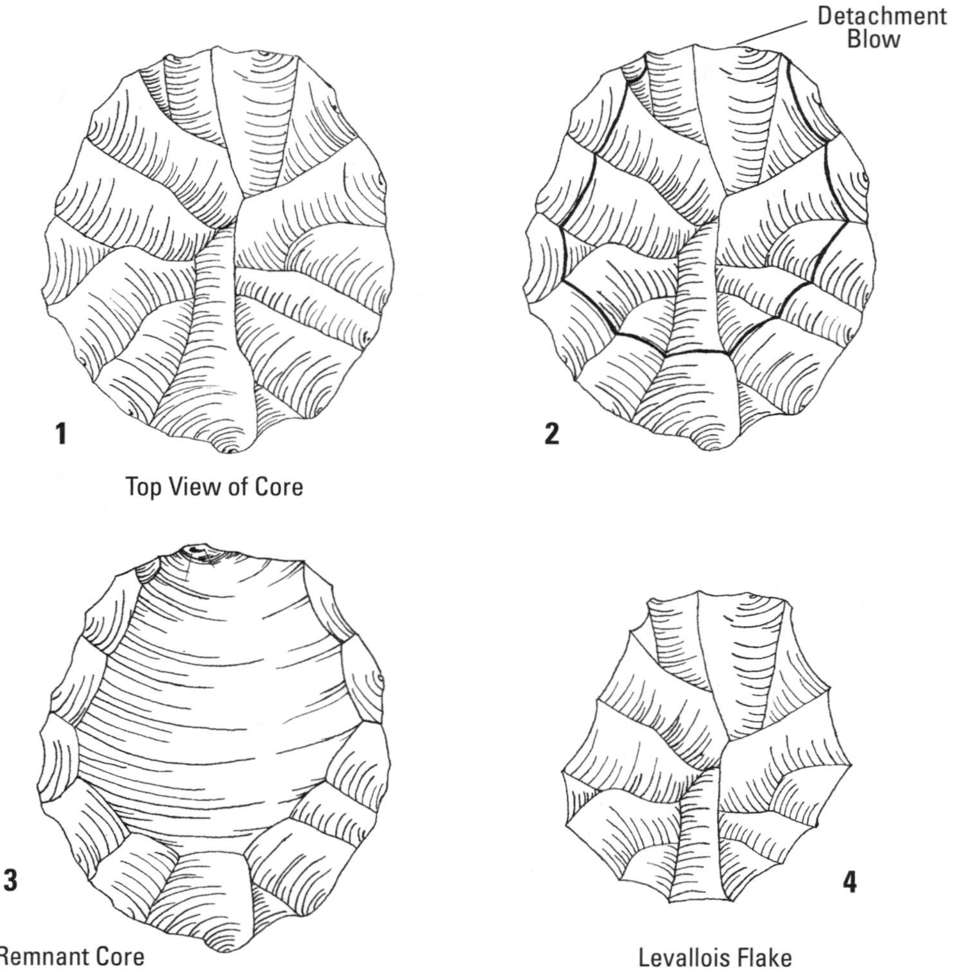

Figure 39: Levallois technique

removal from a core (basically progressing around the circumference of the core/pebble, removing flakes), the core was not prepared in advance.

The outline and the top of the Levallois core were flaked to give a variety of forms; pointed, rectangular, oval, and almost circular. A striking platform was then prepared on the "side" of the core and the "top" was detached as the Levallois flake. This technique allowed the stone worker to predetermine the size and shape of the flake, and to form it to suit the tool being produced. This fact is an important point to remember about the Levallois technique: the idea was to produce a flake of the correct size and shape for a tool *as it was*, with little or no further modification required. This aspect can be seen particularly well in the specific core and procedures used to obtain a flake for a Levallois point; subsequent to the production of the point flake, only minimal edge retouch to smooth the outline was undertaken (Bordes 1988:32–33; Wymer 1982:116). This procedure is the opposite of what we usually think of as the tool making procedure, where a flake of roughly the correct shape and size is produced and then further working of that flake is undertaken to produce the desired form.

One advantage of this technique, in addition to producing a pre-designed flake to fit the task, is that when the tool is produced without the necessity of modifying the flake to produce the final form, the tool has a fresh (produced in the detachment process), unmodified flake edge as its working edge. This edge is as sharp an edge as can be obtained with stone; retouching an edge can never achieve this sharpness again. Hence, in terms of cutting tools (whether as knives or projectile points), the Levallois technique produced superior pieces. This aspect can be seen in the fact that old Levalloisian points were rarely resharpened. They generally appear to have been discarded and new ones manufactured.

Levallois cores tend to be rather flat on top and domed or rounded on the underside, particularly flatter on top once a flake or two has been removed. Not many flakes could be produced from each Levallois core. In fact, when a second flake was removed, it usually went all the way to the edge of the core. The tool resulting was not symmetric and so was not the desired form. The cores have been termed tortoise cores due to this domed shape, and due to the flake scars looking like reptilian scales. Cores frequently have some cortex remaining on the domed base. The flakes themselves are characterized mainly by their dorsal scarring and the scarring or faceting of the striking platform. The flakes can be quite large, with Levallois points frequently about 15 cm in length. The main disadvantage of the Levallois technique was that only one or two flakes could be produced from each core.

During this late stage of the Lower Paleolithic there was a peak in the use of handaxes, followed by a gradual decline (Wymer 1982:115) as they were replaced by large flakes and blade-like flakes produced by the Levallois technique.

It is worth noting that many of the Levallois cores resembled crude bifaces before flake detachment had occurred, so it is easy to see how the technique could have evolved from handaxe technology in the Acheulean. In turn, the production of the elongate blade-like flakes from Levallois cores can be seen to be a logical progression into the next major technological change; blade technology (see also Wymer 1982:116–117).

In terms of lithic technology at this time (Riss glaciation), the Tayacian industry is worthy of mention. The type site is La Micoque near Tayac in the Dordogne (France), and the industry was present in France and Germany (and maybe at one English site). The industry had some handaxes and some Levallois technique represented, but it may also be a separate tradition and its classification has been controversial (Gamble 1986:152). It seems to have had many elements of the later Mousterian tradition and has been called Pre- or Proto-Mousterian (Gamble 1986:150–153, 157; Wymer 1982:121). For example, it had the first leaf-shaped points (unifacially modified and shaped).

6.3 Middle Paleolithic

During the Riss/Würm interglacial (ca. 130,000–85,000 B.P.) bifacial tools became less important, until by 80,000 B.P. it was Levallois flake tools that dominated assemblages. This marks the beginning of the Middle Paleolithic (still Acheulean).

About 60,000 – 50,000 B.P. the Mousterian Industry also arose in the Middle Paleolithic and continued until the Upper Paleolithic ca. 35,000 B.P. The Mousterian (named after the site of Le Moustier in France) was also a flake industry. The core reduction used was different from, though related to, the Levallois technique, and

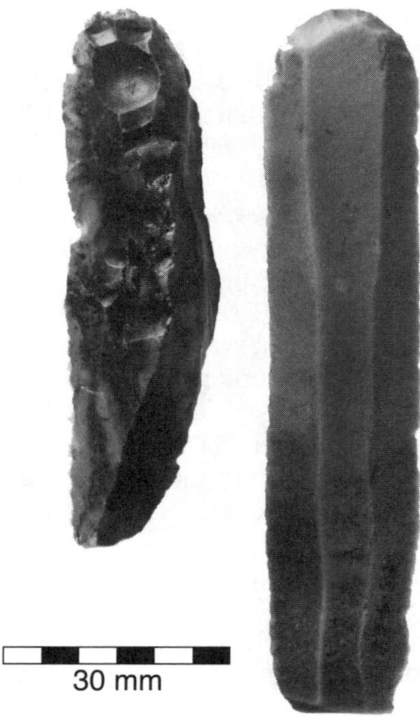

Figure 40: Upper Paleolithic blades

Figure 41: Upper Paleolithic blade core

sometimes even began with a Levallois core. The dischoidal Mousterian core was begun by flaking around the circumference as in the Levallois technique, but then as many flakes as possible were removed by flaking into the center on both faces of the core until the core was exhausted (Bordes 1988:27). This procedure used the material much more efficiently than the Levallois technique; these flakes were then retouched to produce a large variety of formal tool types. Herein lies another advantage to the Mousterian technology relative to the Levalloisian, in addition to the more efficient use of raw material; so long as the Levalloisian makers used little retouching, they could not produce the very intricate tool types that the Mousterian workers produced. There are only so many forms that can be prepared in a core. Scrapers were the most common artifact produced in the Mousterian (Bordes 1988:41), followed by points. Although these points sometimes may have been used as weapon tips, they were probably mainly pointed cutting and scraping tools. Scrapers came in a variety of edge forms (straight, concave, convex), and other tool types such as denticulates ("toothed" or serrated-edged tools) and some backed blade knives (backed means steeply retouch), were also present. During the Mousterian, the Levallois technique was used as well, with the Levallois flakes retouched to produce typical Mousterian tools (Bordes 1988:38, 41).

Sometime during the Middle Paleolithic the first pecked stone implements, including grindstones for paint pigment, appeared.

6.4 Upper Paleolithic

The start of the Upper Paleolithic ca. 35,000 B.P. is marked by a significant increase in specialized tools made on blades (Fig. 40) (Bordaz 1970:51; Gamble 1986:120). The chronology and tool typologies become very complex at this time, especially in Europe (Bordaz 1970:72),

Figure 42: Comparison of Upper Paleolithic blade and bladelet (microblade)

hence they cannot be described here. The Upper Paleolithic ends about 10,000 B.P. Because blade tools tend to be smaller than the tools produced on flakes and cores, the Upper Paleolithic has also been called the Leptolithic (Greek for "lighter stone") (Bordaz 1970:56).

True blades are not simply flakes that are two times as long as they are wide. They must also have approximately parallel sides, be relatively thin, and be produced from specialized cores (Fig. 41). In Europe, small blades less than 5 cm long and 1 cm wide are called bladelets; in North America these pieces are termed microblades (Fig. 42).

A common way to start a blade core was to create a ridge by removing a series of overlapping flakes. The blow was then struck at the top and the ridge guided the long flake, called a "crested blade" (Bordaz 1970:51–53). This utilized the same principle as the Levallois technique. Once the crested blade was removed, two new ridges were created that could similarly be used as guides to remove more blades. If the detachment blow was placed above a single ridge, a triangular cross section blade resulted. If the blow was located between two ridges that both acted as guides, a trapezoidol cross section resulted.

It is generally believed that most of the Upper Paleolithic blades were produced by indirect percussion (Bordaz 1970:55). Experimentally, both hard and soft direct percussion have also been shown to work for blade production.

The origin of the true blade technology has not yet been resolved, but it sometimes pre-dates the local Mousterian in the Middle East. At Mount Carmel (Israel), Jabrud (Syria), Abu Sif Cave (Jordan), and Abri Zumoffen (Lebanon), blades date to at least 80,000 B.P. At Klaises River Mouth in South Africa they date to before 70,000 B.P. (Wymer 1982:149–155).

Some Upper Paleolithic tools were finished by pressure flaking (Whittaker 1994:33). In terms of lithic technology, during the Aurignacian in France (32,000–22,000 B.P.) microblades and microlithic backed blades became common. In the Solutrian, also in France and dated to 21,000–19,000 B.P., elaborate heat treatment was employed prior to the final stage of flaking tools. Pressure flaking also became very important during the Solutrian (Bordes 1968:158–159; Gamble 1986:120). During the Magdalenian, dated to 17,000–11,500 B.P. in France, many microlithic backed blades were used (Bordes 1968:163–164; Bordaz 1970:89–94). Tools with ground edges appear during this period, but only in Japan ca. 20,000 B.P. and in Australia at 25,000–20,000 B.P. (Flood 1990:86). Ground stone tools do not appear in Europe until the succeeding Mesolithic period.

6.5 Mesolithic and Neolithic

The Mesolithic dates ca. 11,000–7000 B.P. in Europe. It is a time of climatic change due to the end of the last glaciation. Culturally, this is the last period before farming developed. The characteristic stone tools are microliths, small blade or flake segments used as insert blades in composite tools. Ground stone tools appear in Europe ca. 9000–8000 B.P. (Bordaz 1970:92–95).

During the Neolithic, the ground stone tools first seen in the European Mesolithic became very important with the introduction of agriculture. The situation in the New World was quite different, with stone tools for processing plant seeds becoming the first common ground stone tools during the Archaic; in the Great Basin these grinding stones probably arise by 10,500–10,000 B.P. On this note it is worth mentioning that the ground stone tools that first appeared in Australia and Japan about 20,000 B.P. give no indication that they had any connection to the later ones in Europe or the New World.

CHAPTER 7

Introduction to the Study of Lithic Production Variables

7.1 Introduction

The technology and procedures used to manufacture stone tools must be reconstructed from the features remaining on lithic tools and debitage. To utilize these features, we must understand how they arise. This has already been discussed in part, but this chapter examines the experiments that have been used to determine what aspects of technology, such as hammer type, produce particular features and forms in tools and debitage. These associations of form with technological production procedures are the basis for understanding how stone tools were produced.

Three basic approaches can be taken toward attempting to define what features of flakes and tools can be used as indicators of how stone tools were produced:

1. laboratory experiments under controlled conditions, breaking lithic materials to "see what happens."
2. experiments by modern-day flintknappers.
3. fracture mechanics theory, used as a predictive model of the features expected.

All of these methods have their strengths, but also their weaknesses. In regards to the weaknesses, for example, in laboratory experiments it is not clear how accurate a model of human flintknapping is achieved by dropping a round steel ball from an electromagnet onto a sawn piece of flat glass held in a vise. This situation cannot reproduce the combination of many factors involved in detaching flakes, so even though these experiments provide valuable controlled observations, they do not reproduce the "real" world and therefore the observed features may not be analytically useful (i.e., no one ever does it that way). Experiments like this also tend to turn each continuous variable into discontinuous, pigeon-hole states. Again, this is not the way it is in the "real" world.

Conversely, a problem with using a flintknapper in the experiment is that there are probably dozens of variables that cannot be controlled and reproduced in a true replication series of experiments. Each time the force of the detaching blow will be different, the angle of the blow will vary, the angle at which the worked piece is held will vary, and so on. It is just not possible to rigidly control the variables. Secondly, the flintknapper is doing "other things" at both the conscious and subconscious levels. These factors (and their variations) may be having a significant effect on the results of flake detachment. In short, one cannot truly have reproducible results, and one cannot be sure that the variables one is "controlling" are even relevant to the feature(s) being studied. Even if the variables are relevant it may be that they cause the observed effect only in combination with other variables not being controlled. As well, flaking techniques that no modern-day flintknapper or scientist has ever thought of may have been used in the past.

Finally, a key issue associated with using fracture mechanics theories is that theories do change. Theories in general usually do not explain and integrate all variations and results, but they seem to explain some major aspects in broad terms based on a limited number of "principal" factors. They have a tendency to "gloss over" the minor inconsistencies. When one tries to use theories to interpret the minutia of material, this critical feature of theories must be borne in mind if one is to avoid extending the theory beyond its experimental data. However, basic fracture mechanics theories, such as the Griffith Crack Theory seem reliable.

The obvious point is that all three of these methods can make contributions and they should be used together rather than separately. Theories should be tested using experiments specifically designed to isolate the relevant factors. The experience of flintknappers can be used to define probable useful features and variables to employ in experiments. If the experiments do not give the same results as the flintknappers' work, the flintknappers' experience and observation of their working techniques can suggest other variations or variables which might be involved. The theory can be used to explain the results in a logical fashion so that we can have confidence that we understand the situation and have eliminated any possible irrelevant or erroneous aspects.

The ideal would be to combine the expertise of the flintknapper with the analytical orientation of the scientist, all in a single person. Fortunately this has started to happen (e.g., Rob Bonnichsen, Bruce Bradley, John Whittaker).

7.2 Manufacturing Techniques: Flintknappers' Experience

The experience acquired by various flintknappers over the years has led them to propose certain features of flakes as being diagnostic, to some degree, of the various manufacturing techniques used (hard and soft hammer percussion, indirect percussion, pressure flaking). There is much disagreement about these features. Most flintknappers will state that any one of these attribute forms can be produced by another technique (Whittaker 1994:187), at least occasionally (cf. Johnson 1978:357–358). Some lithic analysts are extremely skeptical of the subjective nature of the results and are not prepared to employ it.

Results certainly vary to a degree with the individual knapper. If a large sample of material is consulted, it is my opinion that one can use these trends to give a basic idea about the overall type of reduction occurring. After all, these inferences have been proposed by people with a large amount of practical experience and some of their observations must be valid. Not only do these features, frequencies, and attribute configurations probably vary between knappers, they also probably vary with the material type and the type of tool being manufactured. They are summarized in Fig. 43 and are discussed below.

Soft hammerstones allow the objective piece edge to penetrate into the billet, and this results (at least with wooden billets) in a wider striking platform (Crabtree 1970:150). Newcomer (1975:100) found indirect percussion to produce thinner striking platforms than did direct percussion, although this is presumably in part dependent on where the punch is placed in relation to the objective piece surface (Bordes and Crabtree 1969:6–7). Crabtree characterized indirect percussion flakes as having a small striking platform (1972:13; Bordes and Crabtree 1969:1). Hayden and Hutchings (1989:248–252) found that a graph of flake weight to platform surface area produced a slope of about 1 for hard hammer flakes, but either much more positive or much more negative for soft hammer flakes. In their opinion, this situation was the result of two basic soft hammer flakes; small platformed flakes, and flakes in which a bending initiation caused fracture much further back from the objective piece edge, resulting in a larger platform (and a flake form they characterized as "r-shaped"). Stafford (1979)

ATTRIBUTE	HARD HAMMER	SOFT HAMMER	PRESSURE	INDIRECT PERCUSSION
STRIKING PLATFORM				
Width	Narrower	Wider		Small
Size	Never small	Small to large	Small	Small
Thickness	Thicker	Thicker		Thinner
Shape	Tend to triangular	Tend to plano-convex		
Shows impact	Yes (60-80%)	No (only 5-10%)		
Lipped	1% or less	20-60%		Some
BULB OF PERCUSSION				
Prominence*	Salient	Diffuse	Salient or diffuse	Salient
Shape	Tend to taper to top	Tend to truncated top		
Bulbar fissures	May be present	May be present	Rare	Absent
Eraillure**	Common (95%); shallow	Less common (50%); shallow	Rare; deep	Rare - absent
RIPPLE MARKS***				
Prominence	May be prominent	Not prominent	Not prominent; more so as > force	
Frequency	Moderate - common	Moderate - common		Rare
TERMINATION		Feather		
FLAKE				
Thickness	Slightly thicker than soft hammer	Slightly thinner than hard hammer		Thick for size
Size	Larger	Smaller	Much smaller (most <10 mm)	
FLAKE/PIECE BREAKAGE	More common	Less common	Less common	

** When different knappers are compared, result is about 35% prominent for hard hammer and 20% for soft; diffuse includes those absent due to bending initiation*

*** Frequency about 95% on hard hammer vs. about 50% on soft*

**** Highly variable for different knappers (hard and soft both about 45-60% prominent)*

Figure 43: Features associated with various manufacturing techniques based on flintknappers' experience

found hard hammer flakes to have generally larger striking platforms than did soft hammer flakes and also that hard hammer flakes evidenced damage to the striking platform while soft hammer flakes did not. In this latter regard, Hayden and Hutchings (1989:247–248) found almost all instances of point impact marks on striking platforms in their experiments to be the result of hard hammer percussion (79% of hard hammer, versus only 6% of soft hammer) and the incidence of platform crushing was similar (65% of hard hammer, 11% of soft hammer). They also stated that hard hammer flakes never had small striking platforms for their size because if they did, these platforms would collapse and be lost; soft hammer flakes often had a small platform for their size, though not always (1989:248–252). Whittaker (1994:185–187) suggested that soft hammer flakes often have a "small" striking platform and that they are frequently crushed by the blow. In the latter regard, Henry's study (Henry et al. 1976:57) showed equal frequencies of crushed platforms for hard hammer (7.5%) and soft hammer (7.6%), but that soft hammer flakes more frequently evidenced broken platforms (39.1% for soft hammer versus 30% for hard hammer).

Wooden soft hammerstones have been observed to result in a lip forming where the striking platform meets the ventral surface of the flake (Crabtree 1970:150). Stothert attributed lipping to soft hammers (1974:60) as did Whittaker (1994:187). Henry and colleagues (Henry et al. 1976:57) found hard hammer (stone) billets to produced lipped flakes in 1.3% of cases, whereas soft hammer antler billets produced lips in 19.6% of cases. This was in contrast to hard hammers giving unlipped flakes in 52.5% of cases while unlipped soft hammer flakes represented only 25% of soft hammer flakes (both hammer types resulted in about 7.5% crushed platforms and 30-40% broken platforms as well as some indeterminate). Hayden and Hutchings (1989:247) found lipping on 61% of their soft hammer flakes but it did not occur in their hard hammer sample. Crabtree (1972:13) indicated that a lip is often present on indirect percussion flakes.

Crabtree (1970:148; 1972:9) found hard hammerstones produced prominent bulbs of percussion, while antler billets (soft hammer) produced more diffuse bulbs. Whittaker (1994:185) also noted this tendency. Conversely, Hayden and Hutchings (1989:245) did not find bulb prominence to be a useful discriminator between hard and soft hammer percussion, although the tendency was there. In both hard and soft hammer about 45% of the flakes had bulbs with moderate prominence; in addition, about 35% of hard hammer flakes had prominent bulbs and about 33% of soft hammer flakes had diffuse (essentially flat) bulbs (1989:244). Given their definition of the moderate bulbs, these would generally be classified as diffuse in most analyses and so the tendency for soft hammer bulbs to be diffuse is strong (about 80%). Newcomer (1975:100) found direct percussion to produce more salient bulbs than did indirect percussion. Crabtree found flakes detached by wooden billets, still a soft hammerstone, showed even more diffuse bulbs than antler billet produced flakes (1970:150); wooden pressure flakers also produced a diffuse bulb (1970:152). Stothert (1974:60) characterized both soft hammer and pressure flakes as having diffuse bulbs. Bordaz (1970:25) and Whittaker (1994:197) also attributed diffuse bulbs to soft hammer percussion. Young and Bonnichsen found indirect percussion flakes to have prominent bulbs of percussion (1984:144). Patten indicated that pressure flakes could have either diffuse or prominent bulbs, with prominent bulbs being the result of marked outward direction of the detaching force (1978:4).

Bordes and Crabtree found eraillures and bulbar fissures to be rare or absent on indirect percussion flakes (1969). Hayden and Hutchings (1989:244-245) did not find that either of these features reliably separated hard and soft hammer flakes, although they were very common on hard hammer flakes (94%) and only moderately common on soft hammer (56%).

Bordaz (1970:25) found soft hammer flakes to have less prominent ripple marks than did hard hammer flakes, although Hayden and Hutchings (1989:244) did not find this variable useful in separating hard and soft hammer flakes. Hayden and Hutchings found that ripples were more common on hard hammer (59%) than on soft (44%), but that from one knapper to another the frequencies could be reversed. Bordes and Crabtree (1969) found ripple marks to be rare on indirect percussion flakes (see also Crabtree 1972:13). According to Young and Bonnichsen (1984:101) ripple marks become more frequent in pressure flaking as more force is used, although they generally remain indistinct. It is interesting to note that the two knappers in their study showed a consistent difference in the prominence of the ripples they produced in pressure flaking. Their study also found that ripple marks were common even at minimal force levels with a soft hammer billet, but that although they increased in frequency with increased force, they were never prominent (1984:102). Although use of hard hammer was limited in their study, hard hammer percussion resulted in frequent but non-prominent ripple marks (1984:102).

Crabtree noted that although Coutier observed that wooden billets produced thin flat flakes, in his experience not all thin, flat flakes with diffuse bulbs were produced with wooden billets (1970:150). Bordaz (1970:25) suggested that soft hammer percussion produced larger and thinner flakes. Other research (Henry et al. 1976:59-60) suggests that hard hammer flakes are slightly thicker than soft hammer flakes when flakes of similar maximum dimension are compared. The same study found pressure flakes to be significantly thinner than hard and soft hammer flakes. Crabtree found pressure flakes to be small and thin compared to direct and indirect percussion flakes (1972:15). Young and Bonnichsen (1984) found indirect percussion flakes to be thick relative to their size. Whittaker (1994:147) characterizes pressure flakes as short and fragile, the fragility presumably in part related to thinness. He also characterized soft hammer flakes as thin. Although Hayden and Hutchings did not find curvature generally useful in distinguishing between hard and soft hammer flakes, they did find that extreme curvature was only associated with soft hammer flakes (1989:245). Although Whittaker (1994:185) characterized soft hammer flakes as expanding distally, Hayden and Hutchings did not find this a useful criterion to separate hard and soft hammer flakes (1989:245).

Crabtree found that flakes removed with more of an outward component to the force resulted in step terminations (1970:151), apparently the same as what Patten (1978:4) describes as an "abrupt" termination. Crabtree also found that more outward force resulted in a pressure flake that was short (1972:16), an observation supported by Huckell (1978:43). Huckell also suggested that by varying the relative amount of outward force the pressure flake width and thickness might also be varied. Stafford (1979) found soft hammer flakes to be characterized by feather terminations as did Young and Bonnichsen (1984:102). Bordes and Crabtree (1969) found feather terminations to characterize indirect percussion flakes, perhaps because in their experiments the foot was used as a rest and cushioned the blow. In Young and Bonnichsen's study (1984:101) pressure flakes tended to terminate by feathering when lesser amounts of force were applied, but tended to be stepped when increased force was used.

The actual variables that flintknappers can control in addition to material selection, hammer type, etc., and that they generally consider make a difference in the form of the flake produced, are the thickness of the striking platform (dorsal/ventral), the angle from which the detaching blow is struck, the exterior platform angle of the core or tool being flaked (angle between the striking platform and the adjacent exterior surface of the worked piece), and the force of the detaching blow (Whittaker 1994:91). Of these, only the angle of the detaching blow has not been found to have any form characteristics affected by it, although Whittaker still states that he feels the blow angle is a factor (1994:97).

7.3 Controlled Scientific Experiments in Lithic Production Variables

The observations described below are based mainly on controlled experiments using some mechanical fracturing device. Also included are some theoretical data from fracture mechanics research in engineering and related disciplines since that, too, has generally been confirmed by laboratory experiments.

7.3.1 Overall flake form

There are four main factors that appear to govern the overall form of a flake in terms of its length, width, thickness, and generalized shape:

1. *Objective piece surface geometry:* On a flat surface a flake fracture expands radially; much of the force is used in propagation of the fracture laterally as well as in length. As the force of the detachment is consumed, the fracture stops. The more of this force that is consumed in lateral expansion, the shorter will be the final flake length. If the lateral expansion of the fracture intersects a free surface on the objective

piece (core, tool) the fracture ends, so less of the total force is spent or dissipated in the lateral expansion of the flake. Consequently, under such circumstances, more of the force is used in longitudinal propagation of the fracture and so the flake can achieve a greater length before it stops due to lack of force. This is how ridges on the objective piece surface act to "concentrate" the force of detachment.

The use of ridges to guide flake removal is one of the most basic principles of flintknapping. Preparation of isolated platforms, where the platform is separated laterally from the bulk of the objective piece (Whittaker 1994:104–105), similarly helps concentrate the force delivered at impact. Fracture mechanics theory clearly indicates that this should be a major factor in flake form (Bonnichsen 1977:135–136; Cotterell and Kamminga in Hayden 1979:104), and all flintknappers agree. A single ridge should produce a much longer and narrower flake than would be the case of a perfectly flat dorsal surface. A flat surface is expected to result in a strong tendency toward production of a circular flake. This prediction is basically accurate, but because the advancing fracture front encounters microcracks and other flaws in the material the predicted result is often not realized. Rather, the resulting outline form is often quite irregular, though much more rounded than a ridge flake.

It has been argued, with considerable validity, that surface morphology is the single most important aspect in overall flake form. Most importantly, this is clearly a variable over which the flintknapper can exercise considerable control and manipulate as desired. This situation is most obvious in the careful preparation of core form when a specific flake blank type is desired (e.g., blade cores and Levallois cores). But this circumstance potentially carries through to each step in producing a tool, such as trying to create a ridge with a series of flakes to "lead" an ultimate flake to an irregularity that must be removed, or executing a progressive series of overlapping flakes so that longer and longer ridges are produced to "lead" subsequent flakes a greater distance into a tool center. The specific dorsal morphology of debitage flakes may in fact give an important clue to the functions of these flakes, although this has rarely been specifically studied.

2. Initiation type: The next most important variable in flake form is the type of initiation (how the fracture is actually begun). The two main types are "Hertzian" and "bending."

Hertzian initiation, associated with the bulb of percussion feature previously discussed, occurs when there is a large amount of pressure and a hard indentor or fabricator involved. Fracture occurs at the immediate contact area.

Bending initiation occurs when a fracture begins at a distance from the immediate contact area. The flakes that have a prominent lip are the flakes that are begun by bending initiation. In fact, these flakes do not have a true bulb of percussion because Hertzian fracture does not occur. This circumstance arises because although the teardrop-shaped compressive area is present, initial fracture (failure) occurs outside this area (at a distance) and so these compressive stresses do not affect the direction of the fracture.

The implications of these two initiation types are considerable, but the reasons are complex. However, the first important aspect is that the necessary pressure for a Hertzian or conchoidal initiation can only occur with a comparatively hard indentor, such as stone, bone, or antler (wood will not usually cause such initiation). Secondly, the more acute the core or tool edge (exterior platform angle), the more likely it is that the initiation of the fracture will be due to bending rather than Hertzian mechanisms. For acute edges, both hard and soft indentors can cause bending initiations. In the case of nonacute edges, only soft indentors (bone, antler, etc.) can cause bending initiations; hard indentors will cause a Hertzian initiation under these circumstances. The greater the angle, the more likely it is that there will be a Hertzian initiation even with softer indentors. The basic consequence of this is that only rarely will hard hammerstones cause bending initiation and a lipped flake, but bending initiations should be relatively common with the use of soft hammerstones (antler, bone, etc.). However, soft hammerstones can cause either bending or Hertzian initiation. The third significant aspect of initiation type is that there are some features associated with the flakes of these two main initiation types:

(i) because of the way in which there is a change in the fracture from the initiation phase to the propagation phase in bending initiation, bending flakes tend to be "waisted" or constricted just distal to the striking platform.

(ii) the striking platform on a bending flake is very much plano-convex, with the flat side to the dorsal and the convex ventral side quite gradually and evenly rounded, much as an orange segment. This form contrasts with the Hertzian initiation, which tends to be smaller and more triangular. This small triangular form is due to the usual presence of a compressive area to the "outside" of the platform because there is an "outward" component to the force in most cases. The Hertzian cone cannot fracture through this compressive area and there is a more abrupt ending of the force and Hertzian mechanics in this dorsal area.

(iii) a hard hammer initiation often causes secondary ring cracks that result in small additional flakes being detached at the impact point, but this is rare or absent with soft hammer initiation.

(iv) bending initiations usually do not have ripple marks near the proximal end.

3. Exterior platform angle: The next most important variable in overall flake form is the exterior platform angle. This term refers to the angle formed between the dorsal surface of the objective piece and the striking platform. Exterior platform angle effects the following flake features:

(i) termination: based on fracture mechanics, Cotterell and Kamminga (1979:111) concluded that exterior platform angle was one of the two most important factors in flake termination. Experiments by Speth (1981:19) and Bonnichsen (1977:170) showed that a decrease in this angle permitted easier flake removal (Speth used 45° versus 60°, Bonnichsen used 45° versus 90°). In connection with this observation, Bonnichsen found feather terminations were particularly correlated with the lower exterior platform angle (1977:169). Dibble and Whittaker (1981:287–288) found three overlapping exterior platform angle ranges that preferentially resulted in three different termination types as shown in Table 1.

Table 1. Exterior Platform Angle Ranges and Determination Types

Termination	Mean Exterior Platform Angle	Standard Deviation	Range (±2 S.D.)
Feather	41.8°	9.8	22.2–61.4
Hinge	61.5°	14.0	33.5–89.5
Outrepassé	76.7°	9.4	57.9–95.5

Dibble and Whittaker's results confirm Bonnichsen's, although the considerable range overlap limits the practical usefulness of this observation.

(ii) platform lipping: as already noted above, initiation type is effected by the exterior platform angle; hence the "lipping" associated with bending initiations should also be so correlated. Bonnichsen (1977: 85, 165–166) experimented using 90° and 45° exterior platform angles and found that "lipping" was almost exclusively associated with a 45° exterior platform angle.

(iii) flake length and thickness: on theoretical grounds, Speth (1972:53) suggested that an increase in the exterior platform angle should result in an increase in flake length. He later showed this experimentally (1981:17). The experimental work of Bonnichsen (1977:171) and Dibble and Whittaker (1981:291, 293) also corroborated this correlation. Dibble and Whittaker's research also showed an increase in flake thickness with increased exterior platform angle.

4. Platform thickness: Platform thickness is an important variable in flake form. Platform thickness represents the dorsal to ventral dimension of the striking platform itself, not including the bulb of percussion. Dibble and Whittaker noted (1981:294) that it is the combination of platform thickness and exterior platform angle that largely determines flake length and thickness. Similarly, Bonnichsen (1977:171–172) stated that platform thickness was one of the major variables determining flake length and thickness. Experimentally, both flake length and thickness increase as platform thickness increases (Dibble and Whittaker 1981:289). On theoretical grounds, Speth (1972:47–49, 53) showed that flake length should increase with platform thickness.

Cotterell and Kamminga (1979:106) suggested, based on theoretical grounds, that *outrepassé* terminations result when the platform is too thick. Based on these observations about form, platform thickness, and exterior platform angle, it is clear that the flintknapper could vary these two aspects of the striking platform to control flake length and thickness. Isolation of the platform could also have had a role in flake length.

In this regard, Dibble and Whittaker's experiments showed that an increase in the force of the detaching blow resulted in an increase in flake length (1981:289). This, logically speaking, is no surprise. Bonnichsen (1977:114) and Speth (1972:38) noted this should occur based on theoretical considerations. Cotterell and Kamminga said this should be the case in at least some instances (1979:111), although they were speaking of general flake size, not just flake length.

Furthermore, Dibble and Whittaker's work showed that increasing force also increased flake thickness. So in fact, flake length and thickness are affected by three main variables (force, platform thickness, exterior platform angle), and length, at least, is also affected by surface geometry.

The angle or direction of the applied force is also a factor in flake length. Theoretically, a line of force directed into the tool should result in greater flake length than a force directed more outwardly (Bonnichsen 1977:130, 132; Cotterell and Kamminga 1979:103–104). Bonnichsen noted that as a flintknapper he felt that this variable was important (1977:128). Dibble and Whittaker (1981) also felt this variable was an important variable, despite the fact that varying this angle from 50° to 70° made no difference in their experiments. They suggested that it might be that a greater angle difference was necessary to cause a significant effect. In this regard, Speth (1975:207) used angles of 90° and 45° and got slightly larger flakes with the 90° angle. These combined results suggest that this angle does have an effect, but only over a large angle difference.

Cotterell and Kamminga also commented on angle of the loading force (1979:111), noting that in addition to exterior platform angle it was the most important factor in flake termination. Force directed into the objective piece gives more feather terminations. Force directed more out of the tool gives hinge terminations and in extreme examples, directed at right angles to the objective piece on a thinner edge, snap fractures that run right across the piece (1979:104–105).

7.3.2 Other observations

As will have become clear by now, these factors give interesting possible insight into some aspects of how some tools were formed; amount of force used and the angle of that force, platform selection attributes as related to desired flake form, and so on. However, they are not providing much insight about other factors, such as the type of hammer used. Hammerstone type in particular has proven very hard to deal with; as will be seen later, the most useful work on this aspect has been done in the study of microchipping usewear analysis. Some further observations are worth noting, however:

(i) in his experiments, Bonnichsen (1977:164) found that evidence of an impact area on the striking platform (crushing, microflaking, microcracking) was associated with hard hammer percussion.

(ii) Faulkner (1973) found that eraillures were initiated from radial fissures (bulbar fissures) and that they were "deeper" on more salient bulbs of percussion. Concerning the list of useful features based on knappers' experience, the presence of radial fissures and salient bulbs of percussion are supposed to be related to hard hammer percussion. If this is so then hard hammer percussion should also preferentially show deep eraillures. (Note: eraillures form as the last spot on the bulb of percussion that actually "tears" away from the objective piece.)

(iii) step terminations, based on fracture mechanics as shown experimentally, are due to stoppage of the fracture crack. This stoppage is due to a flaw in the material or insufficient force.

(iv) hinge terminations are, at least in some cases, due to an "outward" component in the force angle part way through the fracture process. Usually the time required to detach a flake is so small that no such secondary component can be developed by a flintknapper. However, the velocity of fracture can decrease suddenly. This fact has been documented experimentally just prior to a flake "hinging out." The decrease in velocity can be due to a number of factors. One such example is insufficient force, associated with an outward component to the force; the insufficient force may be due to not enough force being applied at the outset, resulting from circumstances such as a rapidly expanding flake on a flat surface (where much force is consumed in lateral expansion).

(v) feather terminations are the "normal" situation.

7.4 Flintknappers' Replication Studies

The greatest insight into how lithic tools are manufactured, and why they are manufactured in a particular way, comes from lithic analysts who are also themselves skilled flintknappers. The experience of these individuals, combined with their ability to experiment to understand, allows them to probe beyond the basics of typology to truly appreciate the decision-making process past flintknappers engaged in. Although, as already discussed in Chapter 1, there was a number of early works that explored the value of this experience, it is with the studies especially of Ellis, Bordes, Leakey, Tixier, and Crabtree that experimental lithic studies really came to be accepted. Their research has been extended by more recent workers such as Rob Bonnichsen (e.g., Young and Bonnichsen 1984), Bruce Bradley (e.g., Frison and Bradley 1980), Jeffrey Flenniken (e.g., 1981), and John Whittaker (e.g., 1994) among many others. Many replicative studies have been done. An examination of a few of them will indicate how much richer our understanding of lithic reduction is as a result of these many efforts. The best work bringing all this expertise together in one place for archaeologists and flintknappers is Whittaker's excellent recent book (1994).

It should also be kept in mind that, fundamentally, all our modern approaches to lithic analysis come from the research of these expert flintknappers. Without their combined research we would not have developed concepts such as "thinning flake," "bifacial reduction flake," etc., to bring meaning from lithic debitage. In a similar fashion, without their expertise and ability to repeatedly produce similar artifacts, we would not have been able devise schemes to segregate debitage of all types based on scar counts in a meaningful manner. Their research has given lithic analysis the opportunity to have confidence in analytical results in both qualitative (e.g., flake types) and quantitative (e.g., number of scars and flake stage) terms.

In replication studies, as Crabtree noted (1966:9), it is not sufficient to successfully produce a particular flake removal or a finished product resembling the original. These studies must duplicate the results obtained by the original flintknapper or the experiment has not revealed the behavioral processes involved. If the flake scars lack prominent conchoidal ripple marks, a technique that gives prominent ripples to the piece has not succeeded in replicating the technology employed. To accomplish this true replication the flintknapper must study both the tools and the debitage that resulted from their production when both are available (e.g., Bordes and Crabtree 1969:1; Frison and Bradley 1980:47). In this regard, failed tools rejected for some reason during manufacture are particularly important to understanding and reconstructing the entire production process, as so well illustrated by the photographs and descriptions in Frison and Bradley's (1980) study of Folsom point manufacture at the Hanson site. As Bordes and Crabtree noted, not only does the study of such rejects show the stages in the normal production of the tool in question, but study of these pieces can eliminate erroneous interpretations that might otherwise seem equally plausible (1969:2).

An example of the insights of replication studies is Crabtree's study of Folsom point manufacture (1966). He showed that the relative convexity of the preform was critical in producing a channel flake and a resultant flute that was sufficiently wide. Preparation of a preform that was too convex resulted in a channel flake that was too narrow to replicate the form of Folsom points (1966:18–19) (this more ridge-like form directs the force and concentrates the lateral spread of the channel flake [Whittaker 1994:237, 240]). His experiments also even gave an understanding of some of the very minor aspects of motor control involved. For example, a worker removing a channel flake had to employ just the right balance of downward and outward force to successfully remove a channel flake of the correct length for the point. Too much outward pressure resulted in a short channel flake, too little and the platform collapsed or the entire point would be crushed; too little downward pressure produced either a step or a hinge fracture, depending on the nature of the outward pressure, rather than the desired feathering termination (1966:20). These observations allow us to appreciate the skill involved in producing these points and also allow us to understand why failures occurred. In replicating Folsom points, Crabtree noted that although a number of techniques could be used to produce the channel flake that fluted the points, only three of these techniques produced features that were representative of the Folsom points from the Lindenmeier site. For example, direct free-hand percussion resulted in undulations that were too prominent to correctly replicate the Lindenmeier points (1966:10). He also noted that direct percussion required heavier points than typical Folsom points and that the distance between the "tangs" at the base of a Folsom point was not sufficiently great to allow use of a sufficiently heavy hammerstone to accomplish the detachment (1966:10–11). These details would not be appreciated by an individual who lacked the experience of flintknapping to know what was, or was not, possible. This example also shows that although a flintknapper may be able to substantially narrow down the possible techniques that might have been used to produce a particular tool, it is probable that a number of possibilities will still be seen as feasible (see also Crabtree's final comments on this, 1966:22). Frison and Bradley also commented on this aspect of replication studies (1982:211–212), suggesting replication provided limits, but not necessarily proofs, of past behavior.

Frison and Bradley also studied Folsom technology and made many observations in their replication study that provide insight into the process. For example, the removal of the second channel flake in fluting must be done from a much more acute and thinner preform base; hence the second channel flake generally has a markedly lipped platform (1980:48) (for an example of this, see Bradley 1982:188, Fig. 33). Again, this variation would not be understood without the perspective obtained in replication studies, nor would it be possible to place these flakes correctly in the production process. In this same study they noted that individual workers will leave their distinctive mark on stone tools and so some variation seen will relate to individual ancient flintknappers (1980:61) (see also Hill and Gunn 1977). Later, this allowed Bradley to use differences in quality of workmanship to speculate that the worker who had manufactured a particular group of Agate Basin projectile points was not the same as the worker who repaired them once they had been broken at the tips (1982:197). Differences in the style of working also were key to allowing Bradley to identify these reworked points in the first place (1982:195–196). These differences included the pressure retouch scars being deeper, more abrupt, and less carefully spaced. Gunn (1977:169) cites Crabtree as suggesting that the repeated production prehistoric flintknappers had experienced suggested to him that a cluster of variables describing their tools would be tighter than the same variables for tools produced by relatively inexperienced modern flintknappers. Based on flake scar orientation patterns on bifaces, Gunn found this to be true (1977:176). Gunn also found that individual flintknappers were discernible (1977:173–174) (see also Young and Bonnichsen 1984). Given the detail with which specific flaking sequences can be reconstructed (e.g., Bradley and Frison 1987:206), it seems likely to me that individual flintknappers should be definable at any particular site, that they might be traceable from one site to another, and that our regional typology and appreciation of ethnic or other social group differences spatially could be much enhanced by detailed replicative studies and reconstruction of manufacturing sequences for individual tools. Bradley and Stanford (1987:411–412) identified features of Scottsbluff and Eden point manufacture that they felt were under strong social control (general outline and mass distribution, basic reduction system) as opposed to those that were primarily controlled by the individual flintknapper (small variations in proportions, variations in sequence terminations, and variations in edge retouch and finishing techniques). Bradley and Frison (1987:201–218) subjected Eden points to this level of careful study. Not only did they remark on the exceptional level of similarity in manufacturing from point to point in their study, but they even went so far as to suggest that an Eden point from the Horner site in northwestern Wyoming had been made by the same flintknapper who had made a point from the Claypool site in eastern Colorado. They finished by saying: "How they came to be in such widely separated sites is, of course, another matter of conjecture."(1987:217).

Bradley (1982:195–196) identified more general features of reworked projectile points that might allow them to be recognized in most circumstances: an abrupt change in thickness along the longitudinal cross section of the point; irregular flake scar patterns truncating the normal, regular scar patterns; abrupt changes in the outline form of the point; and remnants of the impact breaks. Reworking of broken tools is a very important aspect of assessment of resource scarcity and site type. Knowledge of reworking allows analysts to much more accurately reconstruct site activities. Frequency of tool reworking may even provide insight into attitudes about value. As well, since much comparative work in tool stylistic and functional variation is based on measurements on tools, an understanding of how use and reworking has affected those measurements is central to an accurate analysis. In this regard, it is a flintknapper's appreciation of the workability of different raw materials that also is the basis for allowing researchers to assess to what degree the form of the tool is governed by material quality (Crabtree 1966:9). This understanding in turn allows us to understand why particular lithic materials may be chosen to produce particular tool types. Again, these insights would largely be impossible without the research of replicative studies, and the confidence that comes from long experience with working in the medium.

Replication studies can also be the basis of more general inferences not as narrowly related to manufacture of a specific item. Chlachula and Le Blanc (1996) compared the quartzite tool production technology of a late Holocene site and a site dating to late Wisconsin times. Through a demonstration of technological continuity, the authors greatly strengthened their case for the early site being archaeological rather than being the result of natural glacio-fluvial agents. Bradley and Stanford (1987:417–418) were able to broadly view the variation in Eden and Scottsbluff points to reconstruct a production system that paradoxically allowed maximal standardization of point form through a specifically flexible manufacturing structure. Frison and Bradley (1982:211) noted that fluting of Folsom points could be viewed as not necessary and also very wasteful, particularly given the rejection of apparently very useable preforms, and that this might be a basis for suggesting an artistic or ritual basis to the form. Through contrasting the form of breaks in Folsom bifaces in various stages of reduction and use (perverse breaks, bending breaks, and radial breaks), Frison and Bradley (1980:43–44) were able to demonstrate that the former two were essentially the result of manufacturing errors whereas the latter was, in their opinion, the result of intentional breakage not related to manufacturing. Bradley was able to identify an intentional radial break in another Folsom point at the Agate Basin site (Bradley 1982:192–193), in this case an unusual action since both flutes had been successfully completed. Frison and Bradley's understanding of bifacial technology also allowed them to show that despite the fact that more bifacial reduction flakes were retouched compared to cores (bifaces), many more bifacial reduction flakes were produced in the bifacial reduction process (a ratio of 20:1). This situation indicated that the absolute number of bifacial reduction flakes alone did not certainly mean that the flakes were the primary goal of reduction (1980:21). When Bordes and Crabtree studied blade making technology in both North America and Europe, they found that the relative curvature or straightness of blades was probably dependent on both the use of a rest (which resulted in straight blades) and the form of the core, with some European Paleolithic cores specifically being bidirectional to produce straight blades (1969:7–9). They found Upper Perigordian blades to be distinctively straight, whereas New World Clovis and Old World Aurignacian blades were distinctively curved. The form of blades in turn limited the uses that they could be put to. In particular, Bordes and Crabtree noted that the curvature and size of Clovis blades made them unsuitable as blanks for Clovis point production. These observations on blade form help us to use various archaeological materials as temporal markers and also allow us to more fully understand tool function.

7.5 Analysis Implementation

The experimental data outlined in this chapter provides the basis on which tool production techniques can be inferred. The depth of flake scars on tools can be used to infer if hard hammer percussion was important in all or some stages of tool production, and the size of scars in particular can be used to indicate if pressure flaking was an important technique. These same features can be used to examine associated lithic debitage and so make comparable inferences that should lend support to the inferences based on the tools themselves. Obviously, later flake removals will intersect and partially obliterate earlier flake removal scars on a tool and such intersecting can be used as the basis to determine at what stage in the production process a particular technique was used. Similarly, flaking can be done in different patterns, at times even being quite opportunistic, and the use of such strategies can be related to differing stages in the production based on an assessment of which scars are overlapped and superimposed on others. The sequencing of strategies and the detachment techniques employed in each stage can also give clues about the production process, such as the degree to which mass and bulk are being rather opportunistically removed as opposed to the degree to which very precise, specific goals are being achieved. For example, it can be determined that there was an initial hard hammer thinning and reduction stage, evidenced by large, deep, cross-section flake scars, these scars underlying later small shallow flake scars from final pressure finishing.

Integrating these lines of evidence with evidence on reduction stages and material type sources provides the means to achieve a comprehensive interpretation of stone tool production. For example, an absence of large hard hammer flakes in the debitage of tools made from exotic lithic material could indicate that the hard hammer percussion still visible in some of the tools was something that was done at the quarry and then the preforms were traded as roughouts to other more distant peoples; alternatively this pattern could indicate that the raw material was acquired at the quarry and that the initial preform was produced there. An earlier stage of soft hammer percussion can be identified by larger lipped bifacial reduction flake debitage of the same material type, even if subsequent pressure finishing has obliterated the scars from that earlier step on the finished tools. The critical point to make here is that it is the comparison of the results from these various lines of research that allows the clues from one type of evidence to fill in the gaps in another.

CHAPTER 8

The Meaning of Form in Lithic Tools

8.1 Types of Form

The context in which a lithic tool is found usually reveals some aspect of that tool's function, as for example the finding of incised scrapers preferentially in ritual contexts in the Early Middle Bronze Age in the Levant (Rosen 1997:74-79). Examination of the basic shape of a stone tool, or any other object for that matter, gives some idea of what it is and what it functioned as (i.e., a projectile point, a chair, a pot, etc.). There is generally something basic about the form of an object that relates to its function. The functional aspect of form may not be readily apparent for a number of reasons, such as the following:

1. The observer may not understand or know about the type of function an object serves (e.g., if most people were given a small piece from the inside of a rocket engine, it is unlikely they would know the item's function).

2. A number of more or less identical objects can perform different functions (e.g., nuts and bolts can fasten many things).

3. Different objects can perform the same function (e.g., the many sizes and shapes of containers that can carry water; the many things that serve as doorstops).

In lithic analysis these points might all be issues of concern when looking at retouched flake tools. Function is only one aspect of form, however.

Another aspect of form is that there may be basic ideas about how a particular object should look. This idea need not have any specific relationship to function (e.g., the exact outline form of a projectile point). This aspect of form is very important archaeologically, since it may vary from one culture to another and may be used to define cultural and geographic variants. Such ideas may also change through time, either in a gradual unconscious manner or due to specific conscious decisions about such "style." This circumstance, of course, gives us temporal marks in archaeology. Related to this, an artifact may be made in a style of a particular "school" of craftsmen, etc. (e.g., in wood carving, or in the Crabtree flintknappers versus the Bordes flintknappers).

Another facet of stone tool form is that different raw materials may cause variation in form, as for example, a projectile point made in English flint versus one made in Alberta quartzite. The contrast in form between an axe made in a stone that can be flaked versus one that can only be worked by pecking, grinding, and polishing, is another good example. Certain aspects of the style may be designed to convey a meaning, such as a crest on a shield, the style of projectile point in a dead enemy, and so on. As well, some aspects of the form may relate to the individual worker, in terms of his or her habits or skill.

The meaning of form, and how archaeologists perceive and interpret it, have long been points of debate. The problem is not simply one of lithic analysis, but rather one of archaeology in general. This issue has its inception in some of the original arguments concerning the concept of "type."

As archaeologists, the beginning point of our examination of form in lithic artifacts is with the nature of how we group our material into tool types for analysis. Aspects of this debate in archaeology go back to the late 1930s and Rouse's *Prehistory of Haiti*, but the debate resolved itself into two strong opposing positions in the early 1950s:

1. Types are inherent in the material: they relate to the intended form or mental template of the maker, and archaeologists "discover" them by analysis (e.g., Spaulding 1953). In other words, archaeologically identified types are "real."

2. Types are essentially invented by archaeologists: they are simply arbitrary divisions along a continuum of variation, divisions that are analytically useful but that have no necessary similarity to anything "real" (e.g., Ford 1952).

More recently this has been termed the difference between emic categories (recognized by the informant or culture under study) and etic categories (those imposed or discerned by the outside observer).

Determining the answer to this question about whether types are "real" or only arbitrary analytical divisions is certainly not easy. If the type is a chronological indicator, its absence before and after a certain time clearly suggests it has some validity or "reality." But at the same time, the type definition may still delineate an arbitrary slice of a continuum. The same applies to geographic types having a restricted geographic distribution. The restricted distribution suggests some cultural/ethnic reality, but the cut-off point may still be "unreal." Functional types, "this form is used for this task," are generally based on ethnographic analogy and "common sense." These types are reasonable means to define functional forms, but there is no guarantee that our concepts of what a tool should be like is how such tools were conceived in the past. In a similar vein, there is no guarantee that analogy from the historic period applies in prehistory or in areas far removed geographically.

One approach to this apparent dilemma is to realize that in some sense it is not really an issue. In many aspects of typology it does not matter what the maker thought. As objective, external analysts we study the material in a manner that allows us to see meaning at a level of which even the maker is unaware. As Rosen has noted (1997:25), types need not represent the original producer's conception; their legitimacy is that they are reproducible and are analytically useful. If types can be distinguished analytically, they are real. They are not emic, but they are real all the same. Studying emic categorization (or folk taxonomies, as they are sometimes called) is a specialized area of study within the larger sphere of typological or formal analysis. This level of analysis is popular and somewhat successful in anthropology, where informants can be questioned to elicit their typologies, but in archaeology it can be very problematic (even in anthropology it can be very difficult, as for example when informants do not wish to tell the "anthropologist" for one reason or another). Young and Bonnichsen (1984) have employed a cognitive anthropological approach to study modern flintknapping in this way, although they do not analyze an archaeological sample.

In point of fact, in the archaeological "real" world it is quite probable that most types defined have both an emic and an etic component to them, or more precisely, the etic classification we derive is probably in part correlated with the emic categorization of the maker.

Having circumvented the emic/etic problem, at least for operational purposes, a problem still remains. If a certain number of types or forms can be defined analytically, what do these types or forms mean? Functional differences, ethnic differences, and temporal differences are all possibilities, among others. This problem was at the center of another well known and acrimonious archaeological debate that occurred in the late 1960s: the debate between François Bordes, on the one hand, and Lewis and Sally Binford, on the other, on the meaning of different Mousterian lithic assemblages in France (see Bordes 1968:98–106 for descriptions; also Champion et al. 1984:46–48). There are a number of Mousterian varieties that have no apparent restriction relative to each other in terms of temporal or geographic factors; they are basically present as distinct layers in varying order throughout a region over a particular time span (ca. 80,000–40,000 B.P.). The varieties are defined by differing tool frequencies (scrapers, denticulates, backed blades, handaxes) and the importance of the Levallois technique in tool manufacturing. Bordes saw these assemblages as representing different ethnic or cultural groups inhabiting the same area. The Binfords saw the assemblages as due to different functions in the occupations (e.g., manufacturing non-lithic tools, animal processing, plant processing, etc.); they based this assessment on assumed function of the tools. Although the printed debate ended some 15 years ago for the most part, the question remains unresolved, although current opinion seems to be that neither of these extremes represents the actual situation.

Obviously every tool, more or less, had a function and so likely some aspect of its form may be related to that function. As already noted, ethnographic analogy and "common sense", in terms of what form might have been appropriate for a particular task, are two ways in which function can be assessed. Most basic formal tool types employ this type of analysis (e.g., scraper, projectile point). The obvious other method to define function is through usewear and residue analysis. This area of study has had a significant effect on lithic tool typologies and will be discussed, both its uses and problems, later in the section on usewear and residue analysis.

In this regard, there are three main points to be learned from usewear analysis and the study of functional types:

1. Similar tool types are not necessarily used for the same purpose, and sometimes tools that are formally the same have been used for different tasks.

2. Tools may be used for more than one purpose, sometimes on the same edge area and sometimes on different portions of the same tool. A major problem here is that if an edge is reused, or sharpened and reused, for a different task, usually this new use obliterates traces of the original use. This situation may complicate functional interpretations.

3. Usewear analysis has shown that very simple tools, such as retouched flakes (edge modified flakes), can perform a variety of functions with very little modification and very little formal variation. It is not necessary to have particularly different forms for different tasks.

These comments on form and function apply as much to ground stone tools as they do to flaked stone tools. For example, Horsfall undertook an ethnoarchaeological study of grinding stones, including among other aspects an examination of the form of the grinding stones and their function(s). The study showed that some grinding stones had specific functions and sometimes these functions were well correlated with form, but in other cases they served more than one function (1987:336–340). In some of these latter cases the grinding stones were seen as having a primary function with others secondary. Leach's (1996) examination of historic period European adze form showed that the function of an adze was closely linked to its morphology (e.g., fine trimming versus rough shaping), but that the area in which it was used (e.g., ship building versus barrel making) was not easily defined from form alone without the context (1996:414). There are many variations in form for ground stone tools such as adzes (e.g., Duff 1970, Smith and Leach 1996) but as with flaked stone tools, it is unlikely that form is a straightforward guide to function. Based on Leach's study, however, at least some of the main aspects of form, such as the narrowness of chisels and the hollow bit of gouges, are functional in nature.

Partially in response to questions about the function of various tool types, there has been a concerted effort in the last 25 years or so to gather data about stone tool production and use in cultures that still use such tools, or did until recently. Most of this work has been in Australia and New Guinea, but some has also been undertaken in Mesoamerica, Ethiopia, and Turkey.

An important aspect of the Australian and New Guinea research is that the main focus of emic tool typology is the form of the actual edge portion to be used, with less regard for the more general form. The presence of an appropriate area to grip was also important, and in New Guinea there was also a basic size criterion of "large" for heavy tasks and "small" for lighter. This observation might suggest that most tools were not of a formal type, and it might be cause for wonder at all the elaborate lithic typologies archaeologists have devised over the years. But this observation is particularly true only of New Guinea. Although basically true of Australia as well, Hayden (1979b:14) found that by and large there was a basic recognizable tool morphology for each major type of task (chopping, adzing, sawing, scraping, shaving, cutting). It should also be noted that prehistorically both Australia and New Guinea had few formed tool types; hence the general absence of formal types ethnographically may reflect on Australian and New Guinea tradition that is not characteristic of other regions.

The edge angle of a tool's working edge, that is the angle formed by the two converging faces, is obviously of major functional significance. Australian Aborigines recognized two basic classifications: steep edges for scraping and sharp edges for cutting (Gould et al. 1971). It is obvious even to us that a fairly acute angle is necessary for cutting. Some other ethnoarchaeological data on edge angle and functional tool types (with Wilmsen's [1968] logical or common sense edge angles in brackets) include the following:

1. Flake scrapers (Wilmsen angle for heavy tasks, 66–75°): Hayden (1979b) found that in Australia these tools had edge angles mostly in the range of 60° to 90°. The distribution had peaks at 80°, 90°, and 60° and had a range of 35-95°. Ferguson (1980), also in Australia, obtained a range of 56–113° with a mean of 71°. Gallagher (1977) found that in Ethiopia hide scrapes had an edge angle of 125° +/- 4.72°. These angles and ranges are clearly not the same, but the Ethiopian tools may be a very specialized variant since they were used for a very particular task.

2. Chopping tools (Wilmsen angle for heavy tasks, 66–75°): Hayden (1979b) found the Australian material peaked at 75° and had most of the edges in the 60–90° range, with a total range of 55–115°.

3. Flake adzes (Wilmsen angle for heavy tasks, 66–75°): Hayden (1979b) obtained a peak at 70° for the edge angle of these tools; most had an angle of between 65° and 85° and the angle total range was 30–95°. The material Gould et al. (1971) obtained, also in Australia, showed an edge angle peak at 60° and a total range of 40° to something less than 90°.

4. Cutting knives (Wilmsen angle for cutting, 26–35°): the data Ferguson (1980) obtained in Australia showed an edge angle range of 21–48° for these tools, with a 35° mean. Gould et al. (1971) found all cutting tool edge angles were less than 60° and greater than 18°.

5. Flake saws (Wilmsen angle for general tasks, 46–55°): Hayden's material (1979b) showed no major peaks in its distribution, though a greatest frequency at 50°, but instead found a broad range of edge angles from 25° to 85°.

Other information on stone tool form and function is available from ethnoarchaeological studies of stone tools:

i) Strathern (1969), working in New Guinea, found that there were regular features of polished stone axes. As such, large flake tools were not seen as substitutes for axes or equivalent to them in anyway. In an area where flat-faced axes were made, an axe with a lenticular cross section brought in by the anthropologist was not recognized as an axe because the cross section was inappropriate.

ii) Both Strathern (1969) and White (1967), working in New Guinea, found that flake tools were not initially sharpened by retouch. This was only done later in resharpening. Hayden noted (1979b) that in Australia only the flake adze was flaked over the tool body, rather than just at the edge of the tool. Again, this may have been due to the general absence of formal tool types in the Australian and New Guinean areas.

iii) In terms of resharpening, Gallagher (1977) noted that the hide scrapers he was studying in Ethiopia had to be resharpened every 50-150 strokes. The resharpening was not because the edges became dull, but rather because small nicks and projections had to be removed from the edge so that the tool would not cut or gouge the hide. One result of this frequent resharpening was that tool shape could change rapidly.

iv) Both Strathern and White noted that the same tool could be successfully used for several different tasks. White noted, as an example, that a large piece of chert might serve as a hammer, a core, a scraper, a plane, and a knife. Strathern noted that a flake with a point at the intersection of edges might function in scraping, cutting, gouging, and plant fiber shredding.

v) Backing may be used to remove a sharp area on a tool where it must be held (White and Thomas 1972:279; Gould et al. [1971]) in Australia and New Guinea, but in Australia at least, a gum resin "handle" might also be used to protect the hand. This strategy, of course, leaves no archaeological trace (unless residue analysis is conducted), but the absence of backing could result in an implement being classified in a very different tool type.

vi) Based on Hayden's (1979b) work, chopping implements have a basic functional attribute: they are large (in his study, these tools weighed from 0.25 to 3.0 kg). He found form to be mainly a function of extent of resharpening, ranging from new and unretouched to old and so retouched that the piece had become too small (light) to use anymore.

Overall, then, some aspects of lithic tool form are related to function. In some cases, however, the relationship may be quite minimal, such as general sizes, broad classes of edge angle, and comfort in holding.

Obviously there are other factors that influence the shape of a tool, such as the aspects of form previously mentioned in regards to changes through time and through geographic space or the differing ethnic or cultural groups Bordes saw in the Mousterian assemblages. There are others as well and some are briefly examined below.

In contrast to functional variation, there are two main aspects of what may be termed "style"

(Sackett 1982, 1985, 1986; Weissner 1983, 1985):

1. Formal attributes that are purposefully chosen by the worker to convey a meaning. This has been termed iconic style (icon = symbol). If the message conveyed refers to a person's ethnic or cultural affiliation, this is termed emblemic style (from emblem, as on a shield, flag, etc.). If the message concerns personal identity (e.g., a maker's mark), this is termed assertive style. Hence iconic style has both an ethnic and an individual level.

2. There is a less conscious or totally unconscious level of style that has been termed isochrestic style, literally meaning "equivalent in use." There are almost invariably more than one means to achieve any end result. Where a choice or series of choices are made, consciously or unconsciously, a "style" of the artifact comes into being (Kooyman [1981:32–33, 47–69], Whittaker [1994:289]; but for a comprehensive view that sees this approach as inadequate, see Schiffer and Skibo [1997]). Isochrestic style is visible at many levels of analysis. As an example, there are many ways in which a flake of a general size and shape can be removed from a tool edge. For an individual flintknapper in a particular culture attempting to remove such a flake:

i) members of the flintknapper's culture may only know some of the techniques theoretically possible. Or, members of the culture may have ideas about what technique is appropriate to achieve the end on a particular type of tool (e.g., for aesthetic reasons) (Whittaker 1994:290). One way or another, the technique used gives an unconscious signal of ethnicity because of what is selected from the theoretical universe of possibilities.

ii) similar types of limited knowledge and conventions may operate with a particular subgroup within the worker's ethnic group, as for example his or her residence group, "school" of teaching (Kooyman 1981:47, 61–69; Whittaker 1994:290), or family. Isochrestic variation can be used to isolate these finer divisions of social group (Kooyman 1981:47–53; Whittaker 1994:291). Clearly, iconic style might also operate on this level.

iii) such limited knowledge or preference in techniques and designs can operate at the individual level and so be used to isolate individual style (Kooyman 1981:61–69; Whittaker 1994:290–291). Individual knappers may have a preferred technique to achieve a particular end, simply because it works best for them, out of a number of known techniques. This can be related to a flintknapper's skill in the craft, or the "school" of teaching in which he or she learned. If there is a series of steps in a process, it may be possible to undertake them in various orders, and this can have an effect on the final form since varying the last step (which often obliterates all or some of the previous steps) also varies the final form (contour, flake scar, etc.). Even motor habits of individuals can leave their "mark." Young and Bonnichsen's *Understanding Stone Tools: A Cognitive Approach* (1984) is a good source to illustrate this type of variation, especially Appendices IV and V.

It is necessary to note that the coarse temporal control present in most archaeological records and the many factors that affect where items are deposited and how their context may be further altered, has led researchers such as Rick (1996:247) to doubt that these fine subdivisions of style, individual or social group, will ever be archaeologically visible. It is Rick's view that there is no obvious way to know that any particular aspect of archaeological material culture is related to any specific aspect or scale of human behavior; a style variant can be isolated and defined, but its *specific* social correlate cannot be determined. Although I disagree with this last statement, given that there are "scales" of variation that can be related to individual behavior and that there are others that are clearly choices from among possible alternatives that must relate to cultural knowledge, I agree that once some "social group" patterning has been isolated, the actual nature of that group (ethnic group, work group, etc.) may not be definable. The success that *is* possible with archaeological material, even to the level of the individual flintknapper, is well illustrated by Whittaker's summary (1994:291–297) of his dissertation research. Rick also does see possibilities in this line of inquiry. Where there are many stylistic forms in a given stratigraphic unit, then the forms must be the result of differences between contemporaneous individuals or groups, what he refers to as production units or entities (1996:255). Rick's late preceramic period shows dense occupation with a relatively small number of stylistic entities that are localized to particular sites. Given that they must have had contact in this densely occupied period, yet they maintain integrity, he suggests (albeit tentatively) that the entities were consciously produced as stylistic indicators by the groups involved. His analysis divides his projectile point "type groups" into three finer stylistic groupings (type, then variant, and finally affinity group) and his discussion suggests that these do reflect social group subdivisions, with the variant perhaps related to a local residence social unit (1996:273–275). I suspect that an analysis employing Ricks combination of style subdivisions, spatial localization, and occupation density, with an examination of the association between scales of variation and human behavior and motor habits, could begin to provide us with a much better understanding of the meaning of style.

The discussion above has only barely touched on the kinds of analysis and factors that could be considered in studying iconic and isochrestic style, either at the individual level or on a larger social group or ethnic level. There are too many possibilities to be able to explore them thoroughly here, but modern experimental research (Gunn 1977) has shown that individual flintknappers can be isolated and that these techniques can be applied to archaeological material. More general levels of lithic analysis clearly show that the ethnic level of variation can also be isolated.

One aspect of this type of formal analysis is that if someone wishes to conspicuously display a message, iconic style, then obviously they will choose an artifact type that is likely to be seen by lots of people, both because it is in plain view and possibly also because it has a long uselife. So iconic style is more likely to be present in particular types of artifacts. In lithic analysis, these artifacts would include projectile points (e.g., to indicate who killed an individual or to indicate that a buffalo belongs to a particular hunter), ornaments, war clubs, mortar and pestles, etc. Isochrestic style should be present in all artifacts.

As previously discussed, a particular function for a stone tool can be achieved with a variety of forms. Clearly, isochrestic style can occur in functional form; the simple tool types in Australia and New Guinea are a good example of this. Because of the need for iconic style to be obvious and unambiguous, it is less likely to be manifest in functional form, although it may be so. Hence, function and style need not be mutually exclusive.

Most any other kind of formal variation in lithic artifacts can be encompassed under the banner of isochrestic variation—conscious and unconscious choices from within the sphere of possibilities. One other type of variation is that of the medium the artisan is working in. In lithic artifacts, this medium is the actual type of stone employed. In practice, this defines the limits or realm of possibility. Some stone tools just cannot be made out of poor quality material, and the flakeability of material will have an effect

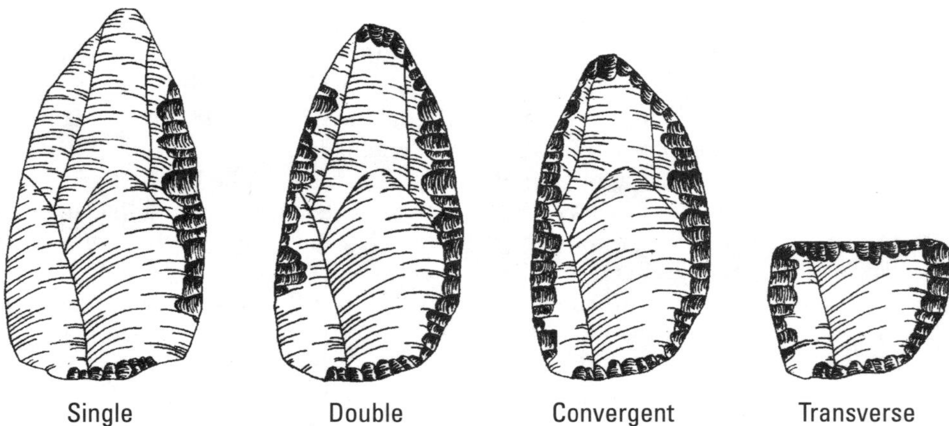

Figure 44: Mousterian scraper types interpreted as rejuvenation stages (after Dibble 1984, 1987)

on the finished form and appearance of a tool. The properties of the stone may limit what is actually possible and what techniques can be used to achieve a desired end. Raw material type can, for example, limit the size of tools that can be made depending on the size of pieces the stone comes in (e.g., river pebbles versus 40 m thick beds). In poor or moderate quality quartzite, flakes simply will not run as far or as predictably as with obsidian, flint, or similar material.

Another type of variation is the form of a tool as it changes due to use and subsequent resharpening, or due to breakage and "retooling" or rejuvenating/fixing. One good example of this type of situation is when a projectile point has its tip broken off. The blunted end can be re-pointed, but the resulting tool is quite a bit more stubby (see also Rondeau's [1996] discussion of Elko point form and Flenniken's [1985] discussion of reworking). Another example comes from a study of Mousterian scrapers by Dibble (1984, 1987). Although 16 types of scrapers are "recognized" in the generalized Mousterian (see also Bordes 1988), this number can be reduced to four basic types:

1. *Simple, single-sided:* retouched on one lateral edge of a flake

2. *Double:* retouched on two non-adjoining edges

3. *Convergent:* retouched on two adjacent edges to form a "point"

4. *Transverse:* retouched on the distal end of a flake

These morphological variants are held to have various functional and chronological implications. Dibble (1984, 1987), however, sees these variants instead as a series of rejuvenation stages, or reduction stages as he terms them (see Fig. 44). As suggested by this conceptualization, there are two reduction routes along which a scraper may go: (1) as a single edged scraper is used up, another edge may be started to give a double scraper, with this tool ultimately being reduced to a convergent scraper, or (2) a single scraper can be gradually reduced down to the point at which it becomes a transverse scraper.

Before applying these ideas to archaeological classification, a final note concerning some problems of the mechanics of classification is warranted. The first issue is concerned with reproducibility. Hopefully each analyst has a classification scheme sufficiently clear that he or she will come up with the same formal types if the material is gone through a second time; i.e., the classification is consistent. In fact, it is not always that easy to achieve this goal, especially if "types" are somewhat vaguely defined.

A more significant problem is whether different workers are classifying artifacts in the same way, so that sites are comparable. This issue is certainly a more common problem, but hopefully expertise and a series of clear definitions can be relied on to minimize this source of inconsistency.

A final point to emphasize is clarity, because a lack of clarity can create significant problems if classifications are not comparable. An aspect of this can be seen in the Upper Paleolithic of France, where the multitude of classifications that have been amalgamated into a more or less single body of types has resulted in different names for the same tool type in some cases. Examples include "frontal long end scraper," which is the same as "blade end scraper," and "borer", which is the same as "straight beak."

8.2 Functional Tool Types

Based on the above discussion, then, in terms of functional types based on tool morphology, first keep in mind that usewear analysis has shown that there will be exceptions to almost any formal type/functional connection (although usewear has its problems too, and may be in error). At the same time there are some trends, some quite strong, that can at least be used as general guidelines. What follows is a list and description of various tool type definitions commonly used in archaeology. Some are felt to have a functional aspect to their form and this aspect is noted. Some have already been covered at least to some extent.

8.2.1 Fabricators

Fabricators are tools that are used to make other tools. The main types include:

Figure 45: Hammerstone

Figure 46: Anvil

1. *Hammerstones ("hard hammer percussors"):* tools used to detach flakes. They comprise rocks of various shapes and sizes depending on the specific tasks for which they are used. A key characteristic that they usually possess is battering and/or crushing on one or more ends or edges (Fig. 45).

2. *Anvils:* function as a resting place for the objective piece during reduction. A characteristic that they usually have is localized pitting/crushing on one or more faces, generally near the center of the face(s) (Fig. 46).

3. *Cores:* already mentioned above, are pieces of lithic material from which flakes have been

Figure 47: Prepared (platform) core (flaked face)

removed with the intention of using those flakes as the starting point for tools.

There are two basic types of cores. Unprepared cores are those that have no striking platform preparation. Prepared cores (or platform cores) have a striking platform that has been prepared prior to flake removal (Fig. 47). Unprepared cores are also referred to as random or amorphous cores (and sometimes as "angular," if they have naturally good edges and platforms). Bipolar cores, which have also already been discussed, are another example of usually unprepared cores.

Cores can also be classified according to where flakes are removed. Unidirectional cores have the flakes detached from one end, bidirectional cores have flakes detached from two different directions (this can be on a tabular core, a dischoidal core, etc.), and multidirectional cores (usually) show flakes removed from three or more directions (some analysts also include bidirectional cores in this last category).

Various other generalized shape or technique terms are employed to describe cores (see Fig. 48). Cylindrical, polyhedral, blade, microblade, and prismatic are used to describe elongate blade cores (Fig. 49). Conical, or cone-shaped, are similar to this first category but are less elongate. Bipolar cores show the opposing battering and other features of bipolar reduction using both a hammerstone and an anvil. Dischoidal cores have a distinct disc shape, often as a result of reduction from multiple directions into the body of the core. Levallois cores result from the use of the Levallois technique to produce formed flake tools directly. Tabular cores have a rectangular, tab-like shape. Tongue-shaped, wedge-shaped, or boat-shaped cores have an upswung, converging form.

8.2.2 Reduction stage tools

Tools associated with various stages in the reduction process have already been discussed, but it is worth reiterating that these are tools as well since they are recognizable stages in the formation of finished tools. The first of these is the blank, basically an unmodified pebble/cobble or flake of suitable size and shape for further reduction to manufacture another tool. Preforms, or roughouts, are another stage in the production process. They represent a blank taken to a particular stage with subsequent work then stopped; "roughout" is usually used to refer to larger axe-like tools (axes, adzes, handaxes). A reject is an unfinished tool, with manufacturing not completed usually due to some manufacturing problem.

8.2.3 Finished tool types: General

The many specialized formed tools will be discussed in the next section, but there are more generalized tools that can also be isolated in analysis. The first of these is the utilized flake. This tool is basically an unmodified flake or piece of shatter that has had a naturally appropriate edge(s) used for some task. Its distinguishing feature is the presence of edge damage from use, but no tool-forming modification or retouch. In a sense these are the "simplest" tool type. Utilized flakes can have various functions.

Edge modified flakes are similar to utilized flakes in that they can have a variety of functions and that they are minimally modified. These tools are flakes or pieces of shatter that have had one or more of the tool edges (only)

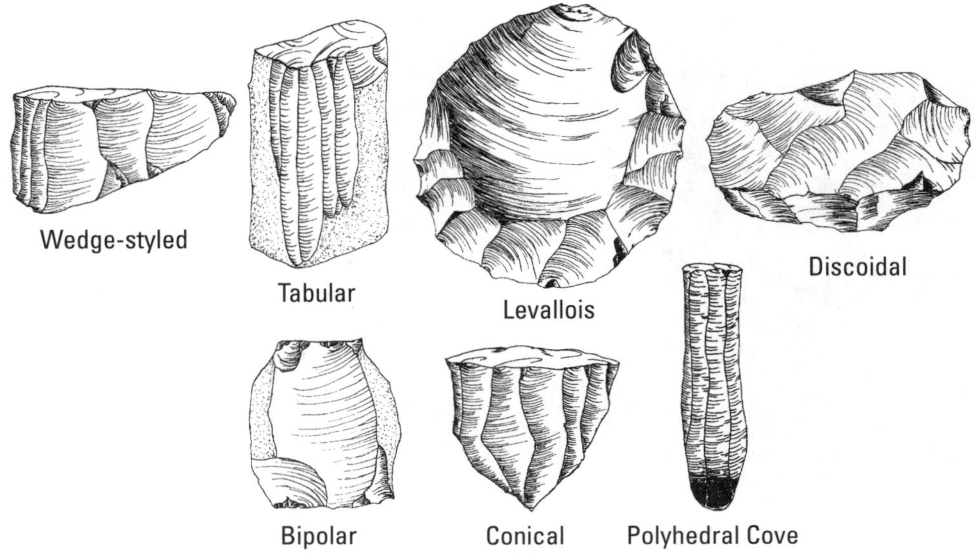

Figure 48: Core types based on shape

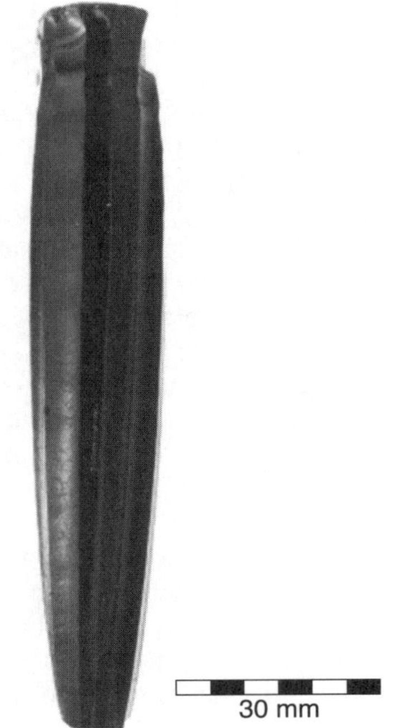

Figure 49: Cylindrical Mesoamerican blade core (lateral view)

retouched to shape that edge for use. These tools may be either unifacially or bifacially worked on the edge. They have also been called retouched flakes, marginally retouched tools or flakes, or flake tools. Utilized flakes and edge modified flakes have also sometimes been referred to jointly as marginally utilized or retouched lithic (MURL), particularly because it can be difficult to distinguish the two tool types in many cases.

Unifaces, discussed before, are tools that have manufacturing flaking extending over all or almost all of one face; again, these tools may have many possible functions. Bifaces, also previously discussed, are similar to unifaces except that the flaking extends over all, or almost all, of both faces of the tool. Again, there are many possible functions for these tools.

8.2.4 Finished tool types: Specific

There are many tool types that are specifically modified and shaped to perform a particular function or a restricted range of functions.

Figure 50: End scraper (dorsal view, working edge to top)

Scrapers are one of the most common of these tool types, their assumed function being for various scraping tasks. The basic distinguishing feature of scrapers is a moderately steep (obtuse) to quite obtuse edge angle (Fig. 50). Most commonly these edges are between 80° and 90°, but scrapers can be found with edge angles between 70° and 125°. In a study of 67 scraping tools (defined based on usewear) from an Alaskan site, Siegel found edge angles to be almost exclusively between 40° and 70° (Siegel 1985). The most common edge profile for these tools is slightly to moderately convex. They are usually unifacial and they may be hafted. There are many types of scrapers, the main ones being the following:

a) *side scraper:* the working edge is on a lateral flake edge (i.e., on the long edge rather than the short edge)

b) *end or transverse scraper:* the working edge is on the short margin, generally either the proximal or distal end of the flake

c) *thumbnail scraper:* these get their name from being approximately the size and shape of a thumbnail

Spokeshaves, also called "notches," are essentially concave-edged scrapers that are generally assumed to be woodworking tools. Certainly this edge form would have been useful for working circular cross sectioned wooden implements such as arrow shafts, but it is very probable that many tools with concave edges were not used to work wood.

Knives are a third specific tool type, more generally called **cutting tools**, with the term "knife" being reserved for thin, extensively worked bifacial cutting tools. The basic feature of knives and other cutting tools is an acute-angled (usually 30–40°) working edge that has a straight to slightly convex outline (Siegel (1985) suggested that cutting tools should have edge angles of 26° to 35° based on his study of scrapers) (Fig. 51). Commonly, the entire tool is quite thin, to aid in depth penetration into the worked material without the central portion of the tool "binding" on the sides of the groove cut into the material worked. These tools may be hafted and often do not have an obvious dorsal and ventral surface, nor an obvious tip and butt. Based on their form they are assumed to have had a cutting function. There are various specialized forms and named types (e.g., Cody knife on the North American Plains; crescentic knife). Cutting tools may also be made of ground stone rather than flaked stone, these often made from slate.

Saws (also called **denticulates**) (Bordaz 1970:19; Bordes 1988:54; Debénath and Dibble 1994:34) are similar to knives, but have either a toothed saw-like edge in outline or a sinuous edge-on or outline profile; this latter form is not as common. It is assumed that these tools were employed in a sawing motion (i.e., more "ripping" than a cutting knife, and in a return stroke action).

Figure 51: Flaked knife

Figure 52: Chopper

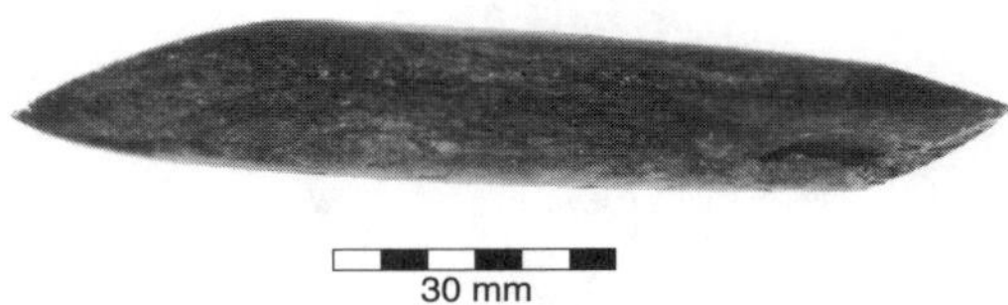

Figure 53: Adze (working edge, bit, to left)

Choppers (unifacial) and **chopping tools** (bifacial) (Bordes 1968:36) are another common tool type discussed previously. These tools are distinguished by their relatively large size (Bordes 1988:69) and usually a moderate edge angle (ca. 50–70°). They are often quite minimally worked (Fig. 52). It is assumed that they are used in chopping tasks where the weight of the tool as it is swung is important in ensuring penetration into the worked material.

There are also more specialized tools that in some respects function as choppers or chopping tools. **Handaxes** (see Fig. 38) are one of these more specialized tools that have already been discussed in some detail. Suffice it to say that handaxes are generally large, pear-shaped, axe-like implements. They have moderately steep edge angles, similar to those for choppers. Handaxes are generally assumed to be chopping tools or multipurpose tools that may have been used in a variety of tasks. Handaxes may have been hafted.

Heavy chopping tasks can be accomplished by other specialized tools, including **axes** and **adzes** (with **celt** [Bordaz 1970:95] being the general, inclusive term for both). Axes have a cutting edge in the plane of the haft and the cutting edge is usually symmetric. In contrast, adzes have a similar overall form but with the working edge at right angles to the haft and often asymmetric (Fig. 53). Axes are assumed to have a chopping function while adzes are generally assumed to act more in a heavy shaving (adzing) manner. Both tool types are generally assumed to have been hafted and many hafted examples are known archaeologically (e.g., Bordaz 1970:95, 99; Sinoto 1982). They usually have a large size and moderate edge angle of about 50-70°. They are often made of ground stone rather than flaked stone. Particularly narrow adzes may be called **chisels** and those with a hollowed, U-shaped bit may be called **gouges** (Bordaz 1970:98).

Figure 54: Drill

Figure 55: Burin

Pièces esquillées are generally made of a rectangular, rather thin but not too thin, piece of lithic material, such as a thicker flake, piece of shatter, bipolar flake, or core. These tools are assumed to have been used in a wedge-like function for working wood or bone, with the material being worked by hammering the tool into the material to wedge off slices. Distinctive features of *pièces esquillées* are a rather stubby but thin cross section and extensive battering and step-flaking at both the hammered and contact ends. Edge angles are somewhat acute to moderate (ca. 40-70°), but the precise angle is often difficult to define due to the extensive damage on the ends. The working edge is rather straight and squared.

"**Perforators**" of various sorts are sharp pointed implements designed to create holes or grooves in various materials. There are a number of quite distinct tools in this category. **Drills** are used in a rotary motion. They generally have a bifacially worked point, may be hafted, and are used on hard material (Fig. 54). Rosen (1997:68) characterizes drills as being manufactured in a relatively standardized form and having bits that are longer, narrower, and thinner than various other boring tools. Perforators are used in a generally back and forth motion through the material. They are frequently minimally altered, or unifacial, on the tip. **Gravers** are similar to perforators, but the tip end is thicker so that it can withstand greater pressure. These tools are used in a somewhat scraping fashion to create narrow grooves and incisions. They are small chisel-like implements. **Burins** are very similar to gravers, but are specifically produced by removing a flake from the working end at a right angle to the long axis of the flake, then usually a second flake (Fig. 55) at more or less a right angle to the first (and parallel to the blade/flake long axis) (see also Bordes 1988:50). The second removed flake is known as a burin spall, which may also be used as a tool. There are a great many types of burins. The burin working edge is thin and chisel-like, used in a motion

Figure 56: Projectile point types (top left is stemmed, corner notched; top right shows side and basal notches; bottom left is lanceolate; middle bottom is basally notched; bottom right is stemmed)

"transverse" to the tool length. Burins are often considered to be particularly bone working tools, although they can also be used on wood.

Points or **projectile points** are basically specialized perforating tools, generally conceived of as having been the penetrating end (tip) of a weapon (arrow, dart, spear). Where this function is fairly certain, these tools are called projectile points; where this use is not so certain, these tools are usually called "points" (many of these latter "points" were probably just gravers or perforators). Their form is pointed, basically symmetrical, and thin. These tools are generally conceived of as having been hafted, especially projectile points. There are huge numbers of varieties of points, basic forms defined on overall shape and on basal area hafting features.

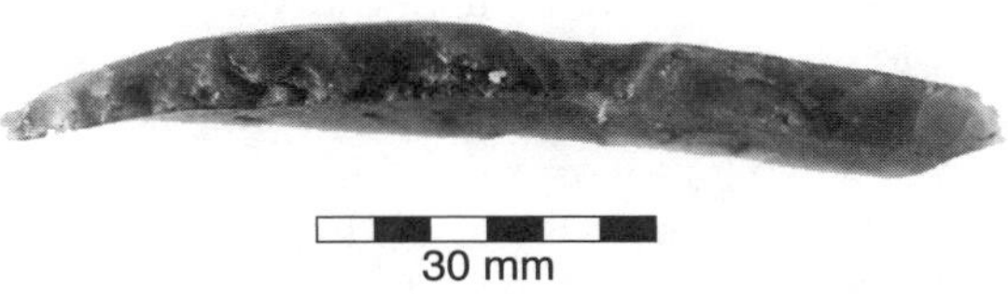

Figure 57: Microlith (backed edge)

Particularly in regards to the haft area there are three main types of projectile points (Fig. 56): (i) unnotched and unstemmed, (ii) stemmed, with a shoulder (a distinct break in the outline shape) dividing the stem from the body, and (iii) notched and stemmed (all notched points must be stemmed, since a notch is an outline break, with the exception of basally notched points). The notches may be basal, side, or corner. The three basic outline forms are: (i) triangular, having a basic three-sided form, (ii) lanceolate, with the lateral sides tapered to a pointed tip but becoming straight and essentially parallel to each other near the base, and (iii) bipointed, with both ends being tapered to a point and no obvious differentiation between a "base" and a "tip".

Microliths are small, geometric pieces each with three or more distinct sides and usually formed from blade fragments (Fig. 57). Microliths are used as side blades or insert blades in composite tools, a series of the individual pieces together being aligned to form a tool edge. Such tools often would also have a terminal microlith that acted as an end blade or point for the tool.

8.3 Analysis Implementation

The beginning point for use of this information is to tabulate the frequencies of different tool types, probably best initially on presumed function and then within each category subdivisions based on other aspects of style that are seen as relevant. These subdivisions could be temporal or cultural styles, or they could be minor variations of a functional category. It is necessary to be aware that, as mentioned before, definition of tool function sometimes may be inaccurate when based on form alone and tools can be multifunctional (see also Chapter 11). Edge angle is an important part of any tool type definition and becomes central for minimally modified tools, such as edge modified or retouched flakes.

Once individual tools have been assessed as best possible, the frequencies of different tools in a site are presumably related to the importance of those activities in the site. The tasks being undertaken, their relative importance, and the variety of tasks overall are excellent indicators of the type of site that is represented. The presence of many cutting and chopping tools, in the absence of scrapers but the presence of much game animal bone, likely indicates a specialized butchering or perhaps kill site. If a site has many tasks represented, such as cores from lithic reduction, cutting tools, scrapers, and grinding implements, it is likely to be some type of habitation site, where a great variety of tasks are commonly performed. There are many other possibilities, of course. Tool information can be compared with lithic types for tools to arrive at ideas about what lithic materials were seen as appropriate for particular tasks. Especially in complex sites with spatial segregation of different styles of functionally equivalent tools, it may be possible to isolate tool styles that are associated with some distinct social group in the site. And, of course, in the absence of the many organic remains that might have been originally deposited in a site, stone tools can give us many clues as to what other items had been there or used in the past (see also Chapter 11).

CHAPTER 9

Northern Plains Stone Tool Cultural History

9.1 Introduction

Earlier chapters have discussed the skills needed to look at and understand stone tools and manufacturing debitage encountered in an archaeological site. Chapter 6 provided a global perspective of the broad patterns of development of stone tool manufacturing technology. As a complement to that perspective, this chapter looks at the detailed patterns of change in one area. The area I have chosen is the Northern Plains of western North America. Although the discussion is mainly for this area, many of the earlier period patterns have strong similarities to the events over much of North America. People working in western North America will find the discussion presents useful insights into classifying tools and manufacturing strategies into different time periods. There have been many characterizations of the pre-European history of the Plains. I will use the one most used, as developed mainly by Reeves for Canada and Frison for the United States (Dyck 1983; Frison 1991b; Reeves 1983; Vickers 1986):

1. Paleoindian or Early Prehistoric, 11,500–7500 B.P.

2. Plains Archaic or Middle Prehistoric, 7500–2000 B.P.

3. Late Prehistoric (Plains Woodland and Plains Village), 2000–250 B.P.

Figure 58: Complete Clovis point

9.2 Clovis

9.2.1 Characteristic lithic tools

Clovis dates from about 11,000 to 11,500 radiocarbon years ago (Taylor et al. 1996:517), or perhaps somewhat later (Frison 1991b:25). Based on our knowledge of how radiocarbon dates should be corrected, this represents the period from about 12,600 to 13,700 calendar years ago (Taylor et al. 1996:523). Clovis points are lanceolate in outline, widest about the middle of the point. They taper gradually toward the tip and, usually, only somewhat toward the

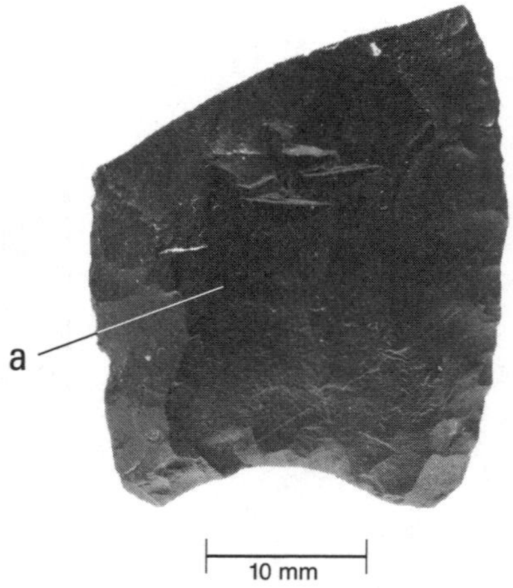

Figure 59: Base of Clovis point ('a' indicates flute)

Figure 60: Paleoindian spurred end scraper ('a' indicates spurs)

base. They are normally characterized by the presence of flutes on one or both faces of the point (Fig. 58 and Fig. 59). Flutes are thinning flakes removed from the base of the point that travel past the haft portion of the point (Bradley 1991:373). In Clovis points, the flutes are created by the removal of the "channel flakes" usually do not progress beyond the basal half of the point and do not expand too far toward the point lateral margins. The basal corners of the points are occasionally worked to give them a more rounded appearance (Frison 1991b:45). The main flaking pattern typically results in flake scars parallel and at right angles to the length of the tool initiated from the lateral margins (parallel collateral), but some examples show diagonal parallel flaking (Frison 1991b:43). Clovis points show considerable variation in length, from about 7 cm to about 20 cm. This variation is due both to resharpening and probably variation in function (including large, ceremonial examples) (Fiedel 1987:56; Titmus and Woods 1991:120, 127; Hofman and Graham 1998:95).

Clovis assemblages may have blades and blade cores, but these are apparently mainly recovered in sites on the Southern Plains and in the Southeast United States (Bradley 1991:373; Frison 1991b:42; Parry 1994:89; Stanford 1991:2, 5). Other tools include large bifaces, cutting and scraping tools made by marginally retouching blades or flakes, gravers (and occasional burins), and a variety of more well formed end scrapers (Stanford 1991:2). Some Clovis end scrapers are made on blades. An end scraper form with a "spur" on the working edge (Fig. 60) is apparently particularly diagnostic of Clovis (Fiedel 1987:63; Goebel et al. 1991:65, 69; Hester 1972:106), or perhaps more so Paleoindian sites (Frison 1991b:128–131; Frison et al. 1996:18). Clovis tools are often made of high quality, non-local lithic material (Frison 1991b:41; Stanford 1991:2). At least some sandstone abrading or grinding tools are known (e.g., Hester 1972:107) but their precise functions have not been determined.

9.2.2 Lithic technology

Clovis lithic manufacturing technology (Bradley 1991:369–373, 1982:203–208) shows a consistent, widespread pattern even though there are some regional variations in projectile point form. This manufacturing technology can be used to recognize Clovis bifaces. Most Clovis tools are bifaces or are made from flakes produced as a result of manufacturing bifaces. Bifaces are generally produced from large fragments of high quality lithic material. In some cases it is clear from the large size of the bifaces and the amount of cortex remaining that they were not made on large flakes, but rather must have been made on unmodified fragments of raw material. Initial biface reduction resulted in a generalized form and proportions, with this piece then being reduced by removal of large thinning flakes.

The Clovis biface thinning process was unique in a number of ways: the flake removal sequence, the spacing of the removals, the platform preparation method, and the flake termination form. The thinning process usually began with the removal of a large thinning flake from near one end of the piece. This step was followed by the removal of a second thinning flake from the same face but the opposite lateral margin and nearer the other end of the piece. Then a third thinning flake removal was initiated, again from the first margin. This last flake was removed from between the first two flake scars, the sequence of these flake removals being evidenced by the earlier scars being transected or interrupted by the later ones in the sequence. If the piece needed more reduction, one or two more thinning flakes were removed from the middle area of the biface, again on the same surface of the biface. Thus, this initial thinning was accomplished very efficiently by the removal of a few large flakes from just one surface. These thinning flakes traveled well across the biface and often carried completely across the face of the tool, removing a portion of the opposite margin in an *outrepassé*. The striking platforms for these thinning flakes were individually prepared to ensure successful removal. The same procedure was then undertaken on the opposite face of the tool; this process was continued until the biface had become regular and narrow. This thinning was by percussion flaking. Bradley has called this initial thinning "alternating opposed biface thinning" (1982:207). Many of the large thinning flakes resulting from this process were used to manufacture other tool types and the function of such bifaces may have been primarily as cores.

Once the biface had become regularized the second stage in the thinning was begun. In this flaking a sequence of thinning flakes initiated from one margin was removed from one face. These were intentionally removed so as to terminate in a diving, hinge fracture at about the midline of the biface. Once this series had been removed, a similar series was initiated from the opposite margin that met the first series and in most cases removed the hinging. Such a use of hinging allowed efficient thinning in the biface midline area since the hinge termination removed a greater thickness of material than a feather termination would have. The debitage flakes produced in this stage are smaller and they are more closely spaced on the biface. The process was repeated on the opposite face as well. This reduction process has been called "opposed diving face thinning" (Bradley 1982:207). If the reduction progressed to this stage then the usual intent was to produce a bifacial projectile point or knife.

Point/knife finishing technologies varied, but the strategies were apparently present throughout the High Plains. Usually the finishing was by percussion with little or no pressure retouch, but sometimes there was a subsequent substantial final marginal pressure flaking and thinning to finish the form (Bradley 1991:371). In the Plateau area it seems that pressure thinning was the rule (Titmus and Woods 1991:125), as demonstrated by the shallow bulb of percussion scar. Here the flaking was collateral but often not regularly spaced and the platforms showing no grinding or abrading (only a few light buffeting strokes with a hammer) although numerous shallow, irregular flake scars along the tool margin showed that the edge was straightened. Close to the end of the manufacturing sequence most Clovis points were basally thinned by the removal of one or more channel flakes to produce the characteristic Clovis fluting. There was usually some final flaking on the lateral margins after the fluting was completed, but it did not remove the flutes (Bradley 1991:373). It was common for this final working to remove the step or hinge fracture at the distal end of the fluting, although this feature is by no means universal (see Fig. 58 and Fig. 59). Bulb of percussion negative impressions adjacent to the proximal end of the flute were commonly removed. Sometimes multiple flutes were removed. Both of these strategies served to better thin the point base and improve contact with the weapon shaft and hence distribute the impact force more efficiently (Titmus and Woods 1991:125). The basal 2–3 cm of the points were almost always dulled, but this dulling progressed into the flute depression and was probably a true polishing rather than just an abrading to protect lashing from being severed by sharp tool margins (some examples show an initial abrading stage)(1991:126–127).

The thinning flakes from Clovis biface production often show distinctive characteristics. Early stage thinning flakes have wide, straight platforms that are faceted and ground, with the grinding often being heavy. These flakes tend to have rectangular outlines, quite parallel lateral margins, low dorsal scar counts with the scars originating from both original biface lateral margins, and an *outrepassé* termination. There is a tendency for these flakes to have a central ridge where the dorsal surface flake scars terminated. These flakes were often used as tool blanks, with unifacial lateral retouch being used to finish them into elongate tools.

Clovis blades were removed from conical cores, probably by indirect percussion (Parry 1994:89).

Figure 61: Goshen-Plainview point

9.3 Goshen-Plainview

9.3.1 Characteristic lithic tools

There has been considerable debate about projectile points variously called Midland, Plainview, and Goshen, both in terms of their taxonomic importance and their dating. Recent work in Wyoming and Montana has now clearly established that the form of the points called Goshen is found below Folsom occupations in a number of sites (Frison et al. 1996:12). In these sites the points seem to date to about 11,300–11,000 B.P., placing them either between Clovis and Folsom or contemporaneous with Clovis. The placement between Clovis and Folsom seems most likely. There is some evidence to indicate that the Midland point is not certainly distinct from Goshen and Plainview; hence Frison has suggested that until further work can clarify these issues, these points should be designated Goshen-Plainview (1996:12–13).

The only certainly distinctive lithic tool of this period is the projectile point itself (Fig. 61).

The lanceolate points are finely pressure flaked and show a basal thinning that distinguishes them from both Clovis and Folsom points. The edges of the point show fine final pressure retouch. Bases are usually concave and the lateral margins are either very straight or slightly convex. They may taper slightly toward the base (Frison 1991a:138–141).

9.3.2 Lithic technology

Frison has remarked that the variation in shape and flaking technology in Goshen points is sufficiently great that it can be difficult or impossible to identify them certainly when not found in a reliable stratigraphic context. Overall the technology is very similar to Folsom technology, particularly the fine pressure retouch to finish the point margins. The distinctive feature compared to Folsom and Clovis is the development of basal thinning rather than fluting to assist in hafting (Frison 1991a:138–141).

9.4 Folsom

9.4.1 Characteristic lithic tools

The definitive tool of the Folsom period, dated to about 10,900–10,200 radiocarbon years ago (Frison 1991b:50)(calibrated about 11,500 to 13,000 calendar years ago [Taylor et al. 1996:523]), is a fluted point, as in Clovis times. However, the Folsom point has a flute that extends all or most of the distance to the distal tip of the point and well out to the lateral edges (Fig. 62). Folsom points are smaller than Clovis points, generally about 3 to 7 cm in length (Titmus and Woods 1991:120; Wilmsen and Roberts 1978:111; Gryba 1988a). Folsom points often taper more abruptly to the tip compared with Clovis points and the widest location is often closer to the tip than to the base. The basal concavity is often quite deep and the basal corners are usually quite pointed and somewhat elongate. The greater uniformity of channel flakes in Folsom fluting means that they are often readily recognizable and so are also a distinctive lithic trait of Folsom sites (see Frison 1991b:54; Frison and Bradley 1982:211; Wilmsen and Roberts 1978:144–145). Many unfluted points are also known from Folsom sites. It is clear that these unfluted points are completed points and in many cases used, based on having been broken in use and/or having basal dulling/grinding (e.g., Frison and Bradley 1980:52–55; Wilmsen and Roberts 1978:112–113).

Figure 62: Folsom point

As in Clovis times, many flake tools were produced from the thinning flakes left from biface manufacture. These are so common in sites such as Hanson that the question has arisen whether the main purpose of bifaces was as tools in their own right or as cores for flake blank production (Bradley 1991:374; Frison and Bradley 1980:20–22). The other main procedure for manufacturing flake blanks for tools was using bifacial, dischoidal cores (Bradley 1991:374; Frison and Bradley 1980:18–20), although other core types are also known (Bradley 1982:183). Both retouched flake tools and utilized flakes are present in Folsom sites (Frison and Bradley 1980:86). A prominent feature of Folsom tools is that different edges on the same tool were used for different tasks, making many of the tools composite or multipurpose (Frison 1982:45; Frison and Bradley 1980:88).

A great variety of other lithic tool types are known from Folsom sites, particularly because of a few well preserved habitation sites such as Hanson (Frison and Bradley 1980) and Lindenmeier (Wilmsen and Roberts 1978). Folsom tools include hammerstones; bifaces; gravers and true burins; various minimally retouched or unretouched notches, denticulates, cutting tools, end and side scrapers, borers, etc.; sandstone abraders; and choppers (Frison 1982: 45–76; Frison and Bradley 1980: 84–112; Wilmsen and Roberts 1978:83–127). Although it has not been seen as a feature of Folsom, there are two examples of scrapers from the Folsom level at the Agate Basin site that might be considered to be spurred (Frison 1982:47, 73). There is another from the Folsom level at Blackwater Draw (Hester 1972:129) and these are also apparently present at the Hanson site (Frison 1991b:128). Blackwater Draw also has an example of a sandstone abrader (Hester 1972:134) and Lindenmeier has examples of sandstone pieces used as abraders, pigment grinding stones, and grooved stones that may have been used for smoothing weapon shafts or sharpening pointed tools of bone or wood (Wilmsen and Roberts 1978:121–125)

9.4.2 Lithic technology

The manufacturing technology for Folsom points has been extensively studied since the 1930s, although there remains much debate about its finer points (e.g., Bradley 1991, Crabtree 1966, Frison and Bradley 1980; Gryba 1988b). The earliest stages of manufacturing have not been reconstructed (Bradley 1991:375, Frison and Bradley 1980:46). After some initial shaping and thinning, there was a stage of pressure flaking, shaping, and thinning. The flakes are shallow and irregularly spaced (Frison and Bradley 1980:46). Flaking is on both faces. The next stage was a series of pressure flakes removed from the lateral margins of one face to prepare it for fluting. These flakes were removed in a manner that produced prominent bulbs of percussion and a deeply hollowed lateral edge on the preform; it was this deep marginal hollowing that constrained the lateral expansion of the channel flake (1980:47). The flakes were removed in a well spaced, regular series, commonly from the base to the tip of the preform. A characteristic feature at this stage was that the preform was thickest at about one-third of the distance from the base to the tip and that the tip was left thick and quite rounded. Small isolated, ground platforms were common on thinning flakes, an aspect quite different from usual Clovis thinning flakes (Bradley 1991:385).

The next stage was the preparation of an isolated platform in the basal concavity of the preform, the platform from which the channel flake would be removed for this first face. This platform was an obvious, beveled tab in the concavity. The channel flake was then removed from this face. Then the second face was similarly prepared and fluted; the platform for this channel flake is much thinner and so the second channel flake platform is usually strongly lipped (Frison and Bradley 1980:48). Even on a finished point there may be a remnant of this platform or an inflection of the basal concavity at this location. Final edge finishing was either by a systematic series of narrow collateral flakes, or by specialized marginal retouch only at the locations where there were projecting areas along the edge between previous flake scars (Frison and Bradley 1980:48–49; Titmus and Woods 1991:125). The basal edges of the point are dulled and sometimes this dulling, again as for Clovis points actually a polishing, extends into the flute cavity (Bradley 1991:374–375; Titmus and Woods 1991:126).

The Hanson site has allowed a detailed reconstruction of how bifaces begun from flake blanks are reduced (Frison and Bradley 1980:31–43). The technique continues into historic times and relies on percussion shaping and thinning until the final stage, when pressure retouch of selected areas is employed to give the final form.

9.5 Agate Basin

9.5.1 Characteristic lithic tools

Agate Basin sites are distinguished by an elongate lanceolate projectile point that tapers toward both the tip and base, yet usually lacks any clear break in the line that might be defined as a shoulder (see Fig. 63). The widest location on the point is between half and three-quarters of the way from the point base to the point tip. The point generally comes to a very flat base, although it may be more rounded/ convex. The points have a thick, lenticular cross section. Agate Basin sites date to about 10,000 to 10,500 radiocarbon years ago (Frison 1991b:57). Spurred end scrapers are apparently present as well (Frison 1991b:128).

Figure 63: Agate Basin point

9.5.2 Lithic technology

Agate Basin points were initially reduced by percussion thinning and then were finished with pressure shaping to produce the final form (Bradley 1991:382, 1982:194–5). It is not uncommon for some of the initial percussion scars to remain visible on the final point. The pressure flaking was highly variable, the process being altered to best achieve the final very regular symmetric point form with very straight, even margins. This marked symmetry and margin straightness, with a smooth lenticular cross section, is characteristic of Agate Basin points. In other words, it was the overall form that took precedence rather than the pattern of the flake scars. Usually the spacing between the pressure flake removals was moderate to wide and the removals were not a regular series. Despite this, the removals were clearly planned and patterned, otherwise the very regular form would not have been attained. When the initial percussion flaking was evenly spaced (but still selective), the subsequent pressure flaking was generally at 90° to the long axis and progressed approximately to the midline; these specimens do have a more regular appearing flaking pattern. Typical thinning flakes had isolated, ground platforms, a continuation of the pattern seen in Folsom times (Bradley 1991:385).

Final point retouch was very selective, confined to locations where ridges between flake scars broke the even straightness of the point margin. The basal margin and lower lateral edges were polished and/or ground in finished points. This dulling generally extended from the base to close to the location of maximum width on the point, with it generally being most intense on the lateral margins (Frison and Stanford

1982:81). Refurbishing of points broken in use is common, especially in the tip area, and is generally evidenced by abrupt changes in the flaking pattern, outline form, and longitudinal and transverse cross section (Bradley 1982:195; Frison and Stanford 1982:80). In many cases the reworking is apparently quite expedient, with little attention to the uniformity of the original working. Another feature of Agate Basin points is that there is no twist or rotation around the long axis of the point, a trait that is relatively common in Hell Gap points.

A number of core types and reduction strategies were used to produce flakes and blades, but dischoidal cores like those in Folsom assemblages are only one of a number of forms and are comparatively uncommon (Bradley 1982:182–184). Most common were bifacial platform cores and multidirectional flake removals. Flake types and the frequency with which they were used for retouched flake tools were very similar for Agate Basin and Folsom sites. About half of the retouched tools were made from bifacial reduction flakes and about another 40% were made from non-specialized secondary flakes. Platform preparation is quite varied, again paralleling the situation in Folsom sites: about 40% of the platforms show grinding and about 30% show faceting (multiple platform scars). The most common retouched flake tools are scrapers of various types; multipurpose tools are also common (Bradley 1982:198–200), both aspects much as in Folsom times. Flake cutting and scraping tools (end scrapers, side scrapers), gravers, notches, and *pièces esquillées* are all represented (Frison and Stanford 1982:107–130). Large tools such as choppers, hammerstones, and bifaces are also present.

9.6 Hell Gap

9.6.1 Characteristic lithic tools

Hell Gap projectile points are similar in outline form to Agate Basin points but they have a distinct shoulder that sets the stem apart from the blade of the point (Fig. 64). The shoulder is often less marked than in later Alberta and Cody Complex times and also shows a distinct taper toward the base that is not usually seen in these later periods. Only occasionally do the flake scars regularly meet at the midline of the point (Frison 1974:72–80; 1991b:61). Hell Gap points have a straight to slightly convex basal edge. There is often quite considerable variation in point length as a result of reworking broken points, a fact shown by significantly different flaking patterns in the repaired area much as seen in Agate Basin points. Dates for Hell Gap are about 9,500–10,000 radiocarbon years ago (Frison 1991b:59).

Figure 64: Hell Gap point

Flake tool and biface tool patterns are as for Agate Basin (Bradley 1991:385). Abrading tools are also known (Frison 1982:138). At the Jones-Miller site many of the projectile points were probably also used as butchering tools (Greiser

Figure 65: Alberta point (missing tip)

1985:69). Frison has experimented with projectile points such as Hell Gap and found that they can be used to butcher animals, but as a point is more specifically designed and hafted to work as a projectile point it becomes less effective as a butchering tool, and vice versa (Frison 1991b:318–321).

9.6.2 Lithic technology

The technology used to manufacture Hell Gap points is a continuation of that used in Agate Basin point manufacture (Bradley 1991:382–383), characterized by percussion thinning and shaping followed by pressure thinning and shaping. Final finishing was either by pressure flaking confined to the margins (progressing into the body of the tool only at the tip and on the stem) or by pressure thinning/shaping that encompassed much of the body of the point. Base and stem grinding is present. Typical thinning flakes had isolated, ground platforms, the common pattern seen since Folsom times (Bradley 1991:385).

9.7 Alberta

9.7.1 Characteristic lithic tools

Alberta projectile points (Fig. 65) have a distinctly stepped, abrupt shoulder and a stem that is usually very straight (untapered) to slightly expanded (Hofman and Graham 1998:111). The stem represents about the basal one-third of the point. The blade is quite broad and often tapers quite rapidly at the tip compared with Agate Basin and Hell Gap points. In some instances the flaking meets along the point midline, apparently this being the result of percussion thinning with only marginal, noninvasive pressure retouch in the finishing stage (Bradley 1991:385). Grinding of the stem and base was usual. The basal margin is usually straight. Alberta sites date to about 9,000 to 9,500 radiocarbon years ago (Frison 1991b:62).

9.7.2 Lithic technology

The only new lithic technology is the serial, regular percussion flaking terminating at the midline that is seen on some Alberta points (Bradley 1991:385–388). This regular, "comedial" pattern (from both margins, meeting opposite each other at the point midline) becomes very important in the Cody Complex (Scottsbluff) projectile point manufacturing procedure.

There is at least one example of a stone lined hearth that dates to this time period (Wilson and Davis 1994:100), although this "stone tool" is apparently very rare until McKean times.

9.8 Cody Complex

9.8.1 Characteristic lithic tools

The division between Cody Complex (sometimes called Scottsbluff) and Alberta material is not yet positively defined. Excavations at the

Figure 66: Cody Complex point, probably Alberta/Cody I

Figure 67: Cody knife

Horner site in Wyoming and the Hudson-Meng site in Nebraska have been central to trying to resolve this issue (Bradley 1991:385–389; Bradley and Frison 1987:204). The Cody Complex materials date to about 8,800 to 9,200 radiocarbon years ago (Frison 1991b:66).

Four projectile point types (Fig. 66) and one "hafted knife" type (Fig. 67) (Cody knife) are typically seen to characterize Cody Complex sites. All the point types are characterized by faces exhibiting transverse series of regular, uniform comedial flakes terminating on the point midline to produce a relatively prominent ridge. The regularity and uniformity of these flakes is especially well defined on Eden points. Eden and Scottsbluff I and II points are narrow and have quite straight lateral blade margins. Scottsbluff III points have a more broad blade, a gradual taper of the blade from base to tip that results in quite a triangular outline, and a more distinct shoulder (see Fig. 66, but also see discussion below). Scottsbluff III points and Cody knives are noticeably thinner than the other Cody Complex points. Scottsbluff II points are not as narrow as Scottsbluff I and Eden points. Compared to Alberta points, all Cody Complex points have a relatively short stem.

Although there is some variation in Cody knives, all are characterized by having a stem and a transverse (diagonal) used edge. In some the stem is quite broad and has been characterized as "shouldered"; others have a narrow or elongate stem and have been termed "stemmed" (Bradley and Frison 1987:220–222, Frison 1991b:66). One example of a Cody knife is known from an Alberta context at the Hudson-Meng site in Nebraska and another is known from an Alberta Cody context at the Horner site in Wyoming (Agenbroad 1978:129, Frison

1991b:126), but otherwise this artifact type is restricted to Cody Complex occupations.

Bifacial drills and knives have been recovered from Cody Complex sites (Bradley 1991:392) as have various types of scrapers, *pièces esquillées*, choppers, gravers, hammerstones, and grooved sandstone abraders (Frison 1987:235–263; Greiser 1985:78; Wedel 1986:69; Wormington and Forbis 1965:120). Grinding slabs may be present in some sites, such as Jurgens (Greiser 1985:75–76) and are present as early as 9,900 years ago at the Medicine Lodge Creek site in Wyoming (Frison 1991b:28).

9.8.2 Lithic technology

It has been suggested that there is an Alberta/Cody cultural manifestation chronologically between Alberta and Cody Complex material. This suggestion is based on a chronologically isolated and apparently short term occupation at the Horner site (Horner II) that evidenced two unique point manufacturing technologies that differed from the two technologies used at Cody Complex sites (Bradley 1991:388–389, Bradley and Frison 1987:199–207). The Fletcher site in Alberta (Vickers 1986:41–44, Wormington and Forbis 1965:119–121) also seems to be from a "mixed" Alberta Cody occupation and lends support to the suggestion of this "mixture" representing a separate tradition.

The transitional Alberta Cody points are of two styles based on form and technology (Bradley 1991:388–391). Alberta Cody I points were produced from a percussion shaped and thinned biface. The finishing was by pressure thinning and shaping, but the removals were not systematically patterned. Pressure thinning was confined to the tip of the point and the earlier percussion scars are often visible on one or both faces. Comedial pressure flaking is present occasionally but it is not well developed and the scars from opposite margins tend to run together rather than meeting at the midline. The points are somewhat thick, often are somewhat asymmetric, and have slightly wavy margins. The clearly visible percussion scars on Fig. 66, combined with the less systematic pressure flaking and the absence of a medial ridge, suggests that this example fits best with Alberta/Cody I in its production technology. The point in Fig. 66 also is not particularly thin as is characteristic of Scottsbluff III points. The second Alberta Cody point type (II) was produced by the same technique but then was taken further. A specialized, alternating series of pressure flakes was removed, giving a pattern of widely spaced collateral scars and a very wavy lateral margin. The stem was then specially pressure retouched to remove this waviness. In outline form these Alberta Cody I and II points look essentially the same as Cody Complex points and this is how they were all classified initially. Some of the Fletcher specimens certainly show the non-patterned flaking of Alberta Cody I (Wormington and Forbis 1965:119).

In Cody Complex points proper, Bradley (1991:389–391) has suggested that the more narrow styles—Scottsbluff I and II, Eden—are related and likely were produced by one technique. The points were initially produced from a biface that had been formed by percussion shaping and thinning. This piece was then selectively shaped by pressure flaking and then was finally finished by removal of one or more series of systematic pressure flakes in a comedial pattern. Three or four sequences of such flaking produced points with well developed, distinctive median ridges on both faces. The difference between Scottsbluff I and II, and Eden, was that Eden points had further fine, well spaced pressure flake removals (Bradley and Frison 1987:212). As well, the lateral margins and stem were then made very regular and straight by removal of very fine noninvasive pressure flakes and the stem margins were lightly polished.

Scottsbluff III and Cody knives are the other highly modified biface types in Cody Complex sites. They, too, were manufactured by

Figure 68: Late Paleoindian Parallel-Oblique point, probably unfinished

percussion thinning followed by pressure thinning and marginal retouch to produce finely finished, medially ridged points, but the points were intentionally manufactured to be very thin. This thinness sets them apart from the other Cody Complex points, which were intentionally manufactured to be relatively thick (Bradley 1991:390–391).

9.9 Late Paleoindian Parallel-Oblique Complex

9.9.1 Characteristic lithic tools

A variety of lanceolate points (Fig. 68), usually with concave bases, and stemmed points, both with parallel oblique flaking, are present on the Plains from about 8,000 to about 9,000 radiocarbon years ago (Bradley 1991:393–394; Frison 1991b:66–73; Hofman and Graham 1998:113–116). These various points and their chronological and geographic relationships are poorly understood and it has been suggested that they are likely all related despite the variation they evidence (Frison et al. 1996:16). One group of these points, Frederick, are lanceolate with basal concavities. These concavities are deeper in some (James Allen and Lusk points) than in others (Frederick) (Frison 1991b:66–67, Hofman and Graham 1998:113–114), but it may be that the Frederick points are really just James Allen points (Frison et al. 1996:16). Angostura points are also part of this complex, characterized by a lanceolate form and concave base but much more regular diagonal flaking that is collateral and meets close to the midline. Their precise relationship to the other parallel-oblique point types is not clear (Hofman and Graham 1998:113–114). Pryor Stemmed points are also from this complex, these showing only a poorly defined stem and quite irregular flaking in terms of size and orientation. Pryor Stemmed point margins tend to be quite irregular (Frison 1991b:72–73). Pryor Stemmed points may have a more restricted distribution, from the northwest of Wyoming into southwestern Alberta (Hofman and Graham 1998:114).

Grinding stones are relatively common, including some at the Betty Greene site in Wyoming and the Ray Long site in South Dakota that are clearly manos and metates (Greiser 1985:79–85; Wedel 1986:70–71; Frison et al. 1996:16). Many other tools are known from the sites in this time period, including choppers, scrapers, drills, knives, bifaces, multipurpose cutting and scraping tools, etc. A grooved stone, perhaps a bola weight, was recovered at the Allen site in Nebraska and ground stone palettes were recovered from the Ray Long site.

9.9.2 Lithic technology

The flaking on the faces of these points is slightly to strongly diagonal in its orientation across the width of the points and tends to be from both margins, meeting somewhere in the middle of the point but often off-center from the midline. The flaking is irregular in size and orientation and the point margins are often wavy irregular (Dyck 1983:83; Frison 1991b:72–73). The transition to this type of flaking seems quite rapid (Frison 1991b:66). Bradley (1991:393–394) has suggested that these various point styles share a common technology. Initial biface reduction was probably by percussion with serial patterned pressure flaking following. The oblique, rather than collateral flaking is a new technology that may have been developed initially in the mountain areas of Wyoming and Montana.

9.10 Mummy Cave/Early Plains Archaic

9.10.1 Characteristic lithic tools

Figure 69: Gowan point (Mummy Cave Series)

The Plains Archaic period (called the Middle Prehistoric period on the Canadian Plains), the time between the end of the Paleoindian period and the introduction of pottery and the bow and arrow in the Late Prehistoric period, is characterized by the appearance (Fig. 69) of side notched projectile points (Frison 1991b:79–111; Reeves 1983:36–37). There are many regional variants of these points. In some areas corner notched points are also present. The introduction of notched points is characteristic of the post-Paleoindian (Archaic) period over most of Canada and the United States. A particularly important site that shows the chronological developments during this time is the Mummy Cave site in Wyoming and, in Canada, the earliest series of points and cultures from this period have been called the Mummy Cave Series (Dyck 1983: 87; Reeves 1969; Vickers 1986:58–59). The Early Plains Archaic or Early Middle Prehistoric begins about 7,500–8,000 radiocarbon years ago and ends about 5000 years ago (Dyck 1983:87; Frison 1991:80, 1998:161; Frison et al. 1996:18; Reeves 1983:36–37; Vickers 1986:58). One of the main problems with understanding this time period is that points from surface and disturbed contexts are often mistaken for those from other time periods, such as late side notched forms (Dyck 1983:92; Vickers 1986:63).

A number of variants of side notched projectile points have been defined for this period. Those seen as most widely distributed include Bitterroot side notched (also called Northern side notched) and Gowan side notched (also called Salmon River side notched). Other relatively well recognized point types are Mount Albion corner notched, Blackwater side notched, and Hawken side notched (Frison 1998:161; Vickers 1986:58–59; Walker 1992:132–142). Bitterroot points date to about 7200–6000 B.P. and are characterized by a side notch that is distinctively high on the base (Walker 1992:137). The Gowan side notched point (Fig. 69) has been described as “relatively nondescript” (1992:141); it has rather broad notches and rounded shoulders and base margins compared to Bitterroot points

(1992:139). Gowan points date to about 6000–5500 B.P. (Kooyman 2000; Walker 1992:141). Both Bitterroot and Gowan points have been found in contexts as recent as 5000–4700 B.P. at the Anderson site and Head-Smashed-In Buffalo Jump in Alberta (Kooyman unpublished data; Quigg 1984; Reeves 1978).

Various tools are present in Mummy Cave sites: bifacial drills, end and side scrapers, choppers, hammerstones, large bifaces, and *pièces esquillées*. Perhaps more distinctive on the Canadian Plains are large side notched bifaces or knives (Dyck 1983:95; Walker 1992:47, 77–78), but similar knives are sometimes found further south, including in McKean contexts (Frison 1991b:133, Frison et al. 1996:18). In Wyoming grinding stones are present (Frison 1991b:84). The Lookingbill site in Wyoming is the last one to retain the spurred end scrapers characteristic of the preceding Paleoindian period (Frison et al. 1996:18).

Although perhaps not what would normally be considered a "stone tool," stone circles may first appear about this time (e.g., Frison 1991b:137). It is generally assumed that these represent the stones used to hold down the edges of tipi-like structures (Frison 1991b:92–96). Stone circles become common sometime about 4,000–5,000 years ago (e.g., Finnigan 1982).

9.10.2 Lithic technology

Bradley (1991:395–396) has characterized all lithic reduction technologies after the Paleoindian period on the Plains as essentially the same: percussion thinning and shaping followed by selective, non-patterned pressure shaping. Great care was taken in some cases, but "...the complex sequences seen in Folsom and Cody technology have never been seen again." (1991:395). The general trend is for increasing reliance on pressure shaping of thin flakes rather than percussion thinning followed by pressure finishing. Most arrow points (from Besant and Avonlea onwards) are made on flake blanks (rather than from larger biface preforms) and the cores employed are increasingly unifacial and multidirectional types, although bifacial cores are still used. Multidirectional cores were common at the Gowan sites in Saskatchewan, but bipolar cores were even more common (Walker 1992:63–64, 89–90). Single platform cores were present but were not common.

Figure 70: Oxbow point

9.11 Oxbow

9.11.1 Characteristic lithic tools

Oxbow projectile points (Fig. 70) have characteristic "ears" formed at the lateral corners of the base as a result of having both side notches and a broad, deep basal concavity. It is often possible to identify even quite small point fragments based on this unique morphology, although care must be exercised since other points can look similar if they are only small fragments (e.g., Hanna points). Oxbow material is

Figure 71: McKean point

Figure 72: Duncan point

widespread, from the northern part of the Canadian Plains south to northern Wyoming, with most dates in the 5000 to 4000 B.P. range. Some sites in Saskatchewan in particular date as recently as about 3000 B.P. (Dyck 1983: 89; Frison 1991b: 86–88; Vickers 1986:66-67).

Other lithic tools are much as the previous Mummy Cave series, but grooved mauls are relatively common (Dyck 1983:96). However, grooved mauls are also common in later contexts (Frison 1991b:136). Both bifacial and unifacial knives are present (Dyck 1983:96).

Stone ceremonial structures, such as cairns and "medicine wheels," date as early as Oxbow times (Vickers 1986:67).

9.11.2 Lithic technology

The basal concavity on Oxbow points is a result of basal thinning. Overall the technology is very similar to that of the preceding Mummy Cave series (Dyck 1983:96).

9.12 McKean

9.12.1 Characteristic lithic tools

There are at least three styles of projectile points associated with this Middle Plains Archaic time period: McKean (Fig. 71), Duncan (Fig. 72), and Hanna (Fig. 73). McKean points are distinctively deeply notched basally, lack side notching, and usually have somewhat convex lateral margins. This point type is truly a lanceolate form, although quite short compared to earlier lanceolate forms. Duncan points are similar but have a distinct stem with a sloping to relatively indistinct shoulder. Hanna points have a stem but also have a very abrupt, distinct shoulder and more of a tendency to have relatively straight lateral margins. Dates for this material are generally between about 3,000 and 5,000 years ago (Dyck 1983:100, Frison 1991b:28–31). A stone pipe is known from the Cactus Flower site in Alberta (Brumley 1975).

Figure 73: Hanna point

A characteristic stone "tool" that becomes relatively common at this time is the use of stone to line hearths or roasting pits (Frison 1991b:89, 93; Frison et al. 1996:21), and this was certainly largely absent until after Paleoindian times (Frison 1991b:137). Although roasting pits are present earlier, these are rarely stone-lined, instead being simple hearths (e.g., at the Barton Gulch site) or hearths containing only firebroken rock (Armstrong 1993:61). Stone linings radiate heat for considerable time after the fire is gone and so constitute a different cooking technology. They are often interpreted as an indication of cooking vegetable foods, although they might also be used to cook meat (Frison 1991b:89).

The increased prominence of grinding stones (Frison 1991b:89) may be related to increased use of plant foods as well. These grinding stones are also increasingly uniform and relatively elaborate in their form and production, the manos becoming quite keel-shaped and the metates having a groove that the mano fits into very well (Frison 1991b:92). These developments occur mainly in the area south of Alberta and Montana; the uniqueness of the Wyoming portion of the Northern Plains is reflected in other aspects of archaeological material, such as the pithouses present in McKean and Early Plains Archaic times (Frison et al. 1996:19–21).

9.12.2 Lithic technology

In some ways the McKean points resemble the lanceolate forms of the Paleoindian period, but they lack basal grinding and the parallel diagonal pressure flaking characteristic of the late Paleoindian forms (Frison et al. 1996:20).

9.13 Pelican Lake

9.13.1 Characteristic lithic tools

Pelican Lake sites date between about 3,300 and 1,800 years ago (Dyck 1983:105, Frison et al. 1996:23). Yonkee projectile points from Wyoming and southern Montana are similar and are probably related, perhaps being a local development from McKean in the area of the Powder River Basin (Frison 1991b:101–105; Frison et al. 1996:22–23). Pelican Lake projectile points (Fig. 74) have sharply barbed corner notching and a triangular form that is much like a stylized Christmas tree; the sharp points on the blade and corner edges of the notches are particularly distinctive. Basal and lateral edges vary from slightly convex to slightly concave. At least in Saskatchewan, points with a convex base appear to be somewhat more recent than those with straight bases (Dyck 1983:105). Pelican Lake points vary considerably in size and the smallest ones (as small as about 2 cm. in length) may be arrow points (1983:107). Early Plains Woodland sites in North and South Dakota have Pelican Lake points that have been linked to the corner notched points commonly associated with Plains Woodland sites further to the south (Johnson and Johnson 1998:201, 218). Bifaces only rarely have modifications such as notching

Figure 74: Pelican Lake point

Figure 75: Besant dart point (short variant)

for hafting (Reeves 1983:83–85). Drills and perforating tools are relatively rare. Grinding stones are mainly present in southern areas, such as Wyoming. Occasional abrading stones and atlatl weights are known.

9.13.2 Lithic technology

Pelican Lake lithic technology has not been well studied, but no particular innovation has been noted. It is seen as a technological continuation of McKean by Reeves (1983:7).

9.14 Besant/Sonata

9.14.1 Characteristic lithic tools

Besant side notched points (Fig. 75 and Fig. 76) are the typical point of this period, along with similar but small Samantha side notched points. These smaller points have sometimes been seen as arrow points, but it has also been suggested that they may represent "...high speed, low impact dart points..." (Gregg et al. 1996:85). Besant

Figure 76: Besant dart point (long variant)

dates from about 1,150 years ago to about 2,000 years ago (Dyck 1983:113; Reeves 1983:93–94; Vickers 1986:81). Some Plains Woodland sites in North and South Dakota have Besant points (Johnson and Johnson 1998:218). Besant point bases are most commonly straight (Frison et al. 1996:24). The notches on Besant points are generally twice as broad as they are deep and the notches are sufficiently low on the point that the lower notch edge is very close to, or even touching, the basal edge of the point (Dyck 1983:115). Points are generally between 3 and 8 cm in length (see Fig. 75 and Fig. 76). The internotch distance is generally between 1.4 and 2.3 cm, but the less common Samantha "arrow" points have an internotch distance of between 1.4 and 1.6 cm.

Grinding stones are relatively rare (Reeves 1983:95–96). Some mauls and abraders are known.

9.14.2 Lithic Technology

At this time there is a return to substantial biface percussion thinning as was common in Paleoindian times (Bradley 1991:395). High quality material and workmanship is common in Besant sites, but certainly there are also a significant number of projectile points that show a lesser concern with uniformity and symmetry (Dyck 1983:116–119; Frison et al. 1996:25; Reeves 1983:329, 341).

9.15 Avonlea

9.15.1 Characteristic lithic tools

Avonlea points (Fig. 77) are typically small, finely worked, flat-surfaced, and very thin compared to other point types. The notches are very shallow and low on the point. The surface flaking is commonly serial and patterned (comedial). The margins are markedly regular and even, the basal margin usually a very regular concave curve. Avonlea points from southern Montana and northern Wyoming are somewhat atypical, but are still clearly morphologically related (Frison 1991b:113). All Avonlea points are small and are assumed to be arrow points.

Figure 77: Avonlea point

The suite of tools present in Avonlea sites is much as previous periods. However, from this time through to the end of the pre-contact period, it may be that large bifacial knives that are flat on one side are characteristic (Dyck 1983:123). This cannot be a blanket statement, however, since asymmetric knives did exist somewhat before this time in Wyoming (Frison 1991b:132–133). In northern Wyoming some ground stone tools are present (1991b:113).

9.15.2 Lithic technology

Avonlea points were manufactured by all over pressure thinning of thin flake blanks, a marked change from previous techniques (Bradley

1991:395; Gregg et al. 1996:85). This combination of thin blanks and fine pressure flaking through the entire reduction sequence has resulted in particularly thin and delicately worked points that are easily recognized. Avonlea projectile point manufacturing exhibits greater technological efficiency than any other Late Prehistoric archaeological time, and perhaps greater efficiency than any other Plains archaeological culture (Stanfill 1988:252). The manufacturing process is basically the same for all Late Prehistoric points, the differences being in degree rather than kind.

Flakes are opportunistically removed from cores, using the natural platforms present on angular raw material pieces. Thin, wide, flat flakes lacking cortex are chosen as blanks (Stanfill 1988:252–255). Wide flakes are chosen to provide the basal expansion area of the point and the use of non-cortical flakes minimizes the need to remove cortex in subsequent stages. These flakes are then pressure flaked into preforms. Thin, flat flakes are chosen to minimize the thinning effort required at this stage. Although a few thinning percussion flakes may be used to reduce thick areas of the blank or render the margins symmetric, ideally all thinning is done by pressure flaking. Essentially the use of percussion is restricted to setting up the preform for systematic pressure shaping. The pre-selection of blanks is the key to the efficiency of the production process. The form of blanks chosen equally minimizes the pressure flaking required, the next stage in the process. Little further edge preparation of these symmetric preforms is undertaken. The thin pieces would easily snap if much force was required at this point in flaking, as might be the case in flaking from a beveled edge. Overhang is removed, particularly weak platforms are strengthened, and the edge is strengthened by relatively heavy grinding. Then a series of flakes are taken from each margin, beginning at the tip and working to the base, using the ridge created by each flake to guide the next removal further into the interior. In this manner, even though the point becomes wider toward the base, each successive flake also progresses a greater absolute distance and so into the center of the expanded portion of the tool. This technique produces the finely flaked, overlapping, patterned scarring characteristic of Avonlea points. The notches are made with a thin, sharp tool by pressure directly on the edge at right angles to the plane of the point. The notches are placed very low on the base, where the greatest mass of the point is situated. This location minimizes the risk of snapping the point because there is resistance to bend here.

Another factor suggesting the particular efficiency of the Avonlea point system is the location of the notches low on the base. This means that the arrow shaft slot can be very shallow and so less effort is needed in its manufacture (Stanfill 1988:255). At the same time the relative lack of protection afforded by a shallow haft might result in an increased frequency of use damage.

In Alberta there is some use of microblades and microblade cores in Avonlea times (Frison et al. 1996:27; Reeves 1983:17).

9.16 Old Women's/ Late Side Notched

9.16.1 Characteristic lithic tools

The projectile points from this time period (Fig. 78) are generally side notched, although some early ones are corner notched (Dyck 1983:126–132, Forbis 1962, Frison 1991b:114; Kehoe 1966; Vickers 1986:95–99). Chronological differences in form during this period from about 1200 to the historic period (about 200 B.P.) have been noted many times and although these vary quite substantially from region to region, on the Canadian Plains these have been found to be consistent over a considerable area. Kehoe (1966), and later Dyck (1983:129), suggested

Figure 78: Old Women's point (late period Cayley, also classifiable as Plains side notched)

Figure 79: Historic period metal point

that there was an earlier (1200–550 B.P.) Prairie side notched point, with the side notch very close to or touching the base of the point, and a later Plains side notched point (550–200 B.P.), with notches well away from the base and an overall very straight triangular outline. Forbis was able to define a number of point forms based on his work at Old Women's Buffalo Jump. Peck (Peck 1996, Peck and Ives in press) has examined all of these ideas with a sample from a larger geographic area and has suggested that two point groups can be defined. The Cayley group, present in southern Saskatchewan, southern Alberta, and northern Montana, dates to about 1250–650 B.P. in Saskatchewan and to the entire time period between 1250 and 200 B.P. in Alberta. Mortlach group points are dated to between 650 B.P. and the historic period and are found in southern Saskatchewan, southwestern Manitoba, northeastern Montana, and northwestern North Dakota. Differences in these points include a high incidence of rectangular bases in Mortlach points compared to more sloped forms in Cayley, mainly broad V-shaped side notches in Cayley versus narrow U-shaped notches in Mortlach, and a much higher incidence of straight basal edges in Mortlach (about 75%) compared to Cayley (about 50%).

A bifacially worked end scraper is found in the Plains Village tradition in the Middle Missouri area and may be diagnostic of it (Gregg et al. 1996:87). Pecked groove mauls are common here and groundstone celts and spherical balls have also been recovered (Winham and Calabrese 1998:295).

The advent of Europeans and their trade goods resulted in the use of trade metal to manufacture projectile points (Fig. 79) at the end of this period, although use of lithic projectile points also continued.

9.16.2 Lithic technology

During this time period there is a shift to use of expedient cores to produce flake tools rather than bifacial reduction of blanks (Bradley 1991:395). On the Canadian Plains there is a change to use of smaller and more regular flaking on the later "Plains" side notched points as compared with the earlier "Prairie" side notched points (Dyck 1983:132). It has been suggested that the "Plains" side notched points have workmanship similar to that of Avonlea people earlier (Kehoe 1966; Dyck 1983:132).

In the Middle Missouri area, about A.D. 1000, the Plains Village period begins. Significantly, these horticulturists had numerous ground stone tools including axes, smoking pipes, and tablets (Gregg et al. 1996:87). Catlinite, a soft red metamorphosed claystone from southwestern Minnesota (Miller 1996:42), was intensively quarried at this time and was used to make groundstone elbow pipes, tubular pipes, incised rectangular tablets, and arrow points (Gregg et al. 1996:87).

CHAPTER 10

Wider Applications of Lithic Analysis

10.1 Introduction

This chapter will shift the focus from the minute details of lithic analysis to larger scale questions of human culture that can be addressed with data from lithic analysis. Lithic technology studies are not undertaken solely to provide information about how tools were manufactured, but also to use that insight to examine questions of human behavior (Carr 1994a). It is time to step back and look at that broader perspective.

10.2 Site Type and Settlement Patterns

The kind of information lithic analysis can supply in this area concerns the activities that occurred at a site. These activities include inferences about the materials worked with the tools, the stages of tool manufacturing that occurred at a site, and the implications these inferences hold for what other types of sites must also have been present to encompass all the activities that a cultural group would need to undertake. These inferences allow definition of a settlement pattern, the location and distribution of sites within a region that allow the people to successfully exploit that environment to obtain their physical and social requirements. These activities can be examined both synchronically, at a single time period, and diachronically, as these activities changed through time. Some aspects of this are also discussed in the section "Sourcing: Defining Contact, Exchange, and Material Transportation."

Habitation sites are likely to have a wide range of tool types because a variety of activities are undertaken there. Much time is spent in such sites so tool manufacturing and repair/maintenance will occur; hence some maintenance debris may be present. Such sites may even have cores and blanks of raw material brought from a quarry elsewhere.

Specialized sites, such as those associated with food getting or obtaining particular resources, will have a restricted range of tools. The tools present will reflect the particular activity undertaken at the site (e.g., projectile points at a hunting stand, axes where clearing agricultural land). Broken and exhausted tools might be found at such specialized sites, as well as resharpening flakes from maintaining the tools during use. The kill area I excavated at Head-Smashed-In Buffalo Jump, Alberta (Kooyman 1992), for example, has a lithic assemblage with projectile points being the main tool. The debitage is dominated by small finishing/resharpening flakes from cutting tools, as identified by the acute exterior platform angle of the flakes.

The most obvious aspect of this area of study is that the process of manufacturing stone tools goes through various stages, and only particular stages or sets of stages would be in evidence at particular types of sites. The lithic variables that can be employed in this type of study include flake debitage type (decortication, BRF, etc.), the dorsal and platform scarring criteria, and the types of tools present (unfinished, finished, broken, and exhausted). It would be unlikely to find any quantity of cores and hammerstones at a specialized fishing camp. Quarries would be characterized by decortication flakes, flakes and shatter with few scars, rejected large flake blanks, and so on. A butchering site of a single, isolated kill of a large game animal might only have a broken or exhausted butchering tool or two (knives, choppers) and some resharpening flakes.

An example of this type of study is the analysis of the results of the 1986 excavation season at the Strathcona site in Alberta (Kooyman et al. 1987:48–60). Based on flake and shatter scarring, it was suggested that there were approximately equal amounts of initial, middle, and late stage lithic reduction represented. In addition, some 5% of the lithic debitage was resharpening flakes. The resharpening flakes showed that tools were being used and resharpened at the site; therefore the site was not strictly a quarry as some researchers had suggested in the past. The presence of all stages in lithic reduction suggested that stone tools were being made and that the raw material was locally quarried. This then suggested the idea of a habitation site of some description where stone was quarried to make tools, perhaps for immediate use. This suggestion was supported by the fact that some three-quarters of the tools were utilized flakes and edge modified flakes, expedient tools made when required and discarded immediately after the task at hand was complete. These were not the types of tools that would be made at a specialized quarry site for subsequent transport elsewhere. Using estimates based on Magne's (1985) work it was also shown that the amount of debitage recovered was probably insufficient even to account for the manufacture of the tools recovered at the site. Clearly, the site was not a specialized lithic workshop, where one would expect much debitage and few tools. The conclusion suggested by this combination of patterns was a habitation site specifically located near a quarry to have a source of tool material while living at that location.

The unspecialized nature of the Strathcona site results make it difficult to visualize what other types of sites might have been present in the area as part of the overall settlement pattern. All sites might have been of this type. Conversely, other types might have also been present, perhaps at different times of the year (e.g., there may have been communal buffalo kills in the fall).

The suggestion that mobile people required tools that could be resharpened many times has been an important basic assumption for interpreting mobility for a decade or more (e.g., Bamforth 1986; Bleed 1986; Magne 1985:250; Kooyman 1985; Walker 1978). The assumption is that mobility means that new lithic material cannot always be acquired as needed and/or that the need of mobile groups to minimize carried goods means that as few lithic tools as possible will be carried. Either circumstance means that the tools to hand will be as intensively used as is feasible. Studies such as Odell's (1994) certainly seem to confirm this suggestion.

Odell's (1994) study also suggested that mobile groups are able to access a wider range of products from more distant locations than are sedentary groups. Conversely, greater sedentism means that task groups are sent to bring resources to the site and that it is most feasible to bring local resources preferentially. This situation means that there is a more marked presence of local resources in a sedentary group, coupled with usual absence of very distant source materials. Linked to the need for mobile groups to have very portable tool kits, it was suggested that mobile groups should evidence a much more standardized core technology to produce the most appropriate blanks for tool production. This constraint would be relaxed for more sedentary groups where there would then be more use of non-standardized "amorphous" core technology. I would see these practices as tendencies and would note that so-called amorphous cores can be very efficient producers of useful, rather standardized flakes. Use of this approach to assessment needs to be carefully considered in each case. Certainly in southern Alberta one would be hard-pressed to describe the core technology as highly standardized, yet there is almost no evidence for marked sedentism. What we truly need to measure is how well the core technology produces appropriate blanks for tool production, blanks that can be used with minimal modification. Edge-modified flakes can easily serve most purposes if they are at least sufficiently large to allow for resharpening and so have extended uselives. In this context it is also relevant to record the opinion of Hayden and his colleagues (Hayden, Franco, and Spafford 1996:17, 27) that some highly standardized prepared cores are actually wasteful of lithic material due to their high rate of failure. If cores can be used to produce appropriate blanks that can be resharpened, and that is the form in which material is transported, such standardized cores may still serve the required purpose (as Hayden Franco, and Spafford [1996] also note).

Seeman's (1994) Paleoindian study at the Nobles Pond site in Ohio adds interesting perspective to this question of the type of lithic material mobile and sedentary groups are expected to utilize. The use of multiple lithic sources by mobile groups is based on the assumption that human groups tend toward one of two extremes: they are either foragers, whose subsistence and other resource procurement activities require them to regularly move their camps from resource to resource, or they are collectors, who have a base camp with resources being brought back to that camp by specialized task groups sent to each resource location to acquire the resource (Binford 1980). By acquiring lithic materials as part of the seasonal round, by "embedding" their acquisition into other resource procurement movements, mobile groups can acquire material from various sources as they need it without any extra "cost" because the lithic material is acquired as part of another activity (Binford 1979) (although obviously they must still spend time to acquire it once they get there). In contrast, Seeman suggests that sedentary groups are more likely to use specialized task groups to acquire lithic material from a limited number of locations. The Nobles Pond occupants were undoubtedly mobile foragers and the lithic material is wholly dominated by non-local lithic material, conforming to the expected pattern of use of non-local material by mobile groups. However, the material for both tools and debitage is almost exclusively from only two high-quality non-local sources to the southwest of the site (70 and 110 km distant from the site), despite the fact that there are numerous high quality lithic sources in all directions from the site that were known in Paleoindian times. Seeman suggests that this unexpected limited diversity in lithic material use is a result of lithic procurement *not* being embedded in the general seasonal round of activities; lithic procurement was a specialized activity with group movement specifically through these source areas to acquire the material.

The ability of a tool to have an extended uselife because it can be resharpened, maintained, reworked, recycled, or transported from one site to another has generally been subsumed under the term "curation." Tools which lack these features, that tend to be made as a need arises and are then discarded immediately after use, have been called "expedient" tools. The various uses and definitions of the term "curated" has rendered its use problematic because its precise meaning can be unclear. A number of participants in a recent lithic analysis conference (Odell 1996b) suggested that more precise specialized terms for the various facets of curation be employed. At the same time, other participants continued to find the term very useful, and so the term is still employed. Regardless of the particular manner in which the term is used, curation was an important consideration for all tool users, but in particular for mobile groups that had to regularly carry belongings. Since curation reduces the need for raw material for tools, many of the consequences and correlates of curation will be similar to those associated with economizing behavior necessitated by the limited availability of lithic raw material (Odell 1996a). Odell goes on to discuss how these two aspects can be distinguished in at least some circumstances. In particular, concentration on preparing tools in advance for use was seen as an indication of curation of tools rather than a response to resource scarcity, with evidence of increased hafting frequency (based on usewear analysis) being an indicator of emphasis on advance preparation. This trend was evident in Odell's material from the Illinois valley. Resource scarcity, as opposed to curation *per se*, was seen in the lithic-poor area of this same study as a decrease in cores, increased reduction of small discarded lithic fragments through bipolar reduction, and a more intense use of tools to exhaustion as seen in a higher frequency of broken tools and a higher frequency of usewear on broken edges. Other indicators of tool exhaustion might also be expected to increase in resource-poor areas, as for example the intensity of retouch as demonstrated in Nash's (1996) study.

The stone tool requirements of mobile groups have also been discussed in terms of the number of utilized edges present on a tool and how versatile, flexible, or multifunctional such a tool is. This versatility is seen as important for mobile groups because they require tools for all or most functional needs they may encounter in a seasonal round, yet they are constrained by the need to transport these tools as they move. If a tool has multiple edges that can be used for a task, this may increase the tool's uselife; if different edges may be used for different tasks, or some of the edges can be reworked to accomplish another task, this flexibility can obviously be very advantageous. Hayden and his colleagues (Hayden, Franco, and Spafford 1996:12–14) discuss this concept and how different researchers have used these various terms. They suggest that the term "multifunctionality" is probably the least ambiguous one to employ. They note that often it can be difficult to determine if multifunctionality is specifically part of tool design or if it arose due to the circumstantial use of a particular tool. They also draw attention to the difficulty of recognizing different functions for different portions of a tool, noting that usewear analysis or distinctive variation in type of retouch are probably the most reliable means to assess this (I presume marked differences in edge configuration, such as edge angle, would also be seen as being as useful).

Examination of usewear and residues on stone tools can be instrumental in defining site activities and site type, as well as isolating multifunctionality as discussed above. The material Vaughan (1981, 1985) analyzed for his PhD dissertation showed a specialized hide working area. Obviously, other site types must have existed in his study area to form an overall settlement pattern, since people would require many other resources in addition to hides to survive.

In my New Zealand work (Kooyman 1985, 1989), which examined the hunting of large flightless birds called moa, I found that the dominant tool type was a woodworking tool (based on usewear analysis). This was the case both in small, apparently specialized short term moa hunting camps, and what seemed to be larger base camps. There were no obvious weapons in these sites, but based on ethnographic analogy it is probable that wooden spears were used. After considering various other possibilities, I concluded that the woodworking focused on making and maintaining wooden spears. This scenario explained the woodworking tool pattern in all sites. Furthermore, there was no evidence for dressing fibrous leaves to produce plant fiber for clothing, thus suggesting that even the large inland sites were not permanent occupations (based on the assumption that, at some stage, people would have to make clothes). Instead, all the sites seemed to be temporary hunting camps, the difference being that some were for small groups of people. Clearly, this then also implied that some other site type or types existed, where clothing manufacture was at least one major activity. This is a good example of how usewear analysis can illuminate specific site function as well as giving insight into the wider settlement pattern.

Just as one can make inferences about what other types of sites are likely to have been present in an area based on what is lacking from a particular site studied, if a number of sites have been studied in a local area it is possible to link them together to encompass the range of activities undertaken over the course of a year or a series of seasons. This linked pattern of sites is the settlement pattern.

These are only a few examples of how lithic analysis can be used in settlement pattern studies. The lithic information also can be correlated with the other remains from sites, such as zooarchaeological remains, to complete the picture and more securely define site activities. Finally, if a site or sites have different time periods represented in them, lithic activity continuities and differences can be traced through time.

10.3 Intra-Site Patterning: Activity Areas

Obviously, clustering of particular types of lithic remains within a site can provide information about how different activities are segregated at a site, how different stages of a process are isolated from each other in conceptual and physical terms, and whether or not certain activities or processes are undertaken together or apart.

For example, one might examine site remains to determine if there is an association of hammerstones, anvils, and cores only with decortication flakes. Such an association would indicate a location where initial core reduction was occurring. It has also been demonstrated by various authors (see studies cited in Healan 1995:689) that small debris, such as lithic microdebitage, remains at the primary refuse locality, the place where it was actually created; larger pieces of material are more likely to be moved to another location, so these larger items are more indicative of the longer use-history of items rather than the location where they were created. As a result, high concentrations of microdebitage (Fladmark 1982) are often seen as a good indicator of areas where lithic reduction occurred. Studies also indicate that larger lithic debitage can be employed in identifying both secondary refuse deposition localities and primary refuse deposition localities; Healan (1995:697) found that probable primary lithic reduction areas were indicated by a marked increase in debitage in size classes of 4.7 mm and smaller (since this size threshold is related to human perception of debitage, it can probably be generally applied across most lithic materials).

Based on usewear analysis, one could examine whether bone working and woodworking were done in separate areas or if there was a single area of a site that was used for such purposes. Similarly based on usewear, but also on tool types, one could study whether the butchering of big game animals, the scraping of flesh from the green hides, and the scraping to soften the dried or tanned hides all occurred in the same area, or whether these activities were spatially segregated. There are many other questions where this level of analysis might be applied.

An example, again from the 1986 field season at the Strathcona site (Kooyman et al. 1987), is the distribution of resharpening flakes in the excavation area (Fig. 80). Resharpening flakes

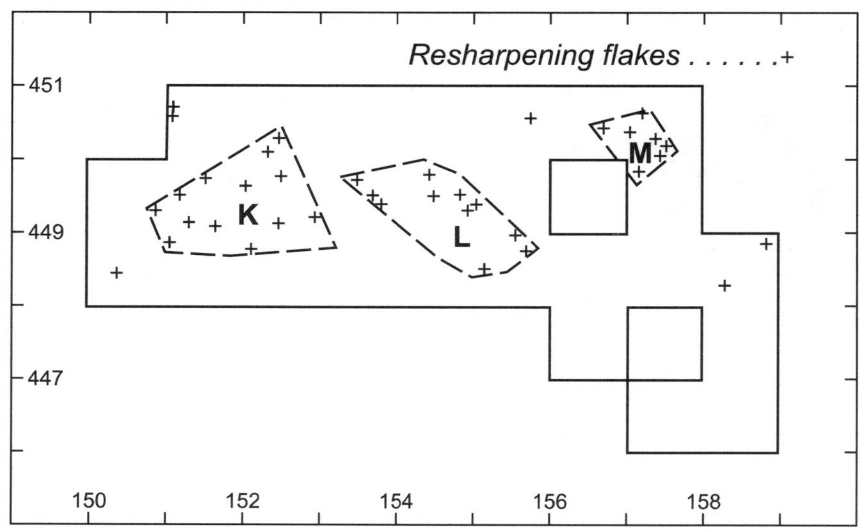

Figure 80: Activity area as seen in distribution of resharpening flakes at the Strathcona site, Alberta (Kooyman et al. 1987)

were present in three fairly tight, restricted clusters, despite the fact that flakes as a whole were evenly distributed over the entire excavation area. The pattern may represent particular areas "designated" for tool maintenance, or localities where particular activities were undertaken that required tool sharpening during the process (e.g., hide scraping, woodworking). The clusters might even represent locations where an individual was working. Obviously a usewear analysis study of the striking platforms of these flakes could assist in determining which particular interpretation is most probable. This analysis was undertaken with the results indicating that there was no particular concentration of worked materials in any one of these areas. These areas might have been tool resharpening areas, or more likely they were just areas where any activity might be undertaken, perhaps specifically away from locations where other activities incompatible with scatters of sharp debris, such as sleeping, occurred.

In a similar manner, Fig. 81a shows the obsidian flake distribution, a generalized scatter, from four layers of my excavations at Head-Smashed-In Buffalo Jump (the blank area is a location where a pothunter's hole disturbed the site so individual flake locations were not plotted). This distribution can be compared to the distribution from just one of these layers, Layer 4 (Fig. 81b). Here an obvious cluster can be seen, probably representing one person sharpening a particular obsidian tool since overall, obsidian is quite uncommon in the site remains.

A rather different example is the study by Hayden and his colleagues (Hayden, Bakewell and Gargett 1996) of the distribution of lithic material types in different house pits at the Keatley Creek site in the Plateau region of interior British Columbia. Each of three large house pits showed a different frequency pattern of lithic material types. This differential patterning suggested that each household unit, as represented by a pithouse, had a different, unique pattern

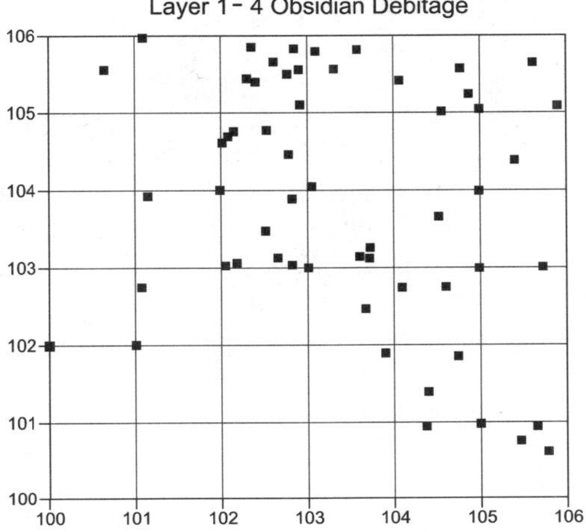

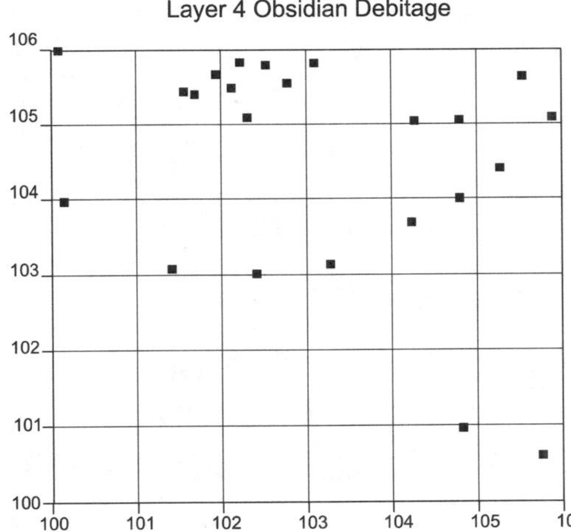

Figure 81: One-metre excavation grid showing obsidian debitage from Layers 1-4 and Layer 4 only at Head-Smashed-In Buffalo Jump, Alberta, showing Layer 4 activity area

of obtaining lithic material and that each was therefore a discrete social unit (residence unit). The authors suggested that this pattern might represent each residence unit dispersing into a different area during the summer season, as was the case historically, each having access to different raw material sources. As well, each of these lithic type patterns was essentially consistent through time within each house pit, indicating that there was continuity of these residence units over time. What was even more significant about this residential unit continuity was that it was over hundreds of years, not just a short time span (their interpretation would have been better illustrated if frequency data were tabulated by level for each housepit, although scrutiny of their other tabulations clearly shows that the interpretation is appropriate). Even with this misgiving, in this instance it is obvious that the lithic materials certainly provide a good deal of insight into past social relations.

10.4 Refitting Analysis

Refitting analysis is comparable to putting a jigsaw puzzle together, but with lithic remains: trying to fit the detached pieces (flakes, cores, and tools) back together. In lithic analysis one of the most obvious uses of refitting analysis is to analyze how the stone was shaped, either to make tools or to produce blanks for tool manufacture. Being able to fit a series of decortication flakes back together may show how a core was initially prepared or how a tool preform was prepared from a cobble. In the adze manufacturing example from New Zealand (Leach 1984) shown in Fig. 30, you can see the pattern of very similar, overlapping flakes that were removed from a face to produce an adze with a triangular cross section; earlier series have cortex, later series do not. Bradley's (1982) refitting of Folsom point manufacturing debitage is another excellent example study.

Refitting analysis can also be employed to define activity areas, locations in a site where lithic reduction of some type was undertaken. A group of flakes that can be refitted to a core found within their midst shows a core reduction area. In the example in Fig. 82 (Leach 1969), again from New Zealand but from a silcrete ("quartzite") quarry and blade manufacturing site, not only can distinct activity areas be seen, but it is also obvious that the reduction of cores here took place in different stages. The working shifted to different areas during the reduction process. Note core reduction group #l is a single area whereas #ll is spread over three locations. In an even more complicated pattern, core reduction group #9 has three main areas and also two more isolated locations. As one can extrapolate from these groupings, widespread patterns of refits can be used to define the various activities in an occupation and hence even the areal extent of a particular occupation. Morrow (1996b) also used refitting to define activity areas, in this case being able to segregate knapping and discard areas (based on differing flake types in each refit area) as well two different occupation episodes. The relatively low frequency of refits of flakes to finished bifaces also caused Morrow to suggest that occupations were of fairly short duration, showing little maintenance of tools. In another study, Seeman (1994) obtained a relatively high frequency of refits. He also obtained four reasonably defined clusters, with refits both supporting their separation and showing some linkage. The flake debitage was very uniform between the clusters, both morphologically and in terms of material type. Together, Seeman took these data to indicate a contemporaneity of the clusters related to a single occupation by presumably related bands, and certainly not indicating a series of non-contemporaneous repeated occupations over an extended period of time. Hence, refit frequency and linkages seem good indicators of occupation duration, a perennially problematic aspect of sites to assess. By further extension, refitting can also be employed to define the areal extent of a site, for one occupation or all occupations.

The vertical distribution of refitted artifacts in a site can be used to define the vertical extent or depth of an occupation. Presumably if the pieces fit together, the pieces relate to (in most cases) "detachment events" that occurred in a relatively short (contemporaneous) time period. The depth dispersal of conjoined pieces can also be an indication of the degree of disturbance a site has undergone. For instance, turning again to the Strathcona site, we found two "bands" of refitting, with no overlapping refits between the two. The lower band comprised roughly the lower 10 cm of the sediments. Above this band there was a "sterile" (in refit terms) zone some 4–5 cm thick. Above that "sterile" zone was a zone of refitting some 20–30 cm thick. Finally, above that refitting band was a zone some 10 cm thick where no refitted material was found. In this case most of the refitting was done with fire broken rock (FBR), the reddened and crazed shattered rock that results from heating and cooling of rock around hearths and in stone boiling, rather than with lithic reduction debitage (although some of this was included). These refitting zones, and associated zones lacking refitting, probably represent three or four major occupations at the site. The large vertical distribution of the middle band is probably due to the considerable disturbance that occurred at the site due to tree roots and burrowing animals (Kooyman et al. 1987).

10.5 Sourcing: Defining Contact, Exchange, and Material Transportation

Patterns of past contact and trade are a major focus of archaeological research and represent a topic to which a great deal of study has been devoted. Moreover, this topic is also one in which lithic analysis, most particularly employing obsidian, has played a major role. A significant problem is that the question of how material moved between different locations prehistorically is very complex. In addition, it must be remembered that there is no guarantee that the exchange system was constant; the type of exchange may have been different at different times, even from day to day, in the past. There are a large number of variables that interact and

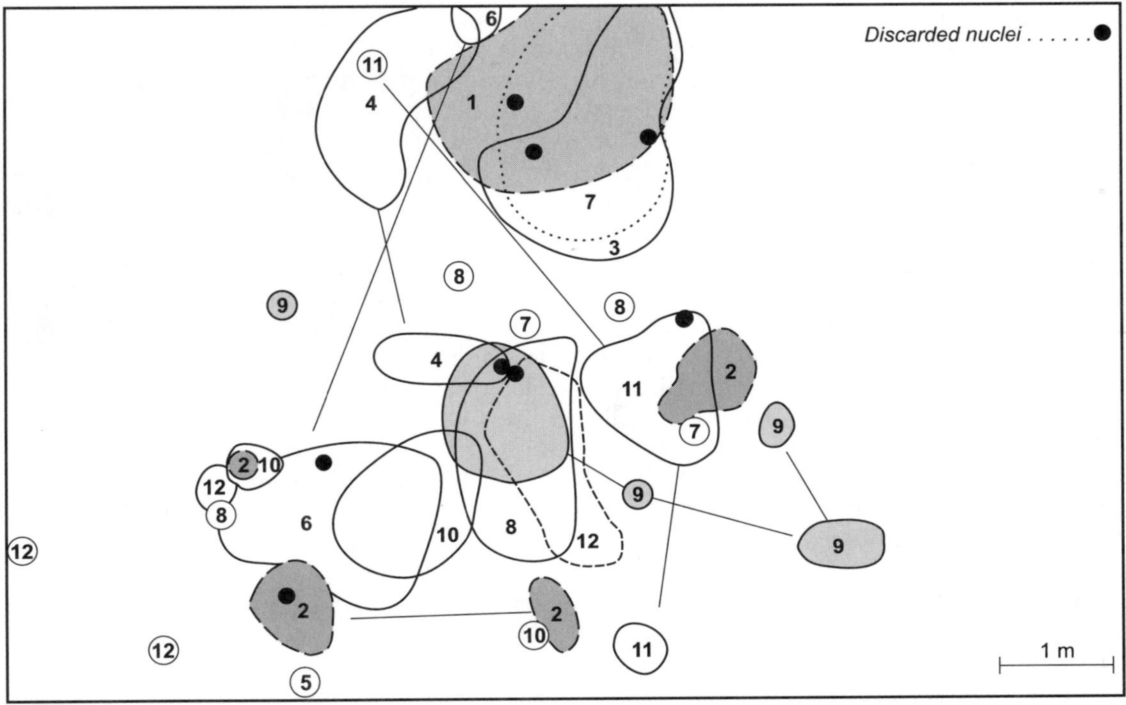

Figure 82: Refitting at a blade manufacturing site in New Zealand showing activity areas and reduction process (adapted from Leach 1969)

many of these variables are ones connected with human behavior patterns. People are notoriously unpredictable and need not act in strictly "optimal" ways, depending on other cultural factors that they see as more important. Furthermore, people often change the "rules" part way through. At the same time, of course, it is exactly these types of non-optimal behavior that make archaeology so interesting and revealing of human culture.

Even before assessing our ability to address the social interactions we wish to study, there are issues with the resolution powers of the techniques used to source stone that must be acknowledged. In the first place, not all materials can be sourced. Even with chemical sourcing, the more reliable method, different sources of a particular lithic material can have considerable overlap in their elemental composition. The meaning of this overlap is that it is not always possible to isolate different sources, nor to always identify the source locality of the archaeological piece being analyzed. Using only the identification of sources macroscopically, employing features visible in hand specimen, can be even more problematic. Macroscopic sourcing is actually impossible in many cases. Despite these types of problems, the results of sourcing analysis are very interesting when applied to the study of trade and exchange and it is worth the effort involved. It is beyond the scope of this book to discuss all the possible means by which trade or exchange occurred and all the models by which this has been analyzed archaeologically. What is feasible is to look at some of the basic factors involved and the patterns that might result.

Some definitions are appropriate first. Direct access occurs when the people being studied obtain the lithic material from the source themselves. Technically, direct access is not trade *per se*. Bilateral reciprocal trade (or balanced reciprocity) occurs when two groups meet and exchange goods deemed to be of equal value (if one side in the exchange does not receive the goods immediately, this is delayed reciprocity). Down-the-line exchange occurs when the goods are traded from a group to an adjacent group, to another adjacent group, and so on, until eventually some of the goods are traded some distance via a number of such intermediate links. In lithic material trade studies, discussions of down-the-line exchange often implicitly or explicitly assume that the exchange is balanced reciprocity (Torrence 1986:106). Trading situations where both parties try to maximize their profit are referred to as negative reciprocity, or sometimes market exchange (Torrence 1986:105–106). Long distance trade is that carried out by freelance traders, sometimes professional, who travel long distances to exchange goods with people removed physically from the source. Trade, of any type, may occur in formal markets or in less formal situations, and it may or may not be under some type of administrative control. This latter situation arises mainly in more complex societies.

A variety of distance decay or distance fall-off models (Fig. 83) have been used to examine lithic exchange. Basically, as a site is more distant from a particular lithic material source, less of the material from that source is found in the site. This situation reflects that fact that as the labor involved in transporting material to a site increases, it becomes more likely that some other, closer source will be used instead (the "costs" increasingly outweigh the "benefits" as the habitation site becomes more distant from the source of the raw material). Both counts of pieces and weight of material have been used to "quantify" this decline, but weight seems best overall since it is the weight of the material that influences how much work/effort/labor is involved. Use of counts might be more appropriate in situations where finished items are traded and the items are deemed essential in some manner (Ericson 1977:120). In such a case, the need for the item may be of much greater concern than a consideration of the effort involved due to its weight. Some models suggest that quantity fall-off is exponential and proportional to distance. There also seems to be a "threshold" distance at which there is a sudden drop-off in quantity, perhaps being the difference between an area of direct access and a wider area where the lithic material is obtained indirectly (i.e., obtained from a neighboring group).

The use of fall-off curves to track trade, particularly obsidian trade, was developed by Colin Renfrew and his colleagues in the late 1960s and early 1970s in their studies of Mediterranean obsidian trade (e.g., Renfrew et al. 1968). Their work was based in part on the studies of distance decay that had been undertaken by geographers (e.g., Olsson 1965; Claeson 1968). By 1977 Renfrew had developed the "Law of Monotonic Decrement" to describe the decreasing quantity of obsidian found in sites as the distance from the obsidian source increased (Renfrew 1977:72–78).

This analysis technique employs a plot of lithic material quantity, usually as a percentage of the total lithic assemblage, at a series of sites, against the distance of each of those sites from the quarry source. Research particularly by Ericson in California (1977:118,124) has shown that the distance measure used must account for the actual distance traveled, in terms of trails used and changes in elevation involved. Torrence has termed this the "effective distance" (1986:122). Plots (see Fig. 83) generally show an area near the source where the decrease in amount of material with distance is only moderate, this distance being up to about 300 km

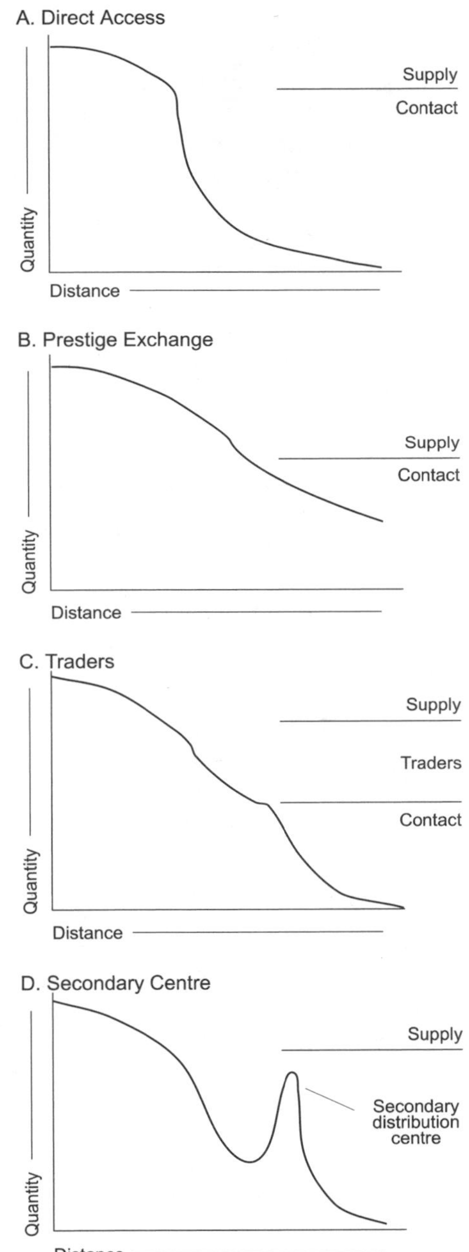

Figure 83: Hypothetical distance decay curves under various conditions (adapted from Torrence 1986)

(but often much less, depending on the transportation system among other factors). Further from the source than this point, the decrease in quantity with distance becomes exponential. The former zone is termed the "supply zone" and is usually seen as the zone where people had direct access to the source quarries. The zone beyond this is called the "contact zone" and is seen as the zone where the lithic material is acquired through trade. This particular pattern is now commonly employed as the "expected" or "normal" pattern, with variations from this baseline pattern interpreted in various manners as other types of exchange (for example, see Torrence 1986).

Obviously, then, idealized types of exchange can be associated with generalized shapes (see Fig. 83) of distance decay curves (Torrence 1986:116–117). As already implied, direct access should result in a slightly curved, almost linear, decline in quantity with distance, as seen in the graph supply zone described above. This shape occurs because it is really only distance and weight of material that can influence the curve, since there is actually no trade (Torrence 1986:118). Down-the-line reciprocal exchange should be similar in shape, since distance and number of exchanges in the chain are really the only factors effecting the exchange, but the decline with distance from the source should be much more rapid and so the slope of the line will be much steeper. If the material being exchanged is very valuable but is still exchanged on a reciprocal basis, as for example ceremonial pieces or absolutely essential materials, the curve should have the same form but the decline in quantity with distance will be much less rapid and so the slope of the curve will be less steep. This is sometimes referred to as prestige-chain exchange. In circumstances where the commodity is being traded by freelance traders, three zones would theoretically be present in the graph. Between the inner supply zone and the outer contact zone there will be a zone where the traders regularly travel. This trader zone will have a less steep slope than the contact zone, since the traders increase the availability of the material in question, but a more steep slope than the supply zone. The contact zone slope will be as in other models, but will begin at a greater distance from the quarry source, outside the zone served by traders. Another situation that may occur is the transportation of quantities of the lithic material to a secondary distribution center at some distance from the quarry. In this context there will be the regular steep decline in the contact zone, but then a rapid rise in quantity in the area surrounding the secondary distribution center. This situation will produce a sharp peak in the graph at this distance from the quarry, the increase being on both the nearer and farther sides of the center from the quarry. Although these generalized models are useful, it is also clear that various circumstances can result in essentially the same plots (Torrence 1986:119). As well as the exchange mechanism *per se*, other important factors include the value of the good, the number and length of the steps between the source and the consumer, the size of the supply zone, economic competition (including alternative sources), and the social and cultural meaning of the goods.

As well as a change in quantity with distance, there is likely to be a change in the form the artifacts take. For example, Nash (1996) used representation of cortex in assemblages as an indication of the frequency with which raw material nodules were brought to Tabun Cave. Within a direct access area, blocks of unmodified material and cores of material are likely to be found. Further away, these relatively unmodified forms are not likely to be common but instead sites may contain more blades, preforms, formed tools, and so on. These formed tools require less effort to transport because more of the excess weight, that material that has to be removed and discarded in the process of making the final tool, has already been removed. No effort is wasted in transporting stone that will be discarded anyway.

A consideration of this aspect, the form the lithic material is in, necessitates a realization that it is not possible to compare a quarry site to a camp site directly when using such distance decay models. Sites also have different types of material based on site function, so site function also needs to be considered in the analysis (e.g., Sidrys 1977:94–97). However, this is not a problem, as it might seem at first, but rather an advantage, since the form of the lithic material can obviously provide information about this functional aspect of the site as well.

When comparing sites, or layers within a site, a basic indication of quantity provides a statement about whether or not a lithic type is important at a site. One gram or one piece probably demonstrates that the material is not important, but it is also necessary to consider the percentage weight or count for the lithic material compared to the total lithic assemblage weight or count. A small or temporary site may have low absolute quantities of everything; hence if only absolute amounts are considered, the variation in use of different lithic materials might be missed. At the same time, then, the absolute frequency of overall lithic material can give an important indication of site inhabitant population, duration of site use, and/or frequency of site use. Comparison of these absolute frequencies between sites, or between layers within a site, can provide insight into changes in site or lithic type use through time and space. It is also important to compare weight and count; a single piece weighing 500 gm suggests very different interpretations compared to 500 one-gram pieces. As already mentioned, quantification by weight is probably the most relevant basic measurement in most cases, since it is the weight of material that determines the effort or cost that was expended in its transportation. All lithic materials used have essentially the same density, so they require a similar transportation space. If the number of pieces a specific weight is divided into varies, there is usually little difference in transportation effort.

Some of these comparison problems can also be addressed by expressing the frequency of lithic material as a "density" per excavated volume (e.g., grams/cubic meter). This allows frequency to be compared realistically between sites having different occupation intensities or functions, as well as to be compared between sites having quite different excavation areas. Examination of changing intensity of use of particular lithic materials, in sites showing simultaneous population increases or decreases, often can be best addressed by expressing lithic material frequency as a ratio to some other artifact type that can be presumed to increase proportionally to population increase (e.g., number of grinding stones, number of pot sherds [Sidrys 1977:100; Torrence 1986:28–29]).

In these comparisons it is also important to examine percent weight and percentage count for various flake and tool categories (BRF, resharpening, shaping, cores, tools, etc.). If the sites or layers being compared have some category frequencies that are quite different for each lithic type, this situation may suggest a change in how lithic types are being exploited. If frequencies are different for different reduction stage categories, there are implications about site function differences, or function differences for different lithic types. For example, if one lithic type largely consists of resharpening flakes, and the percentage by weight is quite low, it may be that this debitage is essentially the result only of resharpening exotic tools. Such a circumstance in turn might suggest that there was some considerable geographic or social distance for that quarry compared to the site, or even both geographic and social distance. Social distance might be due to intervening groups that are enemies of the site occupants, a large number of intervening groups due to great population density, or a variety of other possibilities.

Another area that can be examined is the interplay of tool and debitage frequencies as these reflect site function and duration of occupation. For example, a site probably represents a special purpose occupation function if only a few tool types are recovered. Short term use is suggested if the absolute quantity of material is low. An assemblage consisting mainly of expedient tools is probably due to short term use and/or easy access to the quarry. Short term use, represented by *ad hoc* tool use to accomplish a task with whatever is available, is a reasonable interpretation in such a case if there are a number of lithic types equally represented in the debris and overall the quantity of material is not great. Easy access, perhaps direct access, to the quarry may encourage more "wasteful" use of the particular lithic material; this would include use of minimally formed expedient tools, wasting lithic material rather than time spent in manufacture, since lithic material is easily acquired. Various other methods of assessing efficiency of material use have been employed, such as blank dimensions (giving quantity of lithic material needed per tool produced) and cutting edge to weight ratios (see discussion in Torrence 1986:24–25]). In this regard it is important to remember that when looking at the frequency of lithic material in a site we are actually examining the rate or pattern of *discard* rather than the rate or pattern of use (Torrence 1986:15). More and larger flake debitage would be likely in a case of inefficient material use. If near to a quarry, the assemblage should be largely dominated by this one readily acquired lithic type rather than a variety of lithic types (unless the quarry is a secondary source, such as gravel, that contains multiple lithic types). A special activity site, which might also be a short term occupation, may have expedient tools, but may not if specialized, well formed tools that can be resharpened many times are brought for the specific task (such specialized tools might be advantageous if there is no need to bring anything else to this special purpose site, minimizing transportation effort).

Differential use of specific lithic materials within and between sites can be seen in their varying quantity in different contexts. This can be varying association with status and non-status locations, or varying use for status and non-status items, such as ceremonial objects. Whether objects made of non-local material are imported as finished products or are locally manufactured of imported raw material can be ascertained by examination of the nature of the debitage and whether or not the quantity and type of debitage is sufficient to account for the production of the objects in question (Torrence 1986:30–35).

The interplay of tool form, transportation constraints, and site activities is well exemplified by the debate about whether mobile hunter-gatherers' needs are best fulfilled by having many smaller specialized tools or a few large, multipurpose tools that can be resharpened many times (Kuhn 1994, 1996; Morrow 1996a). Groups that move regularly obviously must concern themselves with the weight of all the material they must move with them, so they should try to minimize the weight they have to transport, including the weight of the stone tools they need. Once tools become too small as a result of use and resharpening they are no longer functional and are discarded. Based on his study, Kuhn (1994) suggested that as tools increase beyond this useful minimum the amount of work that can be completed with them compared to their size increases dramatically, but that as they increase beyond a certain size that increasing amount of work levels off. Based on this situation, he suggested that there was an optimum larger size which allowed the largest amount of additional use value for proportionally the least additional weight of lithic material. His mathematical model, coupled with a recognition that some tools do require a minimum size to function, led him to propose that we should expect that tools should be made about 1.5 to 3 times the size of the minimal useable size. Morrow (1996a) suggested that Kuhn had not considered tool thickness in his model, and that a thicker tool could do more work than a thin tool because there was more edge in contact with the worked material; with thickness included, the rapid increase in work that smaller tools achieved did not occur. Morrow suggested that the most efficient route to go was instead to have a large tool that could be put to many purposes because it could have many useable edge areas of various configurations; this basically allowed one tool to serve for many, reducing the overall weight of stone that had to be carried. Morrow rightly noted that most tasks are accomplished more quickly and with less effort if the tool is quite a bit larger, so that the hand does not tire or experience difficulty in gripping the tool. This aspect, what might be termed a tool's "effective size," coupled with functional needs, clearly dictates that small tools cannot accomplish all tasks. People would have tried to find a minimum size for each tool, even though this minimal size would still have to be a very large tool in absolute terms. Not all tools of mobile people would be small. I would say that Morrow's point about tool thickness is only partially valid. On an edge being used, much of it never does come into contact with the worked material before it is too dull in the contact area and must be resharpened. Kuhn (1996) makes a similar point concerning the fact that at every sharpening there is a thickness of the tool that is removed without having done any work. Morrow makes some other interesting points about time spent in making hafts for small tools requiring extra labor, but I think overall that these issues do not contradict Kuhn's basic point about tools being smaller and having a size beyond which the increased "versatility" is not efficient. For example, if one had a very large tool that might last for several seasons of resharpening, in the first four or five years there would be extra weight to carry that would not be used in the entire year. This seems inherently inefficient. I suspect that the thrust of Morrow's points shows that a more complex, realistic version of Kuhn's model would considerably alter upwards the "optimum" size for mobile peoples' stone tools.

There are also obviously other considerations, such as stone availability and how extreme the transportation constraints are, that will impact on peoples' decisions about tool form, as both Morrow and Kuhn recognized in some manner. Close's study (1996) of Neolithic material in the Sahara region of Africa is a good example of how variation in these other factors can produce some apparently unexpected results. She found some very large blocks of unused lithic material cached in her sites despite the fact that there were no lithic sources for some 10–15 km. People were able to overcome this distance obstacle by using cattle as pack animals to bring the material to where they needed it. Many groups would not have had this means to overcome their transportation constraints. In a similar vein, Odell (1994) explored some ambiguous results from his Illinois Valley study to come to a better appreciation of the actual patterns of lithic material use. He found that decreased residential mobility resulted in more intensive use of tools, this situation being the result of what might be termed a culturally determined unavailability of lithic material; more sedentary groups cannot necessarily travel to distant lithic sources as often or as readily and so they utilize their resources more fully. This situation is seen in intensity of tool use, in this case as measured by number of utilized and retouched portions of a tool. Clearly, better transportation, as in Close's study, or a better ability to send special task groups to bring lithic raw material back to the more sedentary settlement, could mitigate such a material shortage.

Andrefsky's comparison of stone tools in three areas of the western United States (1994) that had very contrasting patterns of raw material availability and quality is also appropriate to consider here. The basic result was that locally available raw material always dominated lithic assemblages if it was also abundant, regardless of whether its quality was good or simply adequate. Andrefsky anticipated this pattern based on ethnoarchaeological research in Australia conducted by Gould (1980) and O'Connell (1977). The same pattern is seen in the prairies of Alberta, Canada, where locally available quartzites tend to dominate tool assemblages even though they are generally difficult to work. Andrefsky found that the difference between poor quality and good quality locally available lithic materials was that if the quality was poor, almost all tools were of an informal type (unretouched flakes and pieces of shatter). On the other hand, if the quality of the raw material was good, both formal and informal tools were manufactured in approximately equal quantities. The other case, where there was little locally available raw material, produced yet a different pattern. Almost all the tools were of non-local material and they were formal types; the few tools manufactured of local material were informal. It is apparent from this evidence that little effort is expended in trying to manufacture intricately formed tools from poor quality material, but presence of abundant local material is an overriding factor in the decision to use this material predominantly regardless of its quality.

A paucity of lithic material in an area should logically result in attempts to maximize the use of that stone. Among the results of this situation is that tools should be extensively resharpened to make maximum use of what is available. Odell's study of the Illinois valley (1994) did demonstrate this in one site in a region with little raw material, but another site did not show this pattern. What this second site did show, however, was a maximization of the lithic material. Old tools were smashed and then these fragments were manufactured into new tools (the breakage would have also decreased the number of modified edges per piece, Odell reasoned, artificially decreasing his values for number of used portions per tool and making it *appear* that use intensity was lower).

Many more examples could be given. The main point is that a careful consideration of the interplay of all the information available ensures as full an interpretation as is possible.

Lithic material quantity fall-off patterns serve as baselines for evaluation purposes. The specific configuration of these distributions depends on variables, such as degree of social stratification that might cause limitation of direct access or that might control the trade further down the line; whether or not craft specialization exists; the transportation system involved; the size of the consumer population (Ericson 1977:120; Torrence 1986:17) (this determining how much material is present in a site and also the extent to which the quantity produced is dispersed through many sites versus being concentrated in a few); whether or not there are alternative sources of lithic material in the area; and so on. Site location, quarry location, and the specific configuration of the fall-off patterns can be evaluated against idealized scenario patterns to ascertain to what extent some of these other social factors may be influencing raw material frequency in a site.

A good example of the use of fall-off patterns and a number of variables to assess the meaning of obsidian distribution patterns is Torrence's study of the Aegean region of the Mediterranean east of Greece (Torrence 1986:127–163, 223–225). The only source of obsidian in the study area was on the island of Melos. The island had a major site on it, Phylakopi, with an associated large obsidian debris pile that had long been used to suggest that the site's wealth came from control of the obsidian source. But careful study of the deposits showed that there was very little obsidian present when the duration of the occupation was considered and that later stages of production (beyond core preparation) were largely unrepresented. These lines of evidence seemed to indicate that there was direct access to the Melos quarries, or purchase of cores from the inhabitants of Phylakopi. The fall-off curves seemed to support this interpretation, showing little decrease in quantity with distance as well as apparent waste of obsidian at considerable distance from the quarry. Torrence then examined the possibility that control of the obsidian was based elsewhere, specifically in the Minoan civilization centered at Knossos on Crete. Even at Knossos, however, there were no great quantities of obsidian debitage as would be expected at a secondary distribution center and there was no specialization or standardization of products as might be expected. Apparently, compared with other products such as wool, obsidian was relatively unimportant and there was no attempt to closely control its production.

Although there are links between raw material geographic distribution and form patterns and various external factors, the interaction of these factors is complex and no one-to-one correlation can be expected (Carr 1994b). Ingbar's (1994) simple simulations that produced dramatically differing raw material frequencies, despite the fact that many of the factors usually discussed in source distribution studies (trade, curation, settlement dispersion, raw material quality, tool uselife, etc.) were not even incorporated, serves as a strong caution against uncritical assessment of archaeological data. At the same time, the fact that Ingbar obtained distinctive patterning with very simple variations in parameters argues for the power of lithic studies to help us understand past human behavior.

An example of the influence of external factors (Fig. 84) is the variability seen in the utilization of different obsidian sources in sites in the Mesoamerican study by Zeitlin (1982). Clearly, Fig. 84 indicates that there is considerable variation in the use of different quarry

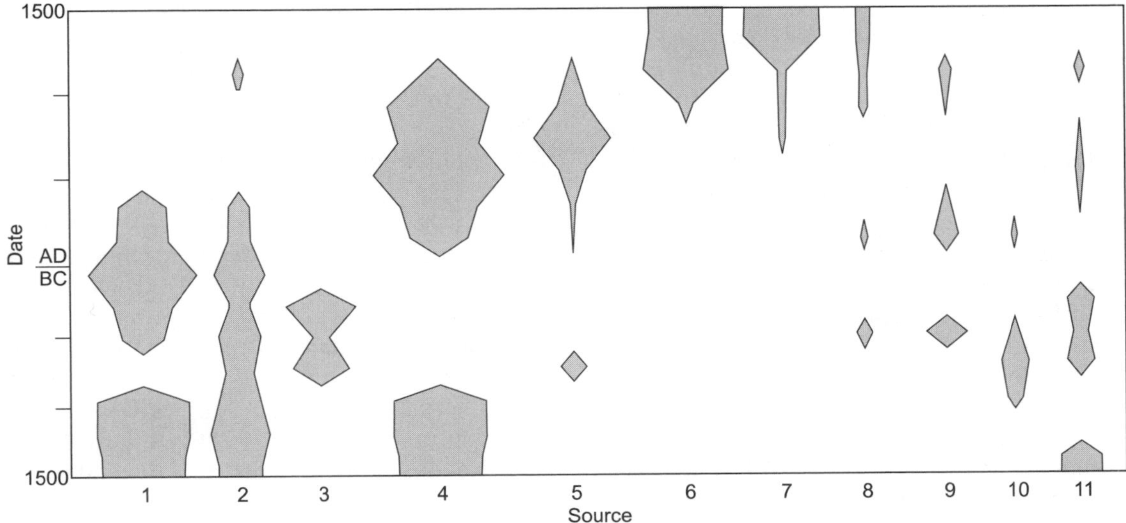

Figure 84: External factors influencing obsidian source use in Mexico (adapted from Zeitlin 1982)

sources through time. This variation is probably due to social and political factors, where each site has varying amounts of material from different sources through time. The quantity is not simply a factor of distance from the source; other possible factors include restricted access, payment of tribute, and so on. Obviously, there may also be circumstances where social boundaries do not affect the movement of trade goods. Ericson's study of obsidian distribution in comparison to historic period ethnic boundaries in California shows no discontinuities in distribution in the boundary areas (1977:118), although other studies do show such patterns (e.g., McBryde 1978). Amick's (1994) comments on variation in lithic material use in Folsom sites in New Mexico and Texas suggest both lithic material quality and patterns of group movement affect the frequency of various lithic materials in archaeological sites.

Another example of how social factors affect lithic material distribution is the case of the "Talasea" obsidian sources from the Willaumez Peninsula of the island of New Britain in western Melanesia (Sheppard 1993:123; Summerhayes and Hotchkis 1992:130; Torrence et al. 1996:213). Studies by Roger Green and his colleagues have long used obsidian sourcing as a basis for assessing patterns of trade in the Lapita Cultural Complex (e.g., Ambrose and Green 1972; Green 1962, 1974, 1982, 1987). Willaumez Peninsula obsidian is present as far east as Fiji, some 3,000 km from the source (Torrence et al. 1996:212). As far east as the Reef and Santa Cruz Islands, about 2000 km from the source, Willaumez Peninsula obsidian is approximately as common as more locally available cherts (Sheppard 1993:123). Further east in Fiji the sites with Willaumez Peninsula obsidian have no more than a few pieces (Allen and Bell 1988:88). Green suggested that different types of exchange might be involved to explain the various differences in exotic materials in Lapita sites (1982:15–17), particularly in regards to these most distant distributions of small amounts of obsidian (1987). It is generally agreed on by other researchers that the long distant distribution of obsidian in Lapita sites has some special significance, although the precise nature of that significance is seen differently by different authors (Kirch 1988:162; Sheppard 1993:135, 1996:108–109; Torrence et al. 1996:220).

Sheppard's study (1993:124–127) of lithic material in the Reef and Santa Cruz Islands showed that Willaumez Peninsula obsidian was a co-dominant material throughout the archaeological sequence despite the much closer presence of reasonable quality cherts and obsidian. He also found that chert from a source about 400 km distance was much more common than good quality chert from only 100–150 km away (Sheppard 1993:124, 1996:108). Size of pieces, utilization, and amount of cortex suggested that there was no special effort to conserve the exotic Willaumez obsidian and that much of it arrived with little prior preparation into blanks, etc. These observations, particularly for the obsidian, were seen as unexpected given that normally the quantity of lithic material is anticipated to be less, and that less cortex is expected in sites at greater distances from the source, and that the use of more distant lithic materials is expected to be associated with more efficient utilization of the material. In both cases, the preferred but more distant lithic material was from sources to the northwest, toward the original area from which the Lapita people colonized eastern Melanesia. Sheppard followed Green and others in suggesting that obsidian had a social function in maintaining ties during colonization (Sheppard 1993:135, 1996:108–109) or that it indicated a significance of place or direction (1996:112). This interpretation was supported by the fact that the amount of these more exotic materials declined through time, presumably as the need to maintain contact declined as the colonies became more established. He also suggested that the contradiction between the supposed special importance of obsidian, yet its use in apparently unspecialized and obviously utilitarian flake and edge-modified flake tools, was a result of its losing its significance once it had been traded. Having served its "ties to the homeland" purpose, it came to be used in a utilitarian manner as it entered the realm of useable commodities. He also indicated that the use of wasteful, expedient tool technology followed the pattern seen elsewhere in sedentary, agricultural societies that could afford to waste material because they could have much on hand in their sedentary communities.

Recently the material Sheppard based his analysis on was re-analyzed to determine which of the specific Willaumez sources were represented (Torrence et al. 1996:230). As part of that analysis these authors noted that the pattern of long distance transport of this obsidian coupled with the apparent wasteful use of it, might be equally well explained by suggesting that the material was acquired by direct access. They noted that the material was transported over water and that even though studies of Mediterranean obsidian transportation over water had seen direct access (supply zones) as up to about 300 km, such transportation might easily be over much greater distances. The authors found the key to supporting Sheppard's original suggestion, rather than direct access, in the specific source present in his samples; all the material was specifically from the Kutau/Bao subgroup. Adjacent to the island of New Britain during the Lapita time period, sites on the island of Garua were dominated by this same Kutau/Bao subgroup, despite the fact that there was a local obsidian source, and the Kutau/Bao material was used in a wasteful manner. Clearly, this obsidian source had special social value or significance.

Support for such significance also comes from research on Paleoindian raw material use in the United States. Tankersley (1989) discussed nonlocal raw material (in his study (1989:265) defined as being from more than 30 km away) in midwestern Paleoindian sites as indicating direct access during the course of a seasonal round of activities if it was the most common material, since presumably people would have to acquire at least some of such a common material themselves (1989:271). Such sources in his study were between 50 and 220 km away from the site. Non-local materials from more distant sources were present in his study, but only represented a few percent of the assemblage at most. He suggested that these materials were indicative of some form of exchange rather than direct access. Goodyear (1989) similarly noted that a number of western Paleoindian sites showed significant quantities of non-local lithic material (e.g., one-third of the material at Blackwater Draw) from up to 200 km away. He, too, suggested such material indicated the size of band territory and that more distant sources likely indicated some form of specialized exchange (1989:5–7). Ellis, working in the Great Lakes area (1989:144–145), suggested that groups might display their cultural identity through the use of highly distinctive, point source lithic raw materials; if a material is distinctive and from (particularly) a geographically restricted bedrock outcrop, no other groups would have access to that material. Such a lithic material could serve as a distinctive signal or marker of the one group. As clear evidence of such behavior, Ellis cites the lithic remains from the Gainey site in Michigan. Although very good quality chert was available (and known) only 130 km away at the Tenmile Creek source, the major source used was Upper Mercer chert that was from 380 km away *in the same direct line* from the Gainey site. This pattern of specialized use of a more distant source when equally useful, closer sources were available parallels the Willaumez obsidian use pattern and supports the idea that lithic material can have special social significance.

Gould and Saggers (1985) also suggested that their research in Australia provided evidence for the special significance of some lithic material. They recovered many flakes of poor quality non-local material at Puntutjara rockshelter despite the fact that better quality local material was available. They argued that this pattern suggested a special ideological significance for this non-local material, although Binford and Stone (1985) suggested that the pattern could be due to long term curation of some specific tool types. Whatever the best interpretation of these data is, there is no question that stone sources associated with Dreamtime Ancestors in Australia are imbued with power and symbolic significance (Taçon 1992). The fact that certain lithic materials are preferentially present as grave goods or are apparently preferentially used to manufacture ceremonial items has also led to them being seen as holding special ceremonial or supernatural significance (e.g., Peterson et al. 1997:235).

In part exchange is about obtaining benefits for effort (i.e., "profit"). In a competitive situation this edge can be maintained by controlling the source of the lithic raw material (with the presence of alternative lithic sources being a factor in the success of the strategy) or by producing the products demanded by more efficient, less "expensive," means (Torrence 1986:41-50). Control of the source quarries is often indicated by the presence of territorial markers or symbols, such as fences. Greater production efficiency can be achieved through more sophisticated, labor-saving technology; simplified or streamlined technology; standardization of form (e.g., variation in blade size in different sites or contexts, as discussed by Torrence 1986:158–159); or specialization in use of raw material resources, tools, techniques, space, and/or labor (e.g., method of applying force as seen in platform facet numbers and orientation, as discussed by Torrence [1986:160]). The latter specialists are either engaged in craft specialization, wherein the knowledge or skills are restricted to a few practitioners, or mass replication, wherein the skills are in easily learned areas that many can master. Craft specialists have a low rate of output of high quality or very individualized products, whereas the "industrial" specialists produce large amounts of goods, generally clearly in excess of local needs. Both of these specializations have important implication for social structure of the group involved, but the implications are quite different. Craftsman skill and efficiency of production are not necessarily the same. Similarly (Torrence 1986:89), it is important to recognize the differing implications of "intensive" production, where a high level of output is achieved, and "efficient" production, where output returns are greater than input costs regardless of the scale (quantity) of production. *Efficiency* of behavior is the only certain indicator of craft specialists. There may be, and often are, other indicators of craft specialists, particularly specialized structures to work in or spatial localization of different stages of the production process. It is common for craft specialists to minimize waste of raw material because they make few errors in production, as has been monitored in lithic analysis by the frequency of hinge fractures (e.g., Torrence 1986:161). Other indicators, such as large dumps of debitage of essentially a single lithic type (1986:146), can be seen as probably necessary, but not sufficient, pieces of evidence for the presence of craft specialists.

An example of a pattern resulting from craft specialization is that at Teotihuacan, where a particular green obsidian was used for some 90% of blades and blade cores manufactured, even though the source was some three times further away than another source. Some of the workshops produced almost exclusively blades, although others produced a wide variety of objects. Here there are some workers, craft specialists, particularly manufacturing blades, and in these circumstances there is also definitely a preferred raw material used. Johnson (1996) also discusses the distinctive features of craft specialization, particularly production on a large scale, production well in access of what is needed locally, and standardization of both method of production and final artifact form. Johnson compared Maya material from Colha to that from the Middle Archaic Benton Period sites of the American Southeast and found some significant parallels in the scale of these attributes in both collections, although cautioning that this was not a claim for craft specialization in the Southeastern Archaic. Although the two sets of material displayed similarities of scale, the Mayan material was produced on a substantially greater scale, included the production of a greater diversity of specialized forms, demonstrated workshops that specialized in specific forms, and revealed all production stages at the quarry source rather than only the initial stages as was the case for the Southeastern material (where later stages were completed in ordinary hunting camps, unlikely locations for craft specialists). Like many aspects of lithic analysis, there were probably degrees of specialization. The patterns seen in the Benton Period sites illustrate this to some extent. Johnson's discussion also clearly indicates that the interplay of elite control, ritual and non-ritual use, and craft specialization can be complex.

Gravity models are another type of model that has been used to examine trade and exchange in lithic studies. Basically, if the relative "attractiveness" of different obsidian sources is the same, two sites with the same quantity of material from that source should be an equal distance from it. There are mathematical equations to make the measurement of this "attractiveness" more objective.

A technological analysis approach has been used to study traded lithics as well. In Sheets' (1978: 85–88, 1983: 283–284) analysis of obsidian in the Zapotitan Valley of El Salvador, he found that all obsidian used in the valley went first to the largest and most important sites and was redistributed from there. These sites in the highest hierarchical level had, for instance, more decortication flakes than other sites, showing that the raw material was brought to them. The flakes also had a greater average size in these largest sites, so the resource was apparently not as scarce as at other sites and more "waste" could be tolerated. Further in this regard, there was a lower cutting edge/weight ratio in the largest sites than in the other sites, again showing a lesser care with this desirable but more available resource at these higher level sites.

The social route by which site occupants obtained their lithic material, and how different households or residence groups within a site specifically obtained their lithic material, introduces other levels of consideration that can be usefully examined for the insight they provide into aspects such as elite control of access. Peterson and her colleagues (Peterson et al. 1997) discuss a number of these factors in light of their study area and previous research, particularly in Mesoamerica and the American Southwest. Based on their discussion and some additional considerations, some tendencies should be observable in the archaeological record. Household groups may obtain their own lithic material, either directly or through trade with kin or other trading partners. Under such circumstances one might anticipate quite different lithic material frequencies in different households (as seen archaeologically in housepits, etc.), since each household might access lithic material in different places or through different social networks (an example of this was previously discussed [Hayden, Bakewell, and Gargett 1996]). This anticipated diversity of lithic material frequency patterns might not pertain if all residence groups in a community obtained their lithic material at the same time or if their trading partners or kin ties were uniformly with the same other groups. A general absence of lithic material variety in a region would also, of course, result in uncharacteristically low variability between household assemblages. In contrast, elite control (through a "big man" or a more formalized class) of access and subsequent redistribution to lower classes might be expected to generally result in a greater uniformity of lithic material type patterns from one household unit to another. Although certain households or kin groups might receive preferential access through their special connections to the elite class, for the most part one would expect that all non-elite households would have approximately equal access to the material and this material would be first "pooled" (and so "homogenized") by the elite class. If a few households are uncharacteristically at variance with the others, it is likely that these represent elite residences. The possibility of specialized traders, rather than a true elite, must also be considered.

10.6 Style and Technology

As form of artifacts and methods of manufacture spread through time and space via contact, their distributions can be used to trace migrations of, origins of, and contact between various peoples and regions. Examples might be the geographic (and temporal) distribution of a method of manufacturing blades or a particular style of projectile point. Based on the aspects of style involved, studies can be used to define prehistoric social, perhaps ethnic, boundaries. Technology, in particular, can be used to trace the evolution of culture, as for instance the change to the Levallois technique or the origin of blade manufacture. This facet of analysis is one of the basic and oldest uses of lithic studies.

The "meaning" of the style has to do with what aspects of style and form are being examined. The various types of style or variation in stone tools previously outlined (isochrestic variation, emblemic variation, etc.) are the variables that are examined in this regard.

Actually isolating an ethnic group, or any other social group, can be difficult because it is not always clear what type of variation is involved for "ethnic" style. But functional variation and individual variation can usually be isolated, with everything of an "intermediate" nature being ascribed to some kind of social group.

Researchers often try to link archaeological variation to known historic ethnic groups. For example, in the Old Man River Dam project in southern Alberta, most of the sites had little lithic material from the interior of British Columbia. Instead, most lithic material was either from southern Alberta or northern Montana. The Smyth site had quite a substantial occupation in Pelican Lake times, about 3,000 years ago. About 30% of the projectile points from the Pelican Lake occupation were made of Kootenai argillite and another 3% were made of Top-of-the-World chert. Both of these lithic sources are from the southeast corner of British Columbia. As well, the Smyth site was almost the only site tested in the project where the use of buffalo was mainly in the summer; all other sites tested showed almost no summer use. Historically, the Kootenai people did undertake summer buffalo hunts in southwestern Alberta where the Smyth site is located, according to tradition this being when the Blackfoot, the usual residents of southwestern Alberta historically, had moved east out onto the open plains (Turney-High 1974). Based on this information, Brumley (1995) has suggested that the Smyth site occupants were interior British Columbia groups. Some of the projectile points are of a rather different style compared to other points of this time period, side notched and not of the Pelican Lake style. These lines of evidence are strongly suggestive of use of the Smyth site by a different ethnic group, probably from the interior of British Columbia. Whether or not these people may have been the ancestors of the historic period Kootenai is rather more difficult to assess with any confidence.

10.7 Summary

It should now be obvious that lithic analysis can make impressive contributions to our understanding of archaeological sites. To be sure, lithic analysis can inform us of past peoples' technological systems, but it can also offer insights into settlement patterns, site functions and activities, trade and social contact, territory, and in some cases, even aspects of social structure and ethnicity. The multiplicity of uses, coupled with the durability and ubiquity of stone tools and lithic debitage, make lithic analysis an extremely important tool in archaeological research.

CHAPTER 11

Lithic Usewear and Residue Analysis

11.1 Introduction

Usewear and residue analysis are the two methods that have been employed to try to obtain an objective assessment of prehistoric stone tool use.

There are three main varieties of usewear analysis:

1. Microchipping: examines the small scars left from flakes that have been knocked off the edge of a tool during use.

2. Micropolish: contact with work material produces a polish on a stone tool just as polishes develop on various surfaces from contact (e.g., polishing glass for windows, gem stones for jewelry, etc.).

3. Striations: contact with the worked material and small fragments of debris results in scratches, striations, on the tool surface.

Residue analysis employs various techniques to analyze the remains of worked material that adhere to the stone tool surface after use. Methods vary from microscopically identifying fragments of plant and animal remains (cells, etc.) left intact on the tool edge, to various chemical and immunological methods (chromatography, electrophoresis, chemical reaction, antigen/antibody reactions) that test the chemical and biochemical properties of the residues rather than their undamaged physical biological structure.

All of these methods of analysis have been criticized for being inaccurate and subjective (e.g., Eisele et al. 1995; Fiedel 1996; Newcomer et al. 1986). They have been seen as particularly problematic because even though modern experiments using stone tools to complete tasks, such as hide scraping, can be used to derive diagnostic analytical criteria, there is always a question about whether or not traces are contaminated, altered, or removed in the archaeological sediment environment and whether the experiments are appropriate analogues for past tool use. Various alternative or modified approaches have been proposed or tested (e.g., Newcomer et al. 1986) and workers in the field have often suggested that multiple approaches are valid or that a combination of approaches is most likely to yield comprehensive and accurate results (e.g., Newman et al. 1997; Odell 1994; Vaughan 1981). Having worked with both polish and microchipping analysis (e.g., Kooyman 1985), as well as residue analysis (e.g., Kooyman et al. 1992), I would certainly agree with those who recognize (e.g., Odell 1994:72) that each method has strengths and weaknesses and that a multifaceted approach is best.

11.2 Historical Development

An examination of the history of the development of usewear and residue analysis, including an examination of the most recent debates, is important since this area of research has the potential to revolutionize our understanding of stone tool use if it provides a truly objective assessment of use tasks.

The first analysis to note in print that wear traces could be used to determine tool function, was the Scandinavian archaeologist Sven Nilsson in the late 1830s, who said: "... through carefully examining how tools were worn, one can often with certainty conclude how they were used" (Vaughan 1981:11).

In 1865 Greenwell, an Englishman, noted that since end scrapers had "... one end smoothed by continual friction, I am inclined to think (it) was used in dressing hides" (Vaughan 1981:11). This is probably the first recording of use polish, along with the observations on striations and polish from use that Rau noted on North American "hoes" in 1864 (Vaughan 1981:12). In 1869 Rau also examined the striations and other damage resulting from manufacturing, specifically that resulting from drilling holes in tools (Vaughan 1981:12).

In 1872 another Englishman, John Evans, did experiments on use damage using a variety of implements such as "hoes," unretouched flakes, scrapers, and knives. He noted that "If long in use, the sides of the blade become rather polished by wear ..." (Vaughan 1981:12) and that he had also observed this on archaeological specimens. He also noted that through use a scraper "... edge will be found to wear away, by extremely minute portions chipping off at nearly right angles to the scraping edge ... The coarseness of those minute chips will vary in accordance with the amount of pressure used, and the material scraped..." (Vaughan 1981:12). He also discussed multiple causes for the same wear traces and similar tool types serving very different functions. He has been termed the father of microwear studies.

The first instance of usewear analysis coming to the forefront of archaeological work was during the sickle gloss debate that began in earnest in the 1890s. Flint tools with a high gloss had been assumed to be tools used for harvesting cereal crops. After experimenting, Spurrell in 1892 suggested that it was the silica particles in grain stalks rubbing on the tool edge that caused the polish (Vaughan 1981: 23). In 1919, Vayson did experiments that produced visible polish from working wood as well as from cereals (Vaughan 1981: 23–24). He concluded that friction alone was the agent of polish formation and that the "sickle gloss" was not proof of cereal harvesting. Between 1930 and 1937, Curwen conducted more experiments that showed polish did form from working straw and wood, but he found that the band of wood polish was much narrower because the tool could not penetrate deeply into this hard material. He attributed the polish to the friction between the tool and the silica particles in both materials (Vaughan 1981:14, 25).

In 1934, Sergei Semenov began his study of usewear striations and polishes in Russia, with his major book ultimately being published in Russian in 1957 and in English translation in 1964. His careful experiments and documentation through photographs mark the start of the modern era of usewear analysis. His work basically showed that striations on tool surfaces were indicative of the action used in the work done (striations from scraping were oriented at approximately 90° to the edge; cutting produced striations parallel to the edge, etc.). The location of striations (and polish) also showed which portion of a tool had been used (or held/hafted). The extent of polishing away from the edge was seen as an indication of how deeply the tool had penetrated the worked material, with working of hard materials, such as wood, having polish confined more to the immediate edge area. The degree to which polish infilled low areas in the microtopography of the tool edge was seen as an indication of the pliability of the worked material. For example, working fresh hides gave more polish in hollows than did dry hides. Use action was also revealed by the differential damage on dorsal and ventral surfaces, with "whittling" having much damage on the ventral surface and less on the dorsal.

Although Western researchers initially had problems trying to replicate and apply Semenov's techniques, these problems were ultimately resolved (e.g., Hayden 1979a). The usewear analysis that developed from Semenov's initial work has tended to relegate striation analysis to a secondary role (as for example in micropolish analysis, where it is used primarily for indicating direction of use), or to having no role at all (as in microchipping analysis). Hay (1977) found different striation morphologies associated with different worked materials by using a scanning electron microscope (SEM). More recently, Mansur-Franchomme (e.g., 1983) has used striation morphology as a clue to the physical conditions produced by working different materials, again using SEM. This approach has in turn allowed her to draw inferences about worked material.

Microchipping usewear analysis was brought to its modern refinement by a group at Harvard University under the direction of Ruth Tringham. In 1974, they published an article (Tringham et al. 1974) describing a large series of use experiments and the characteristics of flake scar form, orientation, and distribution that allowed different materials and use actions to be segregated. The so-called "low power" method, because it uses microscope magnification of up to about 40X, has had problems and is now generally conceded to yield data on relative hardness of worked material rather than on a specific material (e.g., "hard," rather than bone or antler). The main ongoing proponent of this technique is George Odell, a member of the original Harvard group.

Micropolish analysis, also called the "high power" method because it uses magnifications of 100–200X or even greater, was developed by Lawrence Keeley and was first published in 1976, (more completely in 1980). This technique uses polish texture, reflectivity, degree of hollow infilling (low point polish), distribution along the tool edge, and special features of polish to define worked materials. Use action is mainly inferred from striations. Keeley continues to be a major proponent of the technique, but Patricia Anderson-Gerfaud, Emily Moss, and especially Patrick Vaughan have refined and further developed the method. This method, too, has had its problems; not all micropolishes are as distinctive as was once thought (see Grace et al. 1985; Hurcombe 1988; Moss 1987; Newcomer et al. 1986, 1988).

Residue analysis developed from the success achieved in studying blood type and immunological systems in mummified tissue and bone in the late 1960s and early 1970s. This success, coupled with an increasing contact of physical anthropologists (and archaeologists) with forensic experts, was critical in allowing this approach to become successful. The relevance of the techniques of wildlife analysts, who had to identify poached remains, also soon became apparent. Initial work by Briuer in 1976 led to a number of other approaches in the late 1970s, but it was work by Thomas Loy (1983) that really appeared to overcome all barriers. Unfortunately, the particular technique Loy employed has now been shown to be very problematic, but studies more recently undertaken by Margaret Newman (e.g., Newman 1990) and others have been much more successful.

11.3 Results

11.3.1 Microchipping

The following observations on microchipping analysis are tendencies that give an indication of the trend of variables and uses they have been put to. They are based on various authors, but mainly Odell (1981), Vaughan (1981), and my own PhD (Kooyman 1985). There are many other variables involved and numerous exceptions to each tendency.

A first point to be made is that there must be a way in which to define which scars on an edge are usewear scars and which are not. In terms of overall size, Hayden's work (1979b:19) showed that even in chopping actions usewear flake scars rarely exceeded 7 mm in width. Anything larger than this size is probably from retouch rather than usewear. In my work, I found that in non-chopping/adzing tasks usewear scars barely exceeded 3 mm. Hence where one can be reasonably certain that no impact use is involved, anything wider than 3 mm can be viewed as intentional retouch. One problem in this regard, though, is that size is also influenced by lithic type. Lithic types that flake easily, such as obsidian and good quality cherts, also produce larger flakes with any particular applied force than do those that do not flake as readily, such as quartzite. My research used a readily flakeable material, porcellanite, and a less readily flakeable but still high quality quartzite (silcrete), and so probably did test at least the upper size limits of usewear microchipping.

The next problem that requires discussion is what has been termed "spontaneous retouch." When a flake is detached, the "percussor" also contacts the edge of the tool and frequently leaves small scars in the proximal area of the negative flake scar. The detached flake may also "twist" as it is detached and may damage the contact area. The flakes that result are very small, on the same scale as many usewear scars. They do not always occur, but when they do they are usually discontinuously distributed at the impact point and at the "corners" of the flake scar at the edge (see Fig. 85). If this type of pattern is seen, it can be disregarded in the usewear analysis. However, when an edge is used, it takes little time to disguise this non-usewear pattern. Such retouched edges are, in my opinion, impossible to analyze with microchipping analysis. If tools are extensively used so that they have dense scarring, probably these initial spontaneous retouch scars are removed by the subsequent use damage and hence these edges are probably analyzable.

Damage can be added to archaeological tools from non-use taphonomic factors, such as trampling, and movement in soil after burial (Flenniken and Haggarty 1979; Shea and Klenck 1993; Vaughan 1981:117–120). These effects frequently produce random damage which does not affect the overall pattern (i.e., it is "noise" that is lost in analysis), but patterned damage may also result and may be unwittingly interpreted, giving erroneous results. Furthermore, some use also produces almost random damage, such as use on soft materials or very limited use. Due to these types of minimal or random use damage, one cannot truly ignore "random" damage in an analysis. This situation obviously is problematic. "Bagwear," "sieve wear," and "excavation wear" (from trowels, shovels, picks) can occur during archaeological excavation. Handling, even just cleaning with a toothbrush, can cause non-use damage. Again, the damage patterns from these types of damage may or may not be random. Proper procedures and protocols can eliminate most archaeological confusion. Do not use pieces that have "hit" excavation equipment. Put all pieces in their own bags immediately so as to minimize items banging into each other. If necessary use an ultrasonic cleaner to remove sediment from tools without dragging sediment particles across the tool surface, as can easily happen with conventional cleaning procedures.

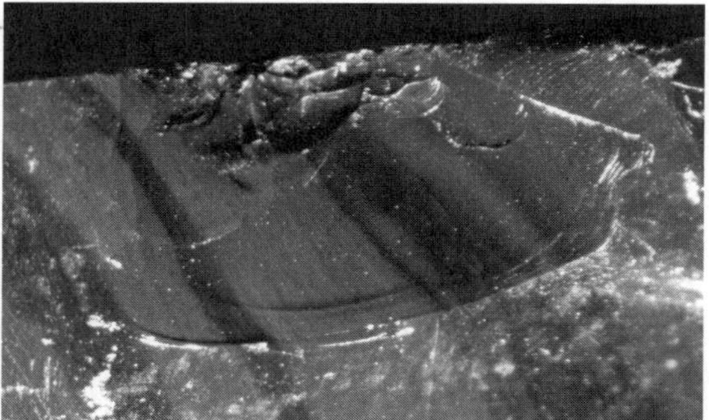

Figure 85: Spontaneous retouch

Various researchers have experimented with trampling damage, trampling being a process

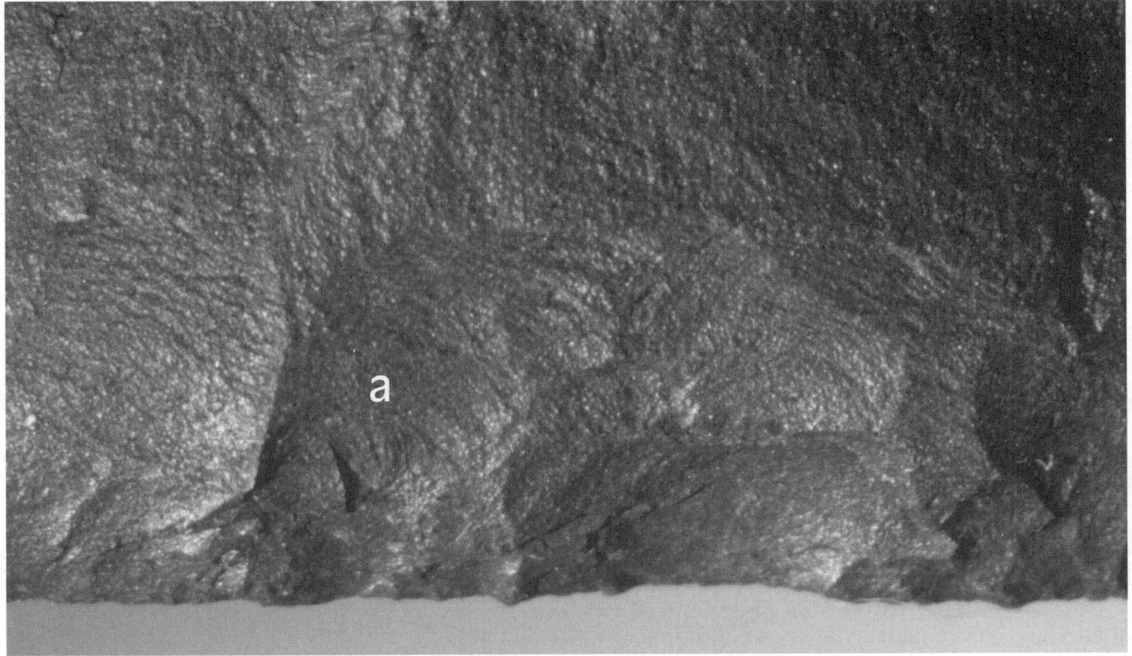

Figure 86: Porcellanite bone scraper showing transverse orientation of usewear scars (indicated by 'a') and edge row (approx. 32X)

that all archaeological tools probably experienced (Tringham et al. 1974; Gifford-Gonzales et al. 1985; Shea and Klenck 1993). The first point to make is that most tools are not effected by trampling chipping, with only about 5% so damaged (Gifford-Gonzales et al. 1985). Most of those that are damaged have only random, isolated damage: a few scars per edge and those not in any one location. About 5% of the *damaged* pieces (0.3% of original number) show patterned damage: denser scarring in only one edge area. Usually the trampling damage flake scars are as wide as, or are wider than, they are long (i.e., they are not invasive into the main body of the tool). Only 20–40% of the *damaged* pieces in the experiments by Gifford-Gonzales (Gifford-Gonzales et al. 1985) were dominated by scars that were longer than they were wide. Because trampled pieces have been stepped on from "above," most trampling damage flake scars are oriented perpendicular to the lithic piece edge (i.e., the dominant scar form for about 70% of the pieces trampled and damaged is scars oriented perpendicularly).

In terms of use action, transverse action, and especially high angle scraping rather than whittling or shaving, produces flake scars whose proximal/distal axis is at right angles to the used edge (Fig. 86). The use damage also tends to be strongly unifacial (flakes on trailing edge, initiated from leading edge). Longitudinal actions, such as cutting and sawing, tend to produce bifacial edge damage, with scars oriented somewhat diagonal to the edge (Fig. 87). Longitudinal actions tend to produce fewer scars than do transverse actions and the scarring can be clumped or discontinuous (compare Fig. 86 and Fig. 87). Transverse actions tend to produce

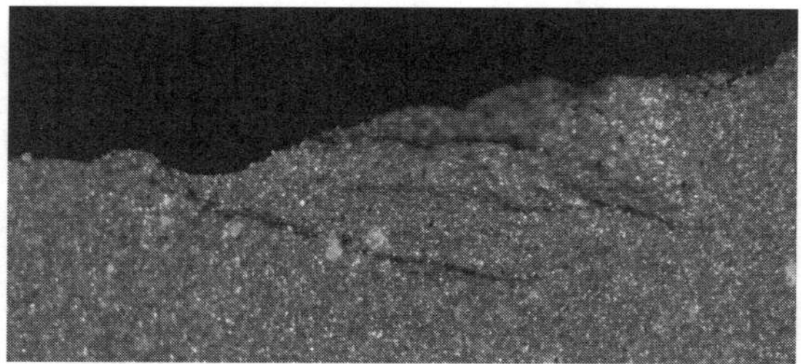

Figure 87: Porcellanite bone cutting tool showing diagonal orientation of usewear scars. Note that the usewear scars are less common than those in Fig. 86 and show a discontinuous distribution (ca. 40X)

continuous scarring. Transverse actions that also have a longitudinal component (e.g., "shaving") tend to a distribution that mixes the other two patterns. Only true scraping stands out as classic transverse action.

Worked material can be broadly split into a number of "hardness" categories for microchipping analysis:

a) *hard:* dry antler, bone, dried wood

b) *medium-hard:* fresh hardwood, fresh antler

c) *medium-soft:* soft woods, dry hides, reeds, grasses (i.e., fibrous plant material, or plants with silica)

d) *soft:* meat, fresh hides, green/soft/non-fibrous plant material

Soft and medium-soft materials tend to produce feather terminations when they are worked, whereas hard materials tend to result in step (and to some extent hinge) terminations (see Fig. 86 and Fig. 87 for hard material usewear scars). Hard materials tend to produce flake scars that have a shallow cross section to the proximal end of the scar, whereas the other materials tend to have deep proximal cross sections or a mix of deep and shallow. Tools used to work hard materials have predominantly large usewear scars, soft materials produce dominantly small scars. Edge rows (Fig. 86), where the used edge has some large usewear scars with many small step scars in their proximal end, are another useful variable. Only hard materials produce edge rows along a complete used portion, although only some 25% show this feature. Partial edge rows are confined to hard and medium-hard worked materials.

Meat and fresh hides are the only materials that can leave tool edges essentially unaltered even after extensive use. This is also the case with micropolish analysis.

Multiple uses of edges can greatly complicate interpretation. This is also a problem in polish analysis, but there are often particular features that can be used to identify particular worked materials in polish analysis so that multiple uses are more likely to be recognized with polish analysis. Otherwise, with both techniques, it is traces of the hardest worked material that are usually recognized (again, this comment is less true of polish analysis, particularly in regards to wood versus bone).

Certain lithic types are very resistant to microchipping. Quartzite is a good case of this and often quartzite cannot be so analyzed. Despite this problem, some success with quartzite can be attained with polish analysis.

11.3.2 Micropolish

These polishes are produced by a combination of abrasion (removal of material) and deposition of silica (taken into solution from the tool surface and any silica in the worked material) (see Anderson 1980, Fullagar 1991, and Unger-Hamilton 1984). Movement in soil can produce an all over, generic weak polish. High pH soils (alkaline) can damage or destroy polishes, sometimes very easily. The following polish descriptions are based on Keeley (1980), Vaughan (1981), and my PhD (Kooyman 1985). As with microchipping, this information alone is not a sufficient basis for analysis; experience obtained

Figure 88: Natural, unpolished porcellanite surface (approx. 320X) (Kooyman 1985)

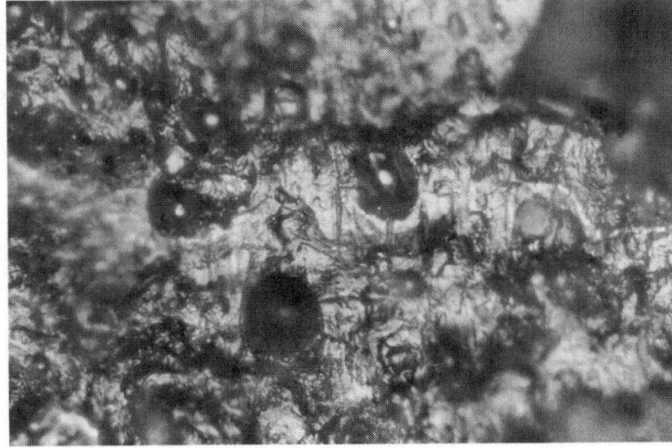

Figure 89: Bone polish on porcellanite showing striations and polish on central, left to right, ridge (approx. 320X) (Kooyman 1985)

with the lithic type being studied is essential, usually through an experimental program. Having said that, micropolish analysis is more able to define a specific worked material than is microchipping analysis (Odell 1994:72), although more so as a result of the specific frictional conditions or forces the worked material provides than as a result of the worked material *per se* (Kay 1996:333–337).

Traces of metal usually remain visible on tool edges damaged by excavation equipment. Minimal tool use produces a somewhat more advanced form of the "generic weak" soil movement polish described above. Use action assessment is primarily based on striation orientation, striations being oriented parallel to the action involved. Longitudinal actions produce striations parallel to the length of the tool edge. Transverse scraping actions produce striations perpendicular to the tool edge.

Bone working generally produces a bright polish (2–3X as reflective as natural surface), but that has a rough texture with pits or bumps (compare Fig. 88 and Fig. 89). Bone polish is located largely on high points of tool topography because the tool surface and edge do not penetrate far into bone. As a result, bone polish tends to be in isolated patches. Striations are common.

Hardwood and softwood basically produce the same polish, but softwood polishes develop more quickly due to the increased contact area between the tool and the more "pliable" softwood. Wood polish (Fig. 90) is very smooth compared to bone polish and similar to somewhat brighter in reflectivity. When well developed, wood polish is very extensive and highly linked rather than being in isolated patches as in bone polish. Wood polish infills hollows much more so than does bone polish; often develops domed, snowbank-like "mounds" of polish; has many striations; and when extreme, can become almost "glassy."

Fibrous and/or silica-rich plant polish (Fig. 91) becomes extremely smooth and glassy when it is well developed; it can appear "flowed". These plant polishes infill low areas extensively. They vary from very highly reflective to somewhat more like bone. Striations are common, but when the polish is well developed striations are absent, probably because they have been infilled. These polishes can have high, arched, and "superimposed" polish domes.

Soft plant polish is less reflective than the preceding polishes and usually is poorly linked. The natural relief or topography of the lithic

Figure 90: Wood polish on porcellanite, best developed in bright linear-domed areas to left of center of photograph (approx. 320X) (Kooyman 1985)

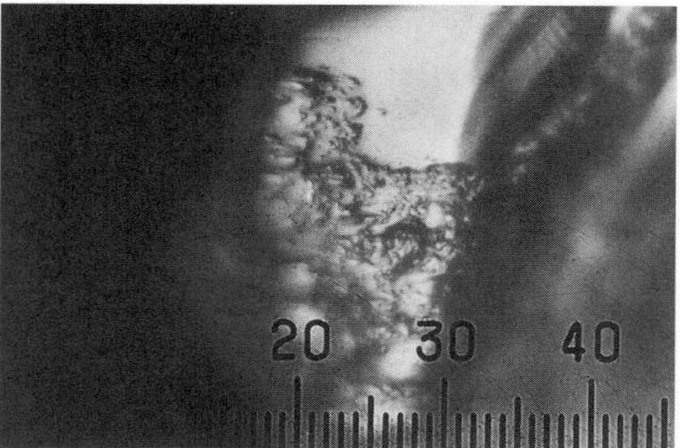

Figure 92: Extreme dry hide polish on quartzite (silcrete), especially well developed at center left of photograph (approx. 320X) (Kooyman 1985)

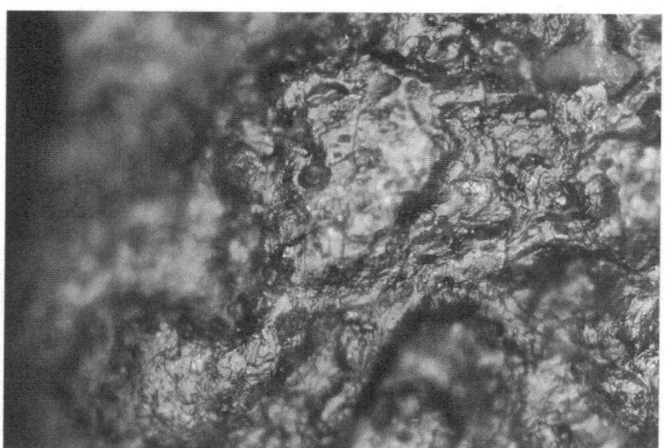

Figure 91: Fibrous vegetable polish on porcellanite, best developed by striation in center of photograph (approx. 320X) (Kooyman 1985)

material surface remains largely unaltered. The polish is smooth but has no rounded domes. Overall these soft plant polishes are quite "grainy" in appearance.

Dry hide polishes (Fig. 92), usually from scraping, have generally been found to be dull and pitted. My work produced polish that was bright and glassy, although with a somewhat "frosted" glassy look to it. Dry hide working produces many striations and extreme edge rounding.

Meat or fresh hide polish (Fig. 93) is dull, being little brighter than the natural surface of the lithic material. Striations are very rare and the topography experiences no rounding and only slight smoothing. The polish is well linked and extensive, much like a generic weak "soil" polish. After much use a tool may develop a bright thin band of polish at the immediate edge (butchering that includes bone contact can make meat polish difficult to interpret).

The most severe criticism of the reliability of micropolish analysis has come from Grace, Newcomer, and their colleagues (Grace et al. 1985; Newcomer et al. 1986; Rees et al. 1991). These researchers have employed computerized analysis of digitized photographic images of polish to suggest that it is not possible to distinguish between polishes derived from working different materials. Conversely, in a reply to this negative assessment, Kimball, Kimball, and Allen (1995) have employed digitized images captured directly by an Atomic Force Microscope (AFM) and have clearly demonstrated that polishes are distinctive, and *quantifiably* so (1995:26). The basic error in the experiments of Grace, New-

Figure 93: Meat polish on porcellanite; more reflective edge area at bottom (approx. 320X) (Kooyman 1985)

comer, and their colleagues is that they viewed polish simplistically as a uniform monolith (Kimball et al. 1995:7–8). Keeley (1980) and all subsequent micropolish analysts (e.g., Vaughan 1981) have clearly shown that worked materials are isolated by a combination of factors that include polish brightness, texture, contour, morphology, distribution, and features such as striations. The use of the Atomic Force Microscope has allowed Kimball and colleagues to produce textural analysis surface plots that allow them to assess the differences in polish in high and low areas of topography which is critical to success in differentiation of polishes (1995:26).

It is clear that Newcomer, Grace, and colleagues do not consider the use of features such as striations. Their approach analyzes complete images in a manner that includes portions of the image that are not part of the tool (Rees et al. 1991:635). The approach also averages peak and valley areas, polished and unpolished portions, and in no manner takes into consideration the distribution of polish in the image and relative to the tool edge (e.g., Newcomer et al. 1986: 208–209, where they illustrate the tool portions employed to produce specific plotted points on their scatter diagram). Reduction of distributional and textural complexity into a single averaged value for comparison does not adequately represent the original surface and almost guarantees each image is reduced to an indistinguishable sameness. Grace and Newcomer have initiated a new and exciting approach to the analysis of micropolishes, but the key is to characterize different portions of the image individually, or to produce a complex textural plot as have Kimbal and colleagues.

11.3.3 Striations

Striation presence and orientation have long been used as indicators of the direction of use of lithic tools, beginning with Semenov's research (1964). The most systematic study of striation morphology, and the causes of that morphology, is the research of Mansur-Franchomme (1983, 1986). Her research was done largely with European flint tools (1986:33). Based on her work (1986:93–102), the immediate cause of striation width is the size of the loose particles involved in the contact area between the tool and the worked material. These particles may come from the tool edge (broken fragments such as microchipping), from deliberately or unintentionally added abrasive material (such as dirt or sand), or from the worked material (such as silica phytoliths). Knutsson (1988:71) suggests that most of the particles are fragments detached from the tool edge). Similarly, the abundance of striations is basically a result of the abundance of these loose particles involved. The depth of striations is a result of the combination of the hardness of the tool lithic material and the amount of pressure exerted on the loose particles (due to use action and presumably the flexibility of the worked material). The morphological type of striation is dependent on the state of the surface of the lithic tool. Basically, this is the degree to which silica from the tool, the abrasive material, and the worked material goes into solution in the water in the contact area, forming a silica gel to varying degrees. The moisture in the worked material, the duration of tool use, and the mode of use are critical variables in this development.

Working harder material results in detachment of more microflakes, so more striations are produced in working material such as bone (when no abrasive material is deliberately added) (Mansur-Franchomme 1986:96). Greater pressure or a more acute working angle also results in detachment of more microflakes. Hide working results in detachment of very few flakes and hence hide working shows very few, or no, striations.

Mansur-Franchomme (1986:97–98) also defined four types of striations. The first were rough-bottomed striations, also characterized as being U-shaped (1986:97). With a regular light microscope, these striations look dark. Deep, narrow (< 2 nm) examples of these were very common on bone working tools. They were present but rare on skin, meat, and antler working tools. The meat and hide striations are short, rare, and difficult to see with the light microscope. Wide (> 2 nm) examples, whether deep or shallow, and shallow narrow striations of this type, were all associated with movement in sediments rather than usewear *per se*. Mansur-Franchomme has also called this general type of striation "rough-bottomed troughs" and has characterized the bottom as "granular" (1983:230).

The second type (1986:98), smooth-bottomed striations, look very bright under regular light microscopes (unless in an area of well developed polish). Their margins may be either regular or irregular. One form, with fern-like ridges in the bottom and irregular margins, is associated with woodworking and working dry hides with abrasives. A second, ribbon-like form with regular margins, is associated with working wood or dry bone if wide (> 2 nm) and deep, but only with dry hide working if narrow. Percussion blow striations (from quartzite and reindeer antler billets) are also ribbon-like, but are generally very long and composed a series of parallel striations. Again, elsewhere (1986:229) Mansur-Franchomme has referred to these striations as "smooth-bottomed troughs."

The third type, additive (1986:98), are very bright and have regular margins but appear to be a deposit on top of the tool edge, much as the micropolish itself (1984:100). Wide examples are associated with woodworking. Narrow ones are rare, but found on tools used to work wood or soaked antler. Long, discontinuous examples are due to percussion in tool manufacture.

The last type, in-filled (1983:229, 1986:98), result from a very liquid gel-like state of the silica solution. They are the result primarily of working plants such as grasses that have a high silica content (e.g., in harvesting grain). Situations with a high water content may produce them as well. The striations are basically filled with liquid silica gel and disappear, so few are visible.

The addition of abrasives such as sand results in many more, very long, striations (1983:227). Addition of water results in striations being more often more smooth-bottomed than in dry hide working, due to their formation in an area of the tool that sees much more silica gel formation due to the presence of water (1983:226). Normally striations resulting from working dry hides have rough bottoms, due to removal of aggregate particles and crystals, and are deep and narrow when viewed with the scanning electron microscope (1983:226).

Knutsson also included striations in his study of quartz (1988:9), finding them to be quite variable (1988:70). However, he did find that well-defined striations with straight sides and parallel sets of vertical cleavage planes were characteristic of working wood, raw hide, and vegetable-tanned hides. Deep, irregular striations composed of lenticular pits were found to be characteristic of working antler, bone, and shell. Poorly defined abrasion tracks were typical of hide working and meat cutting tools. Knutsson's research was undertaken with acetate replicas,

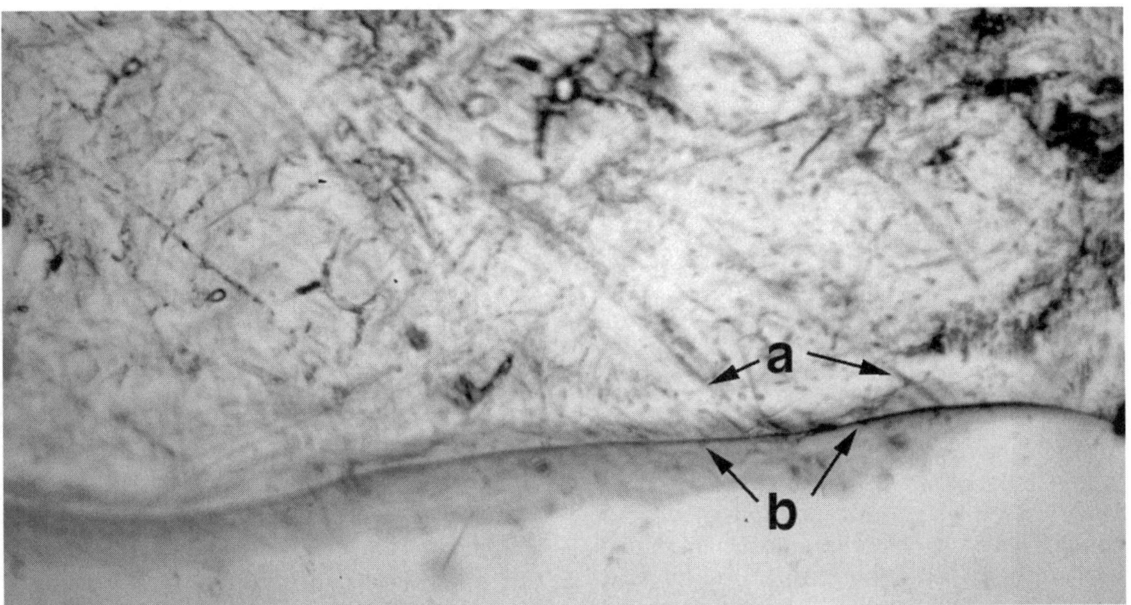

Figure 94: Acetate tape replica of porcellanite tool used to saw bone, showing striations ('a') and polish ('b') on used edge (bottom of photograph) (approx. 500X)

and both polish and striation analysis can be done using this technique (e.g., Fig. 94).

11.3.4 Residues

Residues are actual remains of worked material left on stone tools. In some cases these remains can still be identified by their biological structures as cells or other complex components, but more usually they are a chemical residue that retains some or all of the chemical reactivity of the original worked material. Important early developmental work on residue analysis was undertaken by Briuer (1976), Broderick (1979), and Shafer and Holloway (1979), but it was Loy's paper on blood residue identification by hemoglobin recrystallization (1983) that focused broader attention on the potential of residue analysis. Although the reliability of hemoglobin recrystallization has since been questioned (Hyland et al. 1990; Smith and Wilson 1992), its use has stimulated the development of many more analytical approaches.

The main microscopically identifiable animal remains claimed to have been recovered from tool edges have been animal hairs (e.g., Shafer and Holloway 1979; Loy and Hardy 1992), blood cells, and collagen fibers (e.g., Fullagar et al. 1996; Loy and Hardy 1992). Even at low levels of magnification it has been shown that blood residue deposits have a characteristic form that distinguishes them from other deposits on tool edges (Fullagar et al. 1996). At the same time, not all researchers are convinced that actual red blood cells are likely to be preserved on stone tools (Newman et al. 1997:1025), although in other circumstances, such as mummified tissue, this is possible (Newman et al. 1996).

Some researchers have found plant fibers, cells, starch grains, and other remains such as phytoliths trapped on stone tools (e.g., Shafer and Holloway 1979; Loy et al. 1992). These residues can be identified botanically by examination directly with a microscope. Some researchers have observed plant and animal residue embedded in use polishes (Anderson 1980; Mansur-Franchomme 1983), but others researchers (Unger-Hamilton 1984) have claimed these are actually small fragments of the lithic tool, shatter, and flakes.

Most research on residues has employed chemical or immunochemical characterization of remains that no longer retain visible biologically identifiable structure. Although some analysis of stone tool residues has employed conventional chemical characterization of residues through techniques such as chromatography (e.g., Broderick 1979; Jahren et al. 1997; Loy and Hardy 1992), these methods have more usually been employed in analysis of residues in sediments and ceramic remains (e.g., Evershed and Tuross 1996). Most lithic tool residue analysis has utilized immunological testing using some variation of the antigen-antibody reaction (e.g., Cattaneo et al. 1993; Downs and Lowenstein 1995; Tuross et al. 1996). In these tests, the unknown residue extracted from a tool is allowed to mix individually with a number of antibodies raised to different animal or plant species. If the residue contains antigen from one of these species, the antibody and antigen bind to each other. This compound is then made visible in one of a number of different manners. The "recognition" of an antigen by an antibody may be possible at several "sites" (epitopes) (Newman et al. 1996:678) and these epitopes are sometimes shared by animal species, resulting in "cross reactions" between species. These cross reactions can often be eliminated for a particular antiserum by blocking the shared epitopes or by diluting the antiserum to the point where those relatively uncommon shared epitope reactions are so few as to be essentially undetectable. The configuration stability of these epitopes explains why some will survive in a detectable form for thousands of years.

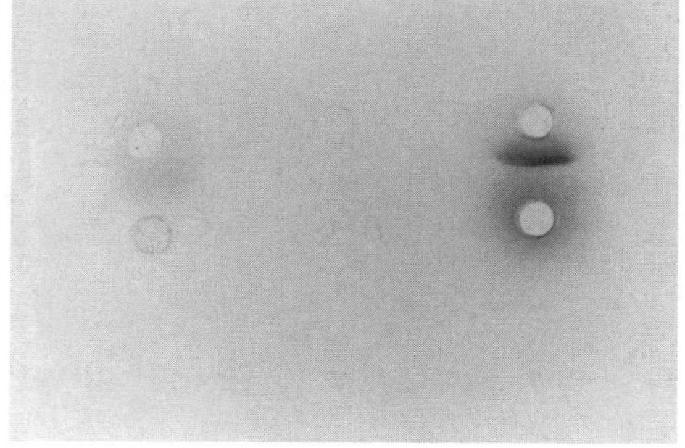

Figure 95: Cross-over immunoelectrophoresis (CIEP) gel stained showing precipitate (courtesy of Margaret Newman)

The three most used immunochemical methods in residue analysis are cross-over immunoelectrophoresis (CIEP), enzyme-linked immunosorbant assay (ELISA), and radioimmune assay (RIA). The most simple of these three techniques is CIEP. In the variation used by Newman (Newman 1990; Kooyman et al. 1992) paired wells are cut into an agar gel and samples of residue extract (containing "antigens") are placed in the wells along one side (Fig. 95). Into the wells opposite this first set are placed individual antisera (antibodies) raised to different plant or (usually) animal species. The antibodies and antigens are electrically charged molecules, and when an electric current is run through the gel, the antigen and antibody molecules migrate with the current toward each other through the gel. Where the antigens and antibodies meet, if the antibody in the antiserum is one raised to an antigen present in the residue, the molecules bind to each other and form a solid precipitate. The precipitate may be visible directly, but is more usually made more readily visible by applying a stain that marks it (e.g., Coomassie Blue). If the antibody is not one raised to an antigen in the residue, the molecules do not combine and no precipitate is formed. Newman removes the residue from the lithic tool by placing 5% ammonia on the tool and agitating the tool in an ultrasonic cleaner.

At Head-Smashed-In Buffalo Jump this technique was used on stone tools dating back as much as over 5,000 years (Kooyman et al. 1992). The goal in this analysis was to "test" the technique in a known case (buffalo blood) that had been subjected to real archaeological conditions for various times up to 5,000 years. The results were positive for buffalo—and only buffalo (except for positive reactions to elk and buffalo antiserum on three tools, but the elk antiserum used was known to cross react with buffalo and so these are almost certainly spurious results), on tools over 5,000 years old. Buffalo residue was also detected in the soil samples that were about 1,000 years old.

The ELISA technique is also based on the antigen-antibody reaction. Cattaneo and colleagues (Cattaneo et al. 1993, 1994) use an inhibition ELISA technique wherein antibodies of the species being tested for are bound to a plate. The residue is mixed with a monoclonal antibody (species specific antibody) and then some of this is placed on the plate. If the monoclonal antibody reacts with an antigen in the residue, there is none of the antibody left to react with the antigen on the plate and so there is no reaction (precipitate); no reaction means the antigen tested for was present in the residue extract. This technique is much more sensitive than CIEP. The most sensitive of these techniques is RIA (Downs and Lowenstein 1995:14), with the particular variation used by Lowenstein being a solid-phase double-antibody method. The residue extract is placed in a plastic well where some of it binds and remains ("solid-state"). Species specific antiserum (antibody) raised in rabbits is then added and some binds to the residue antigens if they are of that species. Then radioactively labeled anti-rabbit antiserum is added (double-antibody); it will react with the first antibody, raised in rabbit, if any of the first antibody reacted with the residue extract. The remnant radioactivity of the bound second antibody is then assessed by computerized counting. This technique is extremely sensitive.

There are also other techniques that can be used to test for residues. Most recently these new approaches have included very promising results employing polymerase chain reaction (PCR) to amplify DNA fragments left on stone tools (Hardy et al. 1997). Only minute amounts of small fragments of DNA are left on tools, but by using PCR to make large numbers of copies of specific portions of these segments there is enough material to subject to analysis to determine the sequence of the base pairs. The portion amplified is chosen to be diagnostic of or within a particular species or other taxonomic group (genus, family, etc.), although such a specific segment may not be found in the particular residue sample. It is quite likely that in the future DNA analysis will become the best and most used technique (Fullagar et al. 1996:743) due to the very specific identifications it permits and the potential for other research (such as evolutionary studies) that it presents.

All residue studies have been criticized because of issues of ancient and modern contamination, false positive identifications due to other materials, and the nature of the preservation process as opposed to natural breakdown and decay; in turn, even many of the critiques have raised the positive evidence for the veracity of the results obtained, at least in some studies (e.g., Cattaneo et al. 1993:41; Downs and Lowenstein 1995:14; Eisele et al. 1995; Fiedel 1996; Fullagar et al. 1996:744; Newman et al. 1996, 1997; Tuross et al. 1996). Almost all authors agree that there is some type of residue preserved on some stone tools and that their study is valuable (e.g., Cattaneo et al. 1993:41; Fullagar et al. 1996:744; Newman et al. 1997), although there are exceptions to this opinion

(Eisele et al. 1995; Fiedel 1996). Contamination can be controlled by careful handling of specimens and can be tested for by parallel testing of soil samples from the immediate context in which each artifact is found (Fullagar et al. 1996:744; Hardy et al. 1997; Newman et al. 1996, 1997). DNA analysis is particularly subject to problems from modern contamination, although careful laboratory procedures and elimination of all larger DNA fragments (likely modern due to their completeness) from extracts probably combine to circumvent concerns on this issue (Hardy et al. 1997:604–605, 609).

Many of the modern experiments that have claimed to show that residues do not preserve (e.g., Cattaneo et al. 1993; Eisele et al. 1995; Tuross et al. 1996) probably do not duplicate the processes that occur in archaeological sites. Given that we do not yet fully understand the mechanisms of the residue preservation process, it is probably best to test techniques with known archaeological samples such as the study of buffalo residues at Head-Smashed-In Buffalo Jump (Fiedel 1996:145–146; Kooyman et al. 1992). Although the various methods employed to date vary in their reliability and sensitivity, within the next few years it seems very probable that the various issues will be resolved and residue analysis will begin to contribute significantly to our understanding of past lithic tool use.

11.4 Analysis Implementation

Obviously residue analysis is basically a technique that cannot be undertaken except in a well equipped research lab. Similarly, conventional micropolish analysis requires a metallurgical microscope and even most "student" metallurgical microscopes used in engineering departments at universities are not adequate for the task. Working with the acetate peel technique does allow both micropolish and striation analysis to be done with a normal transmitted light microscope of the type used commonly for examining material mounted on glass slides in universities, colleges, and high schools. Microchipping analysis requires only a low power (about 40X) binocular "dissecting" microscope, again commonly available even in high schools, and it can be done to a limited extent with a good magnifying glass (10X). This is the only aspect of usewear that can actually be examined in the field.

Using a magnifying glass in the field can allow one to determine if flake scars along a tool edge are from retouch (greater than 3 mm in width) or due to use (less than or equal or 3 mm in width). The distribution of scars along the used edge, their spacing, and their relative frequency on the two faces of the edge can be easily defined. It is usually relatively easy to see the orientation of the scars to the edge long axis so that use action (scraping, cutting/sawing) can be defined. Edge rows and scar termination can also be seen quite easily. Other useful aspects of scar type can be difficult to define without a microscope. The form of the tool, in particular the acuteness of the edge angle, in combination with an assessment of the bifacial distribution of scars and the angle of the scars, can give a good determination of the use action of a tool: acute edged tools with bifacial scars tending to a diagonal angle to the length of the edge are from cutting tasks; steep angled tools showing unifacial scarring oriented transverse to the edge length are scraping tools. Tools used on hard materials are likely to show edge rows, step terminations, and large scars; tools used on soft material are likely to have feather terminations, small scars, and no edge rows.

In any usewear analysis a critical consideration is that it is often impossible to examine all pieces in a collection if the collection is large because of the time required to complete the analysis. It is often necessary to examine only a sample of the total collection. It is important to be sure that the sample chosen adequately represents the collection, specifically as it is important to the questions one asks of the material. It is often useful to examine a very small sample initially to determine the quality and quantity of information one will be able to obtain and then to choose the full sample based on that initial assessment.

CHAPTER 12

Approaches to Analysis and Concluding Remarks

The methods outlined in the preceding eleven chapters have provided the background to interpret lithic remains from archaeological sites, whether an entire collection or only a few scattered lithic fragments on the ground surface. In approaching analysis of a large collection, it is common to initially segregate material into tools, versus debitage, since each must be analyzed differently. In the final interpretation it is important to integrate these data sets again since each will inform and augment the other.

The tools present, and their presumed function, will give a good indication of the activities that occurred at the site. It is important to remember that tools may have had functions we do not recognize from form alone, or that they may have had more than one function, and that often the only manner in which this can be truly assessed is through usewear or residue analysis. Although residue analysis is not normally feasible except in the case of professional excavations, certainly some types of usewear analysis, such as the microchipping and acetate peel techniques, can be undertaken with quite basic equipment. Interpretations about site function are much enhanced by debitage analysis since the lithic reduction stages that occur at various types of sites are often quite restricted. Here the inferences from flake types, even from a very small surface scatter, can be very informative. Together these two lines of evidence provide a very complete picture of site activities. Spatial localization of remains within a site can give an indication of how tasks were accomplished and also cultural perspectives on how activities should be segregated and combined. A determination of the lithic material types in the collection can provide insight into what material types were used for different tool types and functions. Based on what flake types are made of different material types, one can also gain insight into which materials may have been acquired locally and which may have been acquired from some distance and so lack early reduction stages. Obviously this information, coupled with size of lithic pieces at various stages in the reduction and use process of tools, can allow one to speculate about wider contact and trade. Here the models of exchange discussed in Chapter 10 can be implemented and used to test the remains. Trade and exchange are best understood if one can recognize exotic lithic materials, and in most regions there will be some exotic material types that will be recognizable even in hand specimen. Once again, in many cases some more detailed chemical characterization will be necessary to fully understand the role of imported lithic materials in the lithic tool manufacturing at a site and in a region at the particular time involved. This in turn may be the basis from which cultural contact and perhaps conflict can be inferred.

Once these inferences have been made for the site under study, one can begin to put that site into its larger cultural context. What is or is not indicated at the site one studies has implications for what other types of sites must also be present in the region. For example, the absence of early stage reduction suggests that quarry sites must be present. A restricted range of lithic tools, such as only chopping and cutting tools, suggest that the site has a specialized function, such as butchering of game, and that there must be other sites such as habitation sites, located elsewhere. The density and quantity of remains can also contribute to these interpretations.

A final comment is needed on this book and the study of lithic tools. If one glances back over the topics of the chapters and what is presented in them, it becomes very clear that the emphasis has been on the cultural information that can be obtained from individual items. Even in this regard, however, the approaches discussed in debitage and reduction stage analysis clearly cannot be successful without the associated complex of debitage and tools being analyzed as a whole. It is only in such a contextual study that the relative importance of each flake can be assessed. This aspect of archaeological study is also clear from Chapter 10, where inferences from lithic material are applied to larger questions in archaeology, such as past patterns of contact and trade though lithic sourcing studies. Without the provenience data for pieces, the real significance of trade cannot be assessed. It is, in a sense, the responsibility of all of us who want to understand past lifeways to ensure as much as possible that the archaeological record is not lost through development or indiscriminate collecting of archaeological remains. The few professional archaeologists present in any province or state cannot possibly be aware of all the threats to all the sites in their area. It is only through the eyes of interested and knowledgeable non-professionals that the archaeological record can be effectively protected. I hope that this book has given the reader an understanding of, and appreciation for, what is present in the lithic remains in archaeological sites. I hope this knowledge gives enjoyment and also the ability to help protect our heritage for future generations.

Glossary

Acheulean: a period of the Lower Paleolithic from about 1.4 million years ago to about 100,000 years ago, characterized by the use of handaxes and cleavers; in Europe, the term is also sometimes used to refer specifically to later handaxe industries

adze: an axe-like heavy shaving tool (usually for woodworking) with an asymmetric working edge (bit) hafted for use so that the long axis of the working edge is at right angles to the working direction; the more gradually sloped surface of the asymmetric working edge is the one that comes in contact with the worked material and this more gradual slope better allows the working edge to enter the worked material at a more acute angle and so to slice off a thin sliver of material

antibody: a protein produced by animal immune systems in response to, and to defend against, foreign proteins or organisms in the animal's body

antigen: a foreign protein or organism in an animal's body that causes the animal's immune system to protect the animal by producing antibodies to it

anvil: stone used to support a piece of lithic material during working of that piece; the anvil generally actively works in the fracturing process by minimizing loss of the impact force (see also bipolar percussion)

archaeology: the study of the human past through the material remains left behind by past human behavior

arris: the ridge formed on the dorsal surface of lithic material due to the intersection of two or more flake scars, or sometimes the intersection between a flake scar(s) and the original dorsal cortex; often specifically used to designate the one or two main ridges that go from the proximal to the distal end of a flake or blade approximately along the flake/blade midline

assertive style: attributes of form produced by the artisan to specifically convey a message about personal identity; a subdivision of iconic style (see also emblemic style and isochrestic style)

atlatl: a throwing board for dart weapons

atomic absorption spectroscopy: the testing of vaporized samples to determine which light wavelengths they absorb, the ones absorbed being characteristic of the element(s) in the sample

axe: a heavy chopping implement with a symmetric working edge (bit) that is hafted in a handle so that the long axis of the working edge is parallel to the working direction (see also adze); used primarily to chop through large wooden objects, such as trees

backing: removal of flakes and/or grinding of an edge of a tool; generally done so that the tool can be held in the hand without cutting the user, or to aid in hafting

basalt: a dark, fine grained igneous rock, the color of which is due to ferromagnesian minerals; commonly used for both flaked and ground stone tools

bending initiation: the type of flake initiation that arises when there is a significant bending component in the force acting on the objective piece edge and so the fracture begins at a (relatively) great distance from the impact area; the resulting flake has a lip

biface: a lithic tool manufactured by flaking on both major surfaces (see also uniface)

bifacial reduction: the manufacture of a lithic tool by flaking on both major surfaces of the piece or on both surfaces of an edge or edges

bifacial reduction flake: a thin, elongate flake removed in later thinning and reduction of a lithic piece to produce a bifacial tool; characterized by complex scarring on the striking platform (typically three or more flake scars) and dorsal surface and a lip just distal to the striking platform

billet: elongate, rod- or club-like hammer (usually made of antler, bone, or wood)

bipolar percussion: percussion working of lithic material wherein the worked piece is rested on an anvil stone so that the force of the striking blow is reflected back into the worked piece by the anvil; the result is a flake(s) and remaining core that show impact damage at both the proximal and distal ends and often a sheared ventral (flake) or dorsal (core) surface

blade: a flake that is at least twice as long as it is wide with a length greater than 5 cm; it is often also specifically defined as having relatively parallel lateral edges and being produced from a specialized core; it is generally quite thin compared to its overall size

bladelet: a blade less than 5 cm long (also called a microblade)

blank: a useable but unmodified piece of lithic raw material, or a similarly unmodified flake or piece of shatter

block-on-block: the fracturing of lithic material by throwing the piece against an anvil

bulb of percussion: the cone-shaped bulge on the ventral surface of a flake just distal to the striking platform, resulting from Hertzian fracture

burin: a fine chisel tool similar to a graver, but specifically produced by a flake detachment at right angles to the piece's long axis and then a second detachment (burin spall) at an angle to that first detachment to produce a fine, sharp chisel implement

celt: any adze or axe type of implement

chaîne opératoire: idea that in manufacturing there are a series of defined stages and specific goals for each of those stages

chalcedony: as chert, but with a radiating, fibrous texture or structure

chert: any sedimentary mineral composed of microcrystalline (microscopic crystals) quartz (se also flint, chalcedony)

chisel: a narrow adze

chopper: a heavy, relatively thick edged, minimally worked tool presumed to have been used in various heavy chopping and cutting tasks; sometimes a distinction is made between a unifacial tool (a chopper), and a bifacial tool (a chopping tool)

conchoidal ripples: concentric rings (positive relief) radiating out from the striking platform impact point on the ventral surface of a detached flake; comparable features are also produced on the newly created dorsal surface scar on the lithic piece from which the flake is detached, these being the negative impressions of the ripple marks; also called compression rings, compression waves, or ribs

core: any piece of lithic material from which another piece of lithic material has been detached for the purpose of use as a tool or to manufacture into a tool

core tool: a lithic tool made on a large piece of lithic material rather than on a flake

cortex: the naturally altered or weathered (mechanically or chemically) outer surface of lithic material; may be more narrowly used to designate an altered outer surface that forms at the time of the formation of the lithic material (see also patina)

craft specialization: the production of particular material undertaken by individuals who dedicate their work to only, or largely, that task while others supply them with a form of payment

craze: to produce surface fracturing as a result of expansion and contraction caused by heating and cooling

cross-over immunoelectrophoresis (CIEP): a technique for testing residues on lithic tools in which a current is put through an agar gel and an antigen (residue extract from a lithic tool) and an antibody (antiserum) are made to migrate toward each other and where they move past each other, if the antibody in the antiserum is the one for the antigen in the residue extract, the antibody reacts with the residue and forms a precipitate (compound that comes out of solution), which shows that the specific antigen is present in the extract; related techniques are enzyme-linked immunosorbant assay (ELISA) and radioimmune assay (RIA)

curation: maintaining a tool in working condition through resharpening dull tools and reworking broken or damaged tools; although a somewhat misused term, also used in the sense that "curated" tools are those designed to be maintainable over an extended period of use and, often, to be transported from site to site during the course of that uselife

cutting tool: a tool with an acute working edge designed to cut some material (see also knife)

debitage: the discarded garbage or debris resulting from the manufacture of lithic tools

decortication: removal of the outer altered surface (cortex) from a piece of lithic material

decortication flake: a flake whose dorsal surface has some of the altered outer surface (cortex) from the piece of lithic material it was detached from; called a primary decortication flake if the entire dorsal surface is cortex, a secondary decortication flake if only part of the dorsal surface is cortex

denticulate: a sinuous edged or toothed tool presumed to be used in a sawing motion

differential thermal analysis: the heating of lithic material under controlled conditions which results in the take-up or release of heat in a manner characteristic of the minerals present, particularly clay minerals

distal end: the end of the flake where it terminates, where the flake finally detaches from the core or tool; the end opposite the proximal end and the striking platform

DNA: deoxyribonucleic acid, the molecule that contains the coded genes of organisms

dorsal surface: the surface on a piece of lithic material that is created by the removal of other pieces of lithic material (usually flakes) from that surface; characterized by negative flake scars and commonly a ridge (arris) or ridges where flake scars intersect (see also ventral surface)

drill: a perforating tool used in a rotary motion, generally rotated at a high speed, to create a hole in the worked material

edge angle: the angle formed by the two faces or surfaces of the edge of a tool; generally acute for cutting tools and near 90° for scraping tools

edge modified flake: a tool produced from a flake by retouch or modification confined to an immediate edge area(s) rather than being produced by flaking well into the body of the tool

edged blank: a term used by Whittaker (1994) for the first step in making a preform from a blank, wherein a series of flakes confined to the immediate edge of the worked piece are removed (see also preform, blank, and shaping)

electron microscope: a microscope that uses a beam of electrons instead of a beam of light, the advantage being that the de Broglie wavelength of electrons is much less than that of conventional light and so an electron microscope can resolve or differentiate features at a much finer level (magnification of upwards of a million times)

emblemic style: consciously produced features to indicate ethnic or cultural identity; a subdivision of iconic style (see also assertive style and isochrestic style)

emic: style, form, or classification as perceived of and/or defined by an individual(s) of the culture using the artifact; may also be called folk taxonomy (see also etic)

end scraper: a scraper with the working edge on the proximal or distal end of the flake it was produced on, or sometimes just that the working edge is on a short edge of the lithic piece (see also scraper and side scraper)

epitope: a location on a protein where another protein can attach, as for example where an antibody attaches to an antigen

eolith: lithic fragment that has been altered or broken by natural environmental or geological forces such that in some manner it resembles humanly altered lithic material

eraillure: a small flake sometimes detached from the surface of the bulb of percussion; the resulting flake scar is called an eraillure scar or bulbar scar

etic: form, style, or classification as defined by a researcher outside the cultural group being studied (i.e., usually as defined by the archaeological analyst) (see also emic)

expedient: the suggestion that in some cases a tool is manufactured for immediate use only, to be discarded after that specific task is done, and hence that only the minimal amount of modification is done to it to make it adequate for that task; also sometimes termed opportunistic

exterior platform angle: the angle formed by the striking platform and the dorsal surface of the lithic piece (core, tool) being worked or the flake produced in working

fabric: the orientation of particles in a material (e.g., elongate grains in a rock)

fabricator: any object used to work or modify lithic material

fall-off curve: a graph of the decline in frequency of lithic material from a quarry as distance from that quarry increases; the graphs can be of actual changes in frequency or they can be models of how it is assumed the frequency should change under particular circumstances

feather termination: a form of the distal end of a flake where the end gradually thins to a very sharp edge

finishing: a late stage in manufacturing a lithic tool wherein the final regular shape is given to the edge of the tool (see also shaping and thinning)

finishing flake: a small, short flake produced in finishing the shape of a tool edge; characteristically shows complex scarring on the striking platform (typically three or more flake scars) and dorsal surface and, on bifacial tools, commonly has a lip distal to the striking platform

fissures: fine lines or crevices on the fracture surface of lithic material that result from the fracture process; they radiate out from the striking platform impact point and are called bulbar fissures when present on the bulb of percussion and lateral fissures or hackles when they are present on the lateral edges of a flake or flake scar

flake: a piece of lithic material usually intentionally detached from another piece of lithic material (such as a core, a tool, etc.), with a series of features showing that it has a definable original outer surface and a newly created inner surface, as well as a place where the detaching blow was struck (e.g., bulb of percussion, ripple marks, striking platform, arris) (see also shatter)

flaker: a tool used to remove a flake from a piece of lithic material, the term usually being used to describe the tool used in pressure flaking

flint: a dark-colored, nodular form of chert

flintknapper: a person who manufactures lithic tools

flute: a flake removed longitudinally from the base of a projectile point that creates a channel, or flute, along the midline of the point

Folsom: a cultural time period in North America dating to about 10,900–10,200 B.P., characterized by fluted points

gouge: an adze with a U-shaped bit

graver: a fine incising tool with a thick working point that can withstand considerable pressure without collapsing (see also burin)

Griffith Crack Theory: a theory that proposes that when brittle materials (including most lithic materials used in making stone tools) fail or fracture under a load, that fracture normally occurs at an existing flaw or weakness in the material: named for a British scientist, Alan Griffith, who studied material failure in the 1920s (Cotterell and Kamminga 1990:135)

grinding: using abrasive material, such as sand, to remove small amounts of material from a lithic piece to shape it into a tool; also called abrading and the resultant tool is usually called a ground stone tool (see also polishing)

gun flint: flaked squared pieces of flint used in early muskets to give the spark that ignited the gunpowder to shoot the musket ball from the gun

habitation site: a location where people lived, as opposed to where they did specialized activities, such as killing game or quarrying lithic material; a camp or base camp

hammerstone: a stone tool used to detach flakes in working a lithic piece, sometimes indirectly through use of a punch; characteristically has battering and crushing at one or more points on the tool where it has impacted the objective piece or punch (sometimes more loosely used to indicate any percussor, whether of stone or other material, used to strike objective pieces or punches)

handaxe: a lithic tool that is flaked on both main surfaces or faces to produce a biface; it is often a pear-shaped, pointed tool, and it characterizes particularly the Lower Paleolithic and to some extent the Middle Paleolithic of the Old World

hard hammer percussion: detaching flakes from a lithic piece by use of a hard hammer, such as stone; also called direct hard hammer percussion because the hammerstone directly contacts the worked piece (see also soft hammer percussion and indirect percussion)

heat treatment: heating lithic material to make it flake or work in a better or more predictable manner

Hertzian fracture: fracture or breakage in brittle lithic material characterized in part by the fracture front progressing through the lithic material and being deflected around an area of compressive stress just below (distal to) the striking platform, resulting in a bulb or percussion; named for Heinrich Hertz, a German physicist who studies fracture formation in the late 1800s (Cotterell and Kamminga 1990:140)

hinge termination: a form of the distal end of a flake where the fracture "rolls" out to the dorsal surface, producing a rounded or curved distal end

iconic style: attributes of style or form that are chosen and produced by the artisan to convey a specific message, such as ethnic identity (see also assertive style, emblemic style, and isochrestic style)

igneous: rocks formed from molten material (lava)

indentor: the tool that puts pressure on a material to cause it to fail or fracture; blunt indentors (the normal type of indentor in human manufacturing of stone tools) have a circular contact area, sharp indentors have a point contact area

indirect percussion: removal of flakes from a lithic piece by resting a tool, such as a punch, on the piece and striking that punch with the hammer, transferring the force of the detaching blow to the worked piece through that punch (see also hard hammer and soft hammer percussion)

isochrestic style: attributes of style or form that are functionally equivalent but indicative of only certain individuals or cultures because they are only present on the tools of those individuals or cultures, unconsciously chosen from among a suite of possible alternatives, or at least have been chosen without the intention and/or recognition that they are somehow indicative of social group membership

knife: an acute edged cutting implement; often used specifically to refer to a well-worked thin biface with acute edges (see also cutting tool)

Levallois: a technique for manufacturing flake tools particularly characteristic of the Middle Paleolithic (although arising in the Lower Paleolithic) of Europe; characterized by careful preparation of a core such that the flake detached has a predetermined size and shape appropriate for the tool task intended without any, or much, further retouch; the typical domed cores are often called tortoise cores because the flake scars resemble reptile scales

lip: a feature of flakes initiated by a bending initiation wherein there is a discernible "hook" or lip just distal to the striking platform

lithic: having to do with stone

lithomechanics: the physics of how lithic materials fracture

mass analysis: a lithic reduction stage analysis technique that uses weight and count values of lithic fragments of different sizes, as determined by passing debitage through screens of different defined sizes, and cortex cover

maul: a hafted hammer, generally having a hafting mechanism, such as a groove, for the handle

mental template: the idea that an artisan had in mind about what the item being produced would look like

metamorphic: rocks altered by temperature, pressure, or chemical environment from preexisting igneous, sedimentary, or metamorphic rocks

microblade: a small blade, generally less than 5 cm long; also called a bladelet

microchipping: damage or usewear on a tool, the very small flakes removed from a tool edge as a result of use

microdebitage: any lithic debitage less than 1 mm in size

microlith: small geometric lithic pieces usually formed from blade fragments and used as edge pieces in composite tools, a series being mounted in a line to produce the tool working edge

micropolish: damage or usewear on a tool, the (usually) microscopic polishing and smoothing of a tool edge as a result of use; part of the polishing process may be due to removal of material and smoothing of the tool edge, other aspects of the process may involve addition of silica material to the edge

mineral: a naturally occurring inorganic compound with a characteristic internal structure determined by a regular arrangement of the atoms and ions within it, with a chemical composition and physical properties that are either fixed or that vary within a definite range

objective piece: the piece of lithic material being worked with other implements, such as hammerstone; it may be a piece of raw material, a core, a preform, etc.

obsidian: glassy igneous rock of the same chemical composition as granite and rhyolite; most commonly black and used extensively for flaked stone tools

outrepassé: a form of the distal end of a flake where the fracture removes the end or edge of the lithic piece being worked and so this end or edge becomes the termination of the flake; the resultant termination is generally "hooked" and has a portion of both surfaces of the worked piece edge

Paleolithic: the "Old Stone Age," characterized by almost exclusive use of flaked stone tools; the period of time from the first production of stone tools by humans, some two million years ago, through to the end of the last glaciation about 10,000 years ago: divided into Lower Paleolithic (from first tools to about 80,000 years ago), Middle Paleolithic (characterized by use of flake tools primarily), and Upper Paleolithic (beginning about 35,000 years ago and characterized by use of blade tools)

patina: altered outer surface of lithic material that results from chemical or mechanical weathering; also called a weathering rind (see also cortex)

pecking: battering a lithic piece with another stone to pulverize and remove small particles of material to shape that piece into a tool

percussion: flaking a piece of lithic material by directly striking it (dynamic loading) with a hammer of some sort

perforator: a sharp pointed implement used to make holes in worked material

pièces esquillées: thin pieces of lithic material used as a wedge by hammering the piece into the material being worked (e.g., wood or bone); characterized by battering on both the hammered end and the end that entered the worked material

platform remnant bearing flake: a flake that retains the striking platform on its proximal end (i.e., the proximal end has not been lost due to collapse of the platform)

platform thickness: on a flake striking platform, the measurement from the dorsal surface to the ventral surface

polarized light: a beam of light restricted to vibration in only one direction

polishing: using a very fine grained abrasive material to remove minute irregularities on a tool surface to give it a very smooth finish (see also grinding and micropolish)

polymerase chain reaction (PCR): an analysis technique that makes (replicates) many copies of a particular piece of DNA (a segment or gene) present in a residue extract, making enough copies so that it can be chemically analyzed and the specific DNA sequence can be determined; this sequence is unique for particular species or other groupings (e.g., genus, family) of organisms; the technique uses proteins that recognize the ends of this gene or DNA sequence, and protein raw material and RNA, to allow this replication to occur

preform: a blank that has been modified to some extent toward a finished tool, often to the stage where the type of tool is apparent, but that has not yet been completed (see also edged blank)

pressure flaking: removing flakes from a lithic piece by placing a flaking tool on the lithic piece and building up pressure on the tool to the stage where the pressure causes fracture in the lithic piece and the detachment of a flake

projectile point: a weapon tip for an implement such as an arrow, atlatl dart, or spear

proximal end: the end of a flake that has the striking platform; the end opposite the distal end

punch: an elongate tool that is rested on the edge of a lithic piece and struck on the opposing end by a hammer to detach a flake from the lithic piece (see indirect percussion)

quarry: location where lithic raw material is obtained from the earth

quartzite: a metamorphic rock composed of altered sandstone; commonly used for manufacturing flaked and ground stone tools

raw material: any piece of lithic material that has not been modified by humans; sometimes this term is also used to refer to material that has been quarried but has not undergone any further modification

refitting: putting back together pieces of lithic material that have been removed from each other, as for example fitting flakes back onto the core or tool they were removed from

reject: a tool left incomplete and discarded during manufacturing due to a manufacturing problem or error

resharpening: sharpening a stone tool by detaching flakes along the used edge to remove the dull edge portion

resharpening flake: a flake produced when a dull tool edge is flaked to remove the dull area; characterized by the possession of usewear on the striking platform

residue: a portion of worked material left on a tool edge

ring crack: a circular crack that sometimes occurs at the impact point on the striking platform as a result of the fracturing involving the (blunt) indentor (hammerstone)

rock: a naturally formed aggregate composed of one or more minerals in varying proportions

roughout: an early, minimally shaped stage in production of an axe or adze

scraper: a tool designed to be used to scrape material such as wood or bone; the main feature is a steep working edge, often about 80–90° (see also end scraper and side scraper)

secondary flake: a flake on which the dorsal surface has none of the cortex of the lithic piece from which it was detached

sedimentary: rocks formed by cementation of particles broken down by weathering from other, pre-existing rocks

shaping: removal of the first series of flakes from a blank to shape the edge (primarily), give the piece its basic outline form, and prepare the piece for subsequent thinning and reduction (see also thinning and finishing)

shaping flake: a short, small, "rounded" flake from an early step in tool production (shaping) characterized by minimal scarring (typically 2 flake scars) on the striking platform and dorsal surface

shatter: a piece of lithic material generally detached inadvertently from another piece of lithic material (core or other piece of material such as a tool) when intentionally trying to detach another piece of lithic material (a flake); produced by the shattering of the piece from which it was struck

side scraper: a scraper with the working edge on a lateral edge of the flake blank used to manufacture it, or at least on a long edge of the lithic piece (see also scraper and end scraper)

silicate: minerals formed basically of silica and oxygen; they include most of the minerals and rocks used to manufacture stone tools (e.g., chert)

silicified wood: wood replaced by various minerals in the process of fossilization; also called petrified wood

soft hammer percussion: detaching a flake from a lithic piece by impacting the piece with a soft hammer, such as bone, antler, or wood; often called direct soft hammer percussion because the hammer comes into direct contact with the worked piece, rather than through an intermediate tool, such as a punch; soft hammers yield more so than do hard hammers and the worked piece often bites deeply into the soft hammer surface

spokeshave: a tool with a concave working edge presumed to be used mainly to scrape or shave cylindrical material, particularly wood; sometimes called a "notch"

step termination: a form of the distal end of a flake where it ends abruptly in a right angle break (see also hinge and feather terminations)

striation: the scratches produced on a tool edge due to its being used; abrasive particles from fracturing of the tool edge, dirt and dust, and/or particles from the material being worked, are dragged across the tool edge as a result of its use motion and this produces the striations

striking platform: the place on a piece of lithic material (usually a core or tool) that is struck with a hammer to remove a flake; part of this area remains on the detached flake and is referred to as the striking platform of the flake, at its proximal end

thinning: a middle stage in the process of manufacturing a lithic tool, between shaping and finishing, wherein flakes are removed to thin a tool and reduce its thick areas; also sometimes called thinning/reduction

thinning flake: a generally thin and elongate flake removed in middle stages of tool manufacturing to thin a tool and reduce thick areas, characterized by minimally to moderately complex scarring on the striking platform (typically 2 flake scars) and dorsal surface (see also shaping and finishing); sometimes called a thinning/reduction flake

Three Age System: a system developed in Denmark in the early nineteenth century that characterized European archaeological cultures as progressing through three stages: the Stone Age, the Bronze Age, and the Iron Age

type: the classification or division of a tool form into a number of varieties of that form, such as named types of arrow points (Avonlea, Old Women's, etc.)

uniface: a tool manufactured by flaking only on one of the two main faces on the tool (see also biface)

usewear: the damage or wear on the edge of a tool as a result of its being used; such damage commonly includes small flakes being detached from the edge, formation of polish, and abrasion of the edge that rounds the edge and leaves striations

utilized flake: a flake used without any modification, with the only flaking being usewear damage

ventral surface: the surface newly created on a fragment of lithic material (usually a flake) when that fragment is detached (from a core, tool, etc.); commonly has various features, such as a bulb of percussion, ripple marks, hackle marks or fissures (see also dorsal surface)

X-ray diffraction: the manner in which lithic material scatters X-rays, related to crystal structure and hence mineral composition

X-ray fluorescence: a technique of irradiating a lithic sample with X-rays or gamma rays, producing secondarily emitted X-rays that are characteristic of each element present in the sample; related techniques include proton-excited X-ray fluorescence and energy dispersive X-ray fluorescence

References Cited

Agenbroad, L.D. 1978. *The Hudson-Meng site: An Alberta Bison Kill on the Nebraska High Plains*. Washington: University Press of America.

Ahler, Stanley A. 1989. Experimental knapping with KRF and midcontinent cherts: Overview and applications. In *Experiments in Lithic Technology*, International Series 528, ed. Daniel S. Amick and Raymond P. Mauldin, 199–234. Oxford: British Archaeological Reports.

Allen, Melinda S., and Gwen Bell. 1988. Lapita flaked stone assemblages: Sourcing, technological, and functional studies. In *Archaeology of the Lapita Cultural Complex: A Critical Review*, Research Report No.5, ed. Patrick V. Kirch and Terry L. Hunt, 83–98. Seattle: Thomas Burke Memorial Washington State Museum.

Ambrose, W.R., and Roger Green.1972. First millennium B.C. transport of obsidian from New Britain to the Solomon Islands. *Nature* 237:31.

Amick, Daniel S.1994. Technological organization and the structure of inference in lithic analysis: An examination of Folsom hunting behavior in the American Southwest. In *The Organization of North American Prehistoric Chipped Stone Tool Technologies*, Archaeological Series 7, ed. Philip J. Carr, 9–34. Ann Arbor: International Monographs in Prehistory.

Anderson, Patricia C. 1980. A testimony of prehistoric tasks: Diagnostic residues on stone tool working edges. *World Archaeology* 12:181–194.

Andrefsky, William. 1994. Raw-material availability and the organization of technology. *American Antiquity* 59: 21–34.

Armstrong, Steven W. 1993. Alder complex kitchens: Experimental replication of Paleoindian cooking facilities. *Archaeology in Montana* 34(2):1–63.

Bamforth, Douglas. 1986. Technological efficiency and tool curation. *American Antiquity* 51:38–50.

Baumler, Mark F., and Christian E. Downum.1989. Between micro and macro: A study in the interpretation of small-sized lithic debitage. In *Experiments in Lithic Technology*. International Series 528, ed. Daniel S. Amick and Raymond P. Mauldin, 101–116. Oxford: British Archaeological Reports.

Bell, Pat, and David Wright.1985. *Rocks and Minerals*. New York: Macmillan.

Best, Myron G. 1982. *Igneous and Metamorphic Petrology*. San Francisco: W.H. Freeman.

Binford, Lewis R. 1979. Organization and formation processes: Looking at curated technologies. *Journal of Anthropological Research* 35: 255–273.

—— 1980. Willow smoke and dogs' tails: Hunter-gatherer settlement systems and archaeological site formation. *American Antiquity* 45:4–20.

Binford, Lewis R., and Sally R. Binford. 1966. A preliminary analysis of functional variability in the Mousterian of Levallois facies. *American Anthropologist* 68: 238–295.

—— 1969. Stone tools and human behavior. *Scientific American* 220 (4):70–84.

Binford, Lewis R., and N.M. Stone. 1985. "Righteous rocks" and Richard Gould: Some observations on misguided "debate". *American Antiquity* 50:151–153.

Blake, David F. 1990. Scanning electron microscopy. In *Instrumental Surface Analysis of Geological Materials*, ed. Dale L. Perry, 11–43. New York: VCH.

Blatt, Harvey, Gerard Middleton, and Raymond Murray. 1980. *Origin of Sedimentary Rocks*. 2nd ed. Englewood Cliffs: Prentice-Hall.

Bleed, P. 1986. The optimal design of hunting weapons: Maintainability or reliability. *American Antiquity* 51:547–562.

Bonnichsen, Robson. 1977. *Models for Deriving Information from Stone Tools*. Mercury Series, Archaeological Survey of Canada Paper No.60. Ottawa: National Museum of Man.

Bordaz, Jacques. 1969. Flint flaking in Turkey. *Natural History* 78:73–79.

—— 1970. *Tools of the Old and New Stone Age*. Garden City: Natural History Press.

Bordes, François. 1968. *The Old Stone Age*. New York: McGraw-Hill.

—— 1988. *Typologie du Paléolithique ancien et moyen*. Paris: Presses du CNRS.

Bordes, François, and Don E. Crabtree. 1969. The Corbiac blade technique and other experiments. *Tebiwa* 12(2):1–21.

Bordes, François, and Denise de Sonneville-Bordes. 1970. The significance of variability in Palaeolithic assemblages. *World Archaeology* 2:61–73.

Bradbury, Andrew P., and Philip J. Carr. 1999. Examining stage and continuum models of flake debris analysis: An experimental approach. *Journal of Archaeological Science* 26:105–116.

Bradley, Bruce A. 1975. Lithic reduction sequences: A glossary and discussion. In *Lithic Technology: Making and Using Stone Tools*, ed. E. Swanson, 5–14. The Hague: Mouton.

—— 1982. Flaked stone technology and typology. In *The Agate Basin Site: A Record of the Paleoindian Occupation of the Northwestern High Plains*, ed. George C. Frison and Dennis Stanford,181–208. New York: Academic Press.

—— 1991. Flaked stone technology in the Northern High Plains. In *Prehistoric Hunters of the High Plains*, ed. George C. Frison, 369–395. San Diego: Academic Press.

Bradley, Bruce A., and George C. Frison. 1987. Projectile points and specialized bifaces from the Horner site. In *The Horner Site: The Type Site of the Cody Cultural Complex*, ed. George C. Frison and Lawrence C. Todd, 199–231. Orlando: Academic Press.

Bradley, Bruce A., and Dennis J. Stanford. 1987. The Claypool study. In *The Horner Site: The Type Site of the Cody Cultural Complex*, ed. George C. Frison and Lawrence C. Todd, 405–434. Orlando: Academic Press.

Briuer, F.L. 1976. New clues to stone tool function: Plant and animal residues. *American Antiquity* 41:478–484.

Broderick, Michael. 1979. Ascending paper chromatographic technique in archaeology. In *Lithic Use-Wear Analysis*, ed. Brian Hayden, 375–383 New York: Academic Press.

Brumley, John H. 1975. The Cactus Flower Site in Southeastern Alberta: 1972–1974 excavations. National Museum of Man Mercury Series, Archaeological Survey of Canada Paper 46. Ottawa: National Museum of Man.

—— 1995. Prehistoric settlement and subsistence in the Plains of southern Alberta: The seasonality evidence.

Manuscript report on file, Archaeological Survey of Alberta, Provincial Museum of Alberta, Edmonton.

Butler, L.R.P., and M.L. Kokot. 1971. Atomic absorption. In *Modern Methods of Geochemical Analysis*, ed. Richard E. Wainerdi and Ernst A. Uken, 204–243. New York: Plenum Press.

Campling, N.R. 1980. Identification of Swan River chert. In *Directions in Manitoba Prehistory*, ed. L. Pettipas, 291–301. Winnipeg: Manitoba Archaeological Society.

Carr, Philip J. 1994a. The organization of technology: Impact and potential. In *The Organization of North American Prehistoric Chipped Stone Tool Technologies*, Archaeological Series 7, ed. Philip J. Carr, 1–8. Ann Arbor: International Monographs in Prehistory.

—— 1994b. Technological organization and prehistoric hunter-gatherer mobility: Examination of the Hayes site. In *The Organization of North American Prehistoric Chipped Stone Tool Technologies*, Archaeological Series 7, ed. Philip J. Carr, 35–44. Ann Arbor. International Monographs in Prehistory.

Cattaneo, C., K. Gelsthorpe, and R.J. Sokol. 1994. Immunological detection of albumin in ancient human cremations using ELISA and monoclonal antibodies. *Journal of Archaeological Science* 21:565–571.

Cattaneo, C., K. Gelsthorpe, P. Phillips, and R.J. Sokol. 1993. Blood residues on stone tools: Indoor and outdoor experiments. *World Archaeology* 25: 29–43.

Champion, Timothy, Clive Gamble, Stephen Shennan, and Alasdair Whittle. 1984. *Prehistoric Europe*. New York: Academic Press.

Chlachula, Jiri, and Raymond Le Blanc. 1996. Some artifact-diagnostic criteria of quartzite cobble-tool industries from Alberta. *Canadian Journal of Archaeology* 20:61–74.

Claeson, C.F. 1968. Distance and human interaction. *Geografisker Annaler B.* 50:142–161.

Clayton, L., W.B. Bickley Jr., and W.J. Stone. 1970. Knife River flint. *Plains Anthropologist* 15: 282–290.

Cleghorn, Paul. 1982. The Mauna Kea adze quarry: Technological analysis and experimental results. Unpublished PhD dissertation, University of Hawaii, Honolulu.

Close, Angela E. 1996. Carry that weight: The use and transportation of stone tools. *Current Anthropology* 37:545–553.

Collins, Michael B. 1975. Lithic technology as a means of processual inference. In *Lithic Technology: Making and Using Stone Tools*, ed. E. Swanson, 15–34. The Hague: Mouton.

Cotterell, Brian, and Johan Kamminga. 1979. The mechanics of flaking. In *Lithic Use-Wear Analysis,* ed. Brian Hayden, 99–112. New York: Academic Press.

—— 1987. The formation of flakes. *American Antiquity* 52:675–708.

—— 1990. *Mechanics of Pre-Industrial Technology*. Cambridge: Cambridge University Press.

Crabtree, Don E. 1966. A stoneworker's approach to analyzing and replicating the Lindenmeier Folsom. *Tebiwa* 9:3–39.

—— 1967. Notes on experiments in flintknapping: 3 The flintknapper's raw materials. *Tebiwa* 10(1):8–24.

—— 1970. Flaking stone with wooden implements. *Science* 169:146–153.

—— 1972. *An introduction to flintworking.* Occasional Papers of the Idaho State University Museum, Number 28, Pocatello: Idaho State University Museum.

Crabtree, Don E., and B. Robert Butler. 1964. Notes on experiments in flintknapping: 1 Heat treatment of silica materials. *Tebiwa* 7(1):1–6.

—— 1970. Flaking stone with wooden implements. *Science* 169:146–153.

Cullity, B.D. 1978. *Elements of X-Ray Diffraction*. Reading: Addison-Wesley.

Daniel, Glyn. 1967. *The Origins and Growth of Archaeology*. New York: Galahad Books.

Debénath, André, and Harold L. Dibble. 1994. *Handbook of Paleolithic Typology, Volume One: Lower and Middle Paleolithic of Europe*. Philadelphia: University Museum, University of Pennsylvania.

Dibble, Harold L. 1984. Interpreting typological variation of Middle Paleolithic scrapers: Function, style, or sequence of reduction? *Journal of Field Archaeology* 11:431–436.

—— 1987. The interpretation of Middle Paleolithic scraper morphology. *American Antiquity* 52:109–117.

Dibble, Harold L., and John C. Whittaker. 1981. New experimental evidence on the relation between percussion flaking and flake variation. *Journal of Archaeological Science* 8: 283–296.

Dolgoff, Anatole. 1996. *Physical Geology*. Lexington: D.C. Heath.

Domanski, Marian, and John A. Webb. 1992. Effect of heat treatment on siliceous rocks used in prehistoric lithic technology. *Journal of Archaeological Science* 19:601–614.

Dostal, J. and C. Elson. 1980. General principles of neutron activation analysis. In *Short course in neutron activation analysis in the geosciences*, ed. G.K. Muecke, 21–42. Toronto: Mineralogical Association of Canada.

Downs, Elinor F., and Jerold M. Lowenstein. 1995. Identification of archaeological blood proteins: A cautionary note. *Journal of Archaeological Science* 22:11–16.

Duff, Roger. 1970. *Stone Adzes of Southeast Asia: An Illustrated Typology*. Christchurch: Canterbury Museum.

Dyck, Ian. 1983. The prehistory of southern Saskatchewan. In *Tracking Ancient Hunters: Prehistoric Archaeology in Saskatchewan*, Henry T. Epp and Ian Dyck, 63–139. Saskatoon: The Saskatchewan Archaeological Society.

Ehlers, Ernest G., and Harvey Blatt. 1980. *Petrology: Igneous, Sedimentary, and Metamorphic*. San Francisco: W.H. Freeman.

Eisele, J., D.D. Fowler, and R.A. Lewis. 1995. Survival and detection of blood residues on stone tools. *Antiquity* 69:36–46.

Ellis, Christopher J. 1989. The explanation of Northeastern Paleoindian lithic procurement patterns. In *Eastern Paleoindian Lithic Resource Use*, Christopher J. Ellis and Jonathan C. Lothrop, 139–164. Boulder: Westview.

Ericson, Jonathon E. 1977. Egalitarian exchange systems in California: A preliminary view. In *Exchange Systems in Prehistory*, Timothy K. Earle and Jonathon E. Ericson, 109–126. New York: Academic Press.

Ericson, Jonathon E., and Barbara A. Purdy. 1984. *Prehistoric Quarries and Lithic Production*. Cambridge: Cambridge University Press.

Evershed, R.P., and Noreen Tuross. 1996. Proteinaceous material from potsherds and associated soils. *Journal of Archaeological Science* 23:429–436.

Fagan, Brian M. 1978. *In the Beginning: An Introduction to Archaeology*. Boston: Little, Brown and Company.

Faulkner, Aleric. 1972. Mechanical Principles of Flintworking. Unpublished PhD dissertation, Department of Anthropology, Washington State University.

—— 1973. Mechanics of eraillure formation. *Lithic Technology* 2(3):4–11.

Ferguson, W.C. 1980. Edge-angle classification of the Quininup Brok implements: Testing the ethnographic analogy. *Archaeology and Physical Anthropology in Oceania* 15(1):58–72.

Fiedel, Stuart J. 1987. *Prehistory of the Americas*. Cambridge: Cambridge University Press.

—— 1996. Blood from stones? Some methodological and interpretive problems in blood residue analysis. *Journal of Archaeological Science* 23:139–147.

Finnigan, James T. 1982. *Tipi rings and Plains prehistory: A reassessment of their archaeological potential.* Mercury Series, Archaeological Survey of Canada Paper 108. Ottawa: National Museum of Man.

Fite, L.E., E.A. Schweikert, R.E. Wainerdi, and E.A. Uken. 1971. Nuclear activation analysis. In *Modern Methods of Geochemical Analysis*, ed. Richard E. Wainerdi and Ernst A. Uken, 319–350. New York: Plenum Press.

Fladmark, Knut R. 1982. Microdebitage analysis: Initial considerations. *Journal of Archaeological Science* 9: 205–220.

Flenniken, J. Jeffrey. 1981. *Replicative systems analysis: A model applied to the vein quartz artifacts from the Hoko River site.* Reports of Investigations, No.59. Pullman: Washington State University Laboratory of Anthropology.

—— 1985. Stone tool reduction techniques as cultural markers. In *Stone Tool Analysis: Essays in Honor of Don E. Crabtree*, ed. Mark G. Plew, James C. Woods, and Max G. Pavesic, 265–277. Albuquerque: University of New Mexico Press.

Flenniken, J. Jeffrey, and J. Haggarty. 1979. Trampling as an agency in the formation of edge damage: An experiment in lithic technology. *Northwest Anthropological Research Notes* 13: 208–214.

Flood, Josephine.1990. *Archaeology of the Dreamtime: The Story of Prehistoric Australia and its People*. Yale University Press, New Haven.

Forbis, Richard G. 1962. The Old Women's Buffalo Jump, Alberta. *Contributions to Anthropology 1960 Part I*, Bulletin No. 180, 56–123. Ottawa: National Museum of Canada.

Ford, James A. 1952. Measurements of some prehistoric design developments in the Southeastern states. *Anthropological Papers of the American Museum of Natural History* 44(3).

Frison, George C. 1974. Archeology of the Casper Site. In *The Casper Site: A Hell Gap Bison Kill on the High Plains,* ed. George C. Frison, 1–111. New York: Academic Press.

—— 1982. Folsom components. In *The Agate Basin Site: A Record of the Paleoindian Occupation of the Northwestern High Plains*, ed. George C. Frison and Dennis Stanford, 37–76. New York: Academic Press.

—— 1987. The tool assemblage, unfinished bifaces, and stone flaking material sources for the Horner site. In *The Horner Site: The Type Site of the Cody Cultural Complex*, ed. George C. Frison and Lawrence C. Todd, 233–278. Orlando: Academic Press.

—— 1991a. The Goshen Paleoindian complex: New data for Paleoindian research. In *Clovis: Origins and Adaptations*, ed. Robson Bonnichsen and Karen L. Turnmire, 133–151. Corvallis: Center for the Study of the First Americans.

—— 1991b. *Prehistoric Hunters of the High Plains*. San Diego: Academic Press.

—— 1998. The Northwestern and Northern Plains archaic. In *Archaeology on the Great Plains*, ed. W. Raymond Wood, 140–172. Lawrence: University Press of Kansas.

Frison, George C., and Bruce A. Bradley. 1980. *Folsom Tools and Technology at the Hanson Site, Wyoming*. Albuquerque: University of New Mexico Press.

—— 1982. Fluting of Folsom projectile points. In *The Agate Basin Site: A Record of the Paleoindian Occupation of the Northwestern High Plains*, ed. George C. Frison and Dennis Stanford, 209–212. New York: Academic Press.

Frison, George C., and Dennis Stanford. 1982. Agate Basin components. In *The Agate Basin Site: A Record of the Paleoindian Occupation of the Northwestern High Plains*, ed. George C. Frison and Dennis Stanford, 76–135. New York: Academic Press.

Frison, George C., David Schwab, L. Adrien Hannus, Peter Winham, David Walter, and Robert C. Mainfort. 1996. Archeology of the Northwestern Plains. In *Archeological and Bioarcheological Resources on the Northern Plains*, Research Series No. 47, ed. George C. Frison and Robert C. Mainfort, 8–40. Fayetteville: Arkansas Archeological Survey.

Fullagar, Richard L.K. 1991. The role of silica in polish formation. *Journal of Archaeological Science* 18:1–24.

Fullagar, Richard, Judith Furby, and Bruce Hardy. 1996. Residues on stone artefacts: State of a scientific art. *Antiquity* 70:740–745.

Gallagher, James P. 1977. Contemporary stone tools in Ethiopia: Implications for archaeology. *Journal of Field Archaeology* 4:407–414.

Gamble, Clive. 1986. *The Palaeolithic Settlement of Europe*. Cambridge: Cambridge University Press.

Gifford-Gonzales, Diane P., David B. Damrosch, Debra R. Damrosch, John Pryor, and Robert T. Thunen. 1985. The third dimension in site structure: An experiment in trampling and vertical dispersal. *American Antiquity* 50:803–818.

Goebel, Ted, Roger Powers, and Nancy Bigelow. 1991. The Nenana complex of Alaska and Clovis origins. In *Clovis: Origins and Adaptations*, ed. Robson Bonnichsen and Karen L. Turnmire, 49–79. Corvallis: Center for the Study of the First Americans.

Goodyear, Albert C. 1989. A hypothesis for the use of cryptocrystalline raw materials among Paleoindian groups of North America. In *Eastern Paleoindian Lithic Resource Use*, ed. Christopher J. Ellis and Jonathan C. Lothrop, 1–9. Boulder: Westview.

Gould, Richard A. 1980. *Living Archaeology*. Cambridge: Cambridge University Press.

Gould, Richard A., and S. Saggers. 1985. Lithic procurement in central Australia: A closer look at Binford's idea of embeddedness in archaeology. *American Antiquity* 50:117–135.

Gould, Richard A., Dorothy A. Koster, and Ann H. Sontz. 1971. The lithic assemblage of the Western Desert Aborigines of Australia. *American Antiquity* 36:149–169.

Grace, R., I.D.G. Graham, and N.H. Newcomer. 1985. The quantification of microwear polishes. *World Archaeology* 17:112–120.

Green, Roger. 1962. Obsidian: Its application to archaeology. *New Zealand Archaeological Association Newsletter* 5:8–16.

—— 1974. Sites with Lapita pottery: Importing and voyaging. *Mankind* 9: 253–259.

—— 1982. Models for the Lapita cultural complex: An evaluation of some current proposals. *New Zealand Journal of Archaeology* 4:7–19.

—— 1987. Obsidian results from the Lapita sites of the Reef/Santa Cruz Islands. In *Archaeolometry: Further Australian Studies*, Occasional Papers in Prehistory 14, ed. W.R. Ambrose and J.M.J. Mummery, 239–249. Canberra: Australian National University.

Gregg, Michael L. 1987. Knife River flint in the Northeastern Plains. *Plains Anthropologist* 32:367–377.

Gregg, Michael L., David Meyer, Paul R. Picha, and David G. Stanley. 1996. Archeology of the Northeastern Plains. In *Archeological and Bioarcheological Resources on the Northern Plains*, Research Series No.47, ed. George C. Frison and Robert C. Mainfort, 77–90. Fayetteville: Arkansas Archeological Survey.

Greiser, Sally Thompson. 1985. *Predictive Models of Hunter-Gatherer Subsistence and Settlement Strategies on the Central High Plains*. Memoir 20, Lincoln: Plains Anthropologist.

Gryba, Eugene. 1988a. An Inventory of Fluted Point Occurrences in Alberta. Manuscript on file, Archaeological Survey of Alberta, Edmonton.

—— 1988b. A stone age pressure method of Folsom fluting. *Plains Anthropologist* 33:53–66.

Gunn, Joel. 1977. Idiosyncratic chipping style as a demographic indicator: A proposed application to the South Hills region of Idaho and Utah. In *The Individual in Prehistory: Studies of Variability in Style in Prehistoric Technologies*, ed. James N. Hill and Joel Gunn, 167–204. New York: Academic Press.

Hammond, Norman, Arnold Aspinall, Stuart Feather, John Hazelden, Trevor Gazard, and Stuart Agrell. 1977. Maya jade: Source location and analysis. In *Exchange Systems in Prehistory*, ed. Timothy K. Earle and Jonathon E. Ericson, 35–66. New York: Academic Press.

Hardy, Bruce L., Rudolf A. Raff, and Venu Raman. 1997. Recovery of mammalian DNA from Middle Paleolithic stone tools. *Journal of Archaeological Science* 24:601–611.

Harris, Marvin. 1968. *The Rise of Anthropological Theory*. New York: Thomas Y. Crowell.

Hay, Conran A. 1977. Use-scratch morphology: A functionally significant aspect of edge damage on obsidian tools. *Journal of Field Archaeology* 4:491–494.

Hayden, Brian. 1979a. *Lithic Use-Wear Analysis*. New York: Academic Press.

—— 1979b. *Paleolithic Reflections: Lithic Technology and Ethnographic Excavations Among the Australian Aborigines*. Canberra: Australian Institute of Aboriginal Studies.

—— 1987a. *Lithic Studies Among the Contemporary Highland Maya*. Tucson: University of Arizona Press.

—— 1987b. Traditional metate manufacturing in Guatemala using chipped stone tools. In *Lithic Studies Among the Contemporary Highland Maya*, ed. Brian Hayden, 8–119. Tucson: University of Arizona Press.

Hayden, Brian, and W. Karl Hutchings. 1989. Whither the billet flake? In *Experiments in Lithic Technology*, International Series 528, ed. Daniel S. Amick and Raymond P. Mauldin, 235–257. Oxford: British Archaeological Reports.

Hayden, Brian, Edward Bakewell, and Rob Gargett. 1996. The world's longest-lived corporate group: Lithic analysis reveals prehistoric social organization near Lillooet, British Columbia. *American Antiquity* 61:341–356.

Hayden, Brian, Nora Franco, and Jim Spafford. 1996. Evaluating lithic strategies and design criteria. In *Stone Tools: Theoretical Insights into Human Prehistory*, ed. George H. Odell, 9–45. New York: Plenum Press.

Healan, Dan M. 1995. Identifying lithic reduction loci with size-graded macrodebitage: A multivariate approach. *American Antiquity* 60:689–699.

Heider, Karl G. 1967. Archaeological assumptions and ethnographical facts: A cautionary tale from New Guinea. *Southwestern Journal of Anthropology* 23:52–64.

Henry, Donald O. 1989. Correlations between reduction strategies and settlement patterns. In *Alternative Approaches to Lithic Analysis*, Archeological Papers of the American Anthropological Association Number 1, ed. Donald O. Henry and George H. Odell, 139–155. Washington, D.C.

Henry, Donald O., C. Vance Haynes, and Bruce Bradley. 1976. Quantitative variations in flaked stone debitage. *Plains Anthropologist* 21:57–61.

Hester, James J. 1972. *Blackwater Locality No. 1: A Stratified, Early Man Site in Eastern New Mexico*. Fort Burgwin Research Center No. 8. Ranchos de Taos: Southern Methodist University.

Hill, James N., and Joel Gunn (eds) 1977. *The Individual in Prehistory: A Study of Variability in Style in Prehistoric Technologies*. New York: Academic Press.

Hodges, Henry. 1964. *Artifacts: An Introduction to Early Materials and Technology*. London: John Baker.

Hofman, Jack L., and Russell W. Graham. 1998. The Paleo-indian cultures of the Great Plains. In *Archaeology on the Great Plains*, ed. W. Raymond Wood, 87–139. Lawrence: University Press of Kansas.

Horsfall, Gayel. 1987. A design theory perspective on variability in grinding stones. In *Lithic Studies Among the Contemporary Highland Maya*, ed. Brian Hayden, 332–377. Tucson: University of Arizona Press.

Huckell, Bruce B. 1978. "Push" vs. "pull" flaking: A reply to Patten. *Lithic Technology* 7(3):42–43.

Hurcombe, L. 1988. Some criticisms and suggestions in response to Newcomer et al. (1986). *Journal of Archaeological Science* 15:1–10.

Hyland, D.C., J.M. Tersak, J.M. Advasio, and M.I. Siegel 1990. Identification of the species of origin of residual blood on lithic material. *American Antiquity* 55:104–112.

Ingbar, Eric E. 1994. Lithic material selection and technological organization. In *The Organization of North American Prehistoric Chipped Stone Tool Technologies*, Archaeological Series 7, ed. Philip J. Carr, 45–56. Ann Arbor: International Monographs in Prehistory.

Ingbar, Eric E., Mary Lou Larson, and Bruce A. Bradley. 1989. A non-typological approach to debitage analysis. In *Experiments in Lithic Technology*. International Series 528, ed. Daniel S. Amick and Raymond P. Mauldin, 117–136.Oxford: British Archaeological Reports.

Jahren, A.H., N. Toth, K. Schick, J.D. Clark, and R.G. Amundson. 1997. Determining stone tool use: Chemical and morphological analysis of residues on experimentally manufactured stone tools. *Journal of Archaeological Science* 24:245–250.

Johnson, Jay K. 1996. Lithic analysis and questions of cultural complexity: The Maya. In *Stone Tools: Theoretical Insights into Human Prehistory,* ed. George Odell, 159–179. New York: Plenum Press.

Johnson, L. Lewis. 1978. A history of flint-knapping experimentation, 1838–1976. *Current Anthropology* 19:337–372.

Johnson, Ann Mary, and Alfred E. Johnson. 1998. The Plains woodland. In *Archaeology on the Great Plains*, ed. W. Raymond Wood, 201–234. Lawrence: University Press of Kansas.

Julig, Patrick J., L.A. Pavlish, and R.G.V. Hamcock. 1989. Aspects of late Paleoindian lithic technological organization in the northwestern Lake Superior region of Canada. In *Eastern Paleoindian Lithic Resource Use*, ed. Christopher J. Ellis and Jonathan C. Lothrop, 293–322. Boulder: Westview.

Kahn, Jennifer G. 1996. Prehistoric Stone Tool Use and Manufacture at the Ha'atuatua Dune site, Marquesas Islands, French Polynesia. Unpublished M.A. thesis, Department of Archaeology, University of Calgary.

Kay, Marvin. 1996. Microwear analysis of some Clovis and experimental chipped stone tools. In *Stone Tools: Theoretical Insights into Human Prehistory*, ed. George H. Odell, 315–344. New York : Plenum Press.

Keeley, Lawrence H. 1980. *Experimental Determination of Stone Tool Uses.* Chicago: University of Chicago Press.

Keeley, Lawrence H., and M.H. Newcomer. 1976. Microwear analysis of experimental flint tools: A test case. *Journal of Archaeological Science* 4:29–62.

Kehoe, T.F. 1966. The small side-notched point system of the Northern Plains. *American Antiquity* 31:827–841.

Kimball, Larry R., John F. Kimball, and Patricia E. Allen. 1995. Microwear polishes as viewed through the atomic force microscope. *Lithic Technology* 20:6–28.

Kirch, Patrick V. 1988. Problems and issues in Lapita archaeology. In *Archaeology of the Lapita Cultural Complex: A Critical Review*, Research Report No.5, ed. Patrick V. Kirch and Terry L. Hunt, 157–165. Seattle: Thomas Burke Memorial Washington State Museum.

Knutsson, Kjel. 1988. *Patterns of Tool Use: Scanning Electron Microscopy of Experimental Quartz Tools.* Uppsala: Societas Archaeologica Uppsaliensis.

Kooyman, Brian. 1980. Lacandon stoneworking. *Calgary Archaeologist* 8/9:21–22.

—— 1981. Métis Faunal Remains and Variables in Archaeological Butchering Pattern Analysis. Unpublished M.A. thesis, Department of Archaeology, University of Calgary, Calgary.

—— 1985. Moa and Moa Hunting: An Archaeological Analysis of Big Game Hunting in New Zealand. Unpublished PhD dissertation, Department of Anthropology, University of Otago, Dunedin.

—— 1989. Moa hunting: Communal or individual hunting? In *Hunters of the Recent Past*, ed. L.B. Davis and Brian O.K. Reeves, 327–351. London: Unwin and Hyman.

—— 1992. Preliminary report of the 1991 excavations in the North Kill at Head-Smashed-In Buffalo Jump (DkPj-1). Manuscript on file, Social Sciences and Humanities Research Council of Canada, Ottawa.

—— 2000. 1994 excavations at the Spring Kill site (EgPs-51) near Exshaw, Alberta. Report on file, Archaeological Survey of Alberta, Edmonton.

Kooyman, Brian, Tom Arnold, Don Boras, and Maria Teresa Garcia. 1987. Final report of the 1986 University of Calgary Archaeology Field School at the Strathcona Site (FjPi-29). Manuscript report on file, Archaeological Survey of Alberta, Provincial Museum of Alberta, Edmonton.

Kooyman, Brian, Margaret E. Newman, and Howard Ceri. 1992. Verifying the reliability of blood residue analysis on archaeological tools. *Journal of Archaeological Science* 19:265–269.

Kuhn, Steven L. 1994. A formal approach to the design and assembly of mobile toolkits. *American Antiquity* 59:426–442.

—— 1996. The trouble with ham steaks: A reply to Morrow. *American Antiquity* 61:591–595.

Lawn, B.R., and D.B. Marshall. 1979. Mechanisms of microcontact fracture in brittle solids. In *Lithic Use-Wear Analysis*, ed. Brian Hayden, 63–82. New York: Academic Press.

Leach, B. Foss. 1969. *The concept of similarity in prehistoric studies*. Studies in Prehistoric Anthropology 1. Dunedin: Anthropology Department, University of Otago.

Leach, Helen M. 1984. Jigsaw: Reconstructive lithic technology. In *Prehistoric Quarries and Lithic Production*, ed. Jonathon E. Ericson and Barbara A. Purdy, 107–118. Cambridge: Cambridge University Press.

—— 1996. Of steel and stone adzes and typological tests. In *Oceanic Culture History: Essays in Honour of Roger Green*, J.M. Davidson, G. Irwin, B.F. Leach, A. Pawley, and D. Brown, 411–420. Dunedin North: New Zealand Journal of Archaeology.

Leach, Helen M., and B. Foss Leach. 1980. The Riverton site: An Archaic adze manufactory in western Southland, New Zealand. *New Zealand Journal of Archaeology* 2:99–140.

Le Moine, Genevieve M. 1991. Experimental Analysis of the Manufacture and Use of Bone and Antler Tools Among the Mackenzie Inuit. Unpublished PhD dissertation, Department of Archaeology, University of Calgary, Calgary.

—— 1994. Use wear on bone and antler tools from the Mackenzie delta, Northwest Territories. *American Antiquity* 59:316–334.

Liebhafsky, H.A., and H.G. Pfeiffer. 1971. X-ray techniques. In *Modern Methods of Geochemical Analysis*, ed. Richard E. Wainerdi and Ernst A. Uken, 245–270. New York: Plenum Press.

Loy, Thomas H. 1983. Prehistoric blood residues: Detection on tool surfaces and identification of species of origin. *Science* 220:1269–1271.

Loy, Thomas H., and Bruce L. Hardy. 1992. Blood residue analysis of 90,000–year-old stone tools from Tabun Cave, Israel. *Antiquity* 66:24–35.

Loy, Thomas H., Matthew Spriggs, and Stephen Wickler. 1992. Direct evidence for human use of plants 28,000 years ago: Starch residues on stone artifacts from the northern Solomon Islands. *Antiquity* 66:898–912.

Luedtke, Barbara E. 1992. *An Archaeologist's Guide to Chert and Flint*. Los Angeles: Institute of Archaeology, University of California.

Magne, Martin P.R. 1985. *Lithics and Livelihood: Stone Tool Technologies of Central and Southern Interior British Columbia*. Mercury Series, Archaeological Survey of Canada Paper No.133, Ottawa: National Museum of Man.

Mansur-Franchomme, Maria Estela. 1983. Scanning electron microscopy of dry hide working tools: The role of abrasives and humidity in microwear polish formation. *Journal of Archaeological Science* 10:223–230.

—— 1986. *Microscopie du matériel lithique préhistorique: Traces d'utilisation, altérations naturelles, accidentelles et technologiques*. Centre National de la Recherche Scientifique, Cahiers du Quaternaire No.9, Paris: Centre

Mauldin, Raymond P., and Daniel S. Amick. 1989. Investigating patterning in debitage from experimental bifacial core reduction. In *Experiments in Lithic Technology*, International Series 528, ed. Daniel S. Amick and Raymond P. Mauldin, 67–88. Oxford: British Archaeological Reports.

McBryde, I. 1978. Wil-im-ee moor-ing: Or, where do axes come from? *Mankind* 11:354–382.

Miller, James C. 1996. Lithic sources on the Northwestern Plains. In *Archeological and Bioarcheological Resources on the Northern Plains*, Research Series No. 47, ed. George C. Frison and Robert C. Mainfort, 41–49. Fayetteville: Arkansas Archeological Survey.

Monroe, James S., and Reed Wicander. 1995. *Physical Geology: Exploring the Earth*. Minneapolis/St. Paul: West Publishing.

Morrow, Toby A. 1996a. Bigger is better: Comments on Kuhn's formal approach to mobile tool kits. *American Antiquity* 61:581–590.

—— 1996b. Lithic refitting and archaeological site formation processes. In *Stone Tools: Theoretical Insights into Human Prehistory*, ed. George H. Odell, 345–373. New York: Plenum Press.

Moss, Emily H. 1983. *The functional analysis of flint implements. Pincevent and Pont d'Ambon: Two case studies from the French Final Palaeolithic*. International Series 177. Oxford: British Archaeological Reports.

—— 1987. A review of "Investigating microwear polishes with blind tests". *Journal of Archaeological Science* 14:473–481.

Muto, Guy R. 1971a. A stage analysis of the manufacture of stone tools. *Anthropological Papers, Department of Anthropology, University of Oregon* 1:109–117.

—— 1971b. A technological analysis of the early stages in the manufacture of lithic artifacts. Unpublished M.A. thesis, Idaho State Univeristy.

Nash, Stephen. 1996. Is curation a useful heuristic? In *Stone Tools: Theoretical Insights into Human Prehistory*, ed. George H. Odell, 81–99. New York: Plenum Press.

Newcomer, Mark H. 1975. Punch technique. In *Lithic Technology: Making and Using Stone Tools*, ed. E. Swanson, 97–102. The Hague: Mounton.

Newcomer, Mark H., Roger Grace, and Romana Unger-Hamilton. 1986. Investigating microwear polishes with blind tests. *Journal of Archaeological Science* 13:203–217.

—— 1988. Microwear methodology: A reply to Moss, Hurcombe, and Bamforth. *Journal of Archaeological Science* 15:25–33.

Newman, Margaret. 1990. The hidden evidence from Hidden Cave, Nevada. Unpublished PhD dissertation, Department of Anthropology, University of Toronto, Toronto.

Newman, Margaret E., Howard Ceri, and Brian Kooyman. 1996. The use of immunological techniques in the analysis of archaeological materials — a response to Eisele; With report of studies at Head-Smashed-In Buffalo Jump. *Antiquity* 70:677–682.

Newman, Margaret E., Robert M. Yohe II, Brian Kooyman, and Howard Ceri. 1997. "Blood" from stones? Probably: A response to Fiedel. *Journal of Archaeological Science* 24:1023–1027.

O'Connell, James F. 1977. Aspects of variation in central Australian lithic assemblages. In *Stone Tools as Cultural Markers: Change, Evolution and Complexity,* ed. R.V.S. Wright, 269–281. Canberra: Australian Institute of Aboriginal Studies.

Odell, George H. 1981. The mechanics of use-breakage of stone tools: Some testable hypothesis. *Journal of Field Archaeology* 8:197–204.

—— 1989. Experiments in lithic reduction. In *Experiments in Lithic Technology,* International Series 528, ed. Daniel S. Amick and Raymond P. Mauldin, 163–198. Oxford: British Archaeological Reports.

—— 1994. Assessing hunter-gatherer mobility in the Illinois valley: Exploring ambiguous results. In *The Organization of North American Prehistoric Chipped Stone Tool Technologies*, Archaeology Series 7, ed. Philip J. Carr, 70–86. Ann Arbor: International Monographs in Prehistory.

—— 1996a. Economizing behavior and the concept of "curation". In *Stone Tools: Theoretical Insights into Human Prehistory*, ed. George H. Odell, 51–80. New York: Plenum Press.

—— 1996b. ed. *Stone tools: Theoretical Insights into Human Prehistory*, New York: Plenum Press.

Odell, George H., and Frieda Odell-Vereecken. 1980. Verifying the reliability of lithic use-wear assessments by 'blind tests': The low-power approach. *Journal of Field Archaeology* 7:87–120.

Olausson, Deborah Seitzer. 1983. Experiments to investigate the effects of heat-treatment on use-wear on flint tools. *Proceedings of the Prehistoric Society* 49:1–13.

Olsson, G. 1965. Distance and human interaction: A review and bibliography. *Regional Science Research Institute Bibliography Series 2.*

Parry, William J. 1994. Prismatic blade technologies in North America. In *The Organization of North American Prehistoric Chipped Stone Tool Technologies*, Archaeological Series 7, ed. Philip J. Carr, 87–98. Ann Arbor: International Monographs in Prehistory.

Patten, Robert J. 1978. "Push" vs. "pull" flaking. *Lithic Technology* 7(1):3–4.

Patterson, Leland W. 1984. Comments on studies of thermal alteration of central Pennsylvania jasper. *American Antiquity* 49:168–173.

Peck, Trevor. 1996. Late side-notched projectile points on the Northwestern Plains. Unpublished M.A. thesis, Department of Anthropology, University of Alberta, Edmonton.

Peck, Trevor, and John W. Ives. In press. Late side-notched projectile points on the Northern Plains. *Plains Anthropologist*.

Peterson, Jane, Douglas R. Mitchell, and M. Steven Shackley. 1997. The social and economic contexts of lithic procurement: Obsidian from Classic-period Hohokam sites. *American Antiquity* 62:231–259.

Plummer, Charles C., and David McGeary. 1991. *Physical Geology* (5th ed.). Dubuque: Wm. C. Brown.

Prentiss, William C., and Eugene J. Romanski. 1989. Experimental evaluation of

Sullivan and Rozen's debitage typology. In *Experiments in Lithic Technology*, International Series 528, ed. Daniel S. Amick and Raymond P. Mauldin, 89–99. Oxford: British Archaeological Reports.

Price, T.D., S. Chappell, and D.J. Ives. 1982. Thermal alteration in Mesolithic assemblages. *Proceedings of the Prehistoric Society* 48:467–485.

Purdy, Barbara, and H. K. Brooks. 1971. Thermal alteration of silica materials: An archaeological approach. *Science* 173:322–325.

Quigg, J. Michael.1984. A 4700–year-old tool assemblage from east-central Alberta. Plains *Anthropologist* 29:151–159.

Rees, D., G.G. Wilkinson, R. Grace, and C.R. Orton. 1991. An investigation of the fractile properties of flint microwear images. *Journal of Archaeological Science* 18:629–640.

Reeves, Brian O.K. 1969. The southern Alberta paleo-cultural — paleoenvironmental sequence. In *Post-Pleistocene Man and his Environment on the Northern Plains*, ed. R.G. Forbis, L.B. Davis, O.A Christensen, and G. Fedirchuk, 4–46. Calgary: Chacmool.

—— 1978. Head-Smashed-In: 5500 years of bison jumping in the Alberta Plains. In *Bison Procurement and Utilization: A Symposium*, Memoir 14, ed. Leslie B. Davis and Michael Wilson, 151–174. Lincoln: Plains Anthropologist.

—— 1983 *Culture change in the Northern Plains: 1000 B.C. - A.D. 1000*. Archaeological Survey of Alberta Occasional Paper No. 20. Edmonton.

Renfrew, Colin. 1977. Alternative models for exchange and spatial distribution. In *Exchange Systems in Prehistory*, ed. Timothy K. Earle and Jonathon E. Ericson, 71–90. New York: Academic Press.

Renfrew, Colin, J.E. Dixon, and J.R. Cann. 1968. Further analysis of Near Eastern obsidians. *Proceedings of the Prehistoric Society* 34:319–331.

Rick, John W. 1996. Projectile points, style, and social process in the preceramic of central Peru. In *Stone Tools: Theoretical Insights into Human Prehistory*, ed. George H. Odell, 245–278. New York: Plenum Press.

Rondeau, Michael F. 1996. When is an Elko? In *Stone Tools: Theoretical Insights into Human Prehistory*, ed. George H. Odell, 229–243. New York: Plenum Press.

Rosen, Steven A. 1996. The decline and fall of flint. In *Stone Tools: Theoretical Insights into Human Prehistory*, ed. George H. Odell, 129–158. New York: Plenum Press.

—— 1997. *Lithics after the Stone Age: A Handbook of Stone Tools from the Levant*. Walnut Creek: Altamira.

Rouse, Irving. 1964. *Prehistory in Haiti: A Study in Method*. Yale University Publications in Anthropology Number 21, reprinted by Burns and MacEachern, Toronto.

Sackett, James R. 1982. Approaches to style in lithic archaeology. *Journal of Anthropological Archaeology* 1:59–112.

—— 1985. Style and ethnicity in the Kalahari: A reply to Wiessner. *American Antiquity* 50:154–159.

—— 1986. Style, function, and assemblage variability: A reply to Binford. *American Antiquity* 51:628–634.

Schiffer, Michael Brian, and James M. Skibo. 1997. The explanation of artifact variability. *American Antiquity* 62:27–50.

Schindler, Debra, James W. Hatch, Conran A. Hay, and Richard C. Bradt. 1982. Aboriginal thermal alteration of a central Pennsylvania jasper: Analytical and behavioral implications. *American Antiquity* 47:526–544.

—— 1984. Thermal alteration of Bald Eagle jasper: Authors' reply to Patterson. *American Antiquity* 49:173–177.

Schüler, V.C.O. 1971. Chemical analysis and sample preparation. In *Modern Methods of Geochemical Analysis*, ed. Richard E. Wainerdi and Ernst A. Uken, 53–71. New York: Plenum Press.

Seeman, Mark F. 1994. Intercluster lithic patterning at Nobles Pond: A case for "disembedded" procurement among early Paleoindian societies. *American Antiquity* 59:273–288.

Semenov, Sergei A. 1964. *Prehistoric Technology: An Experimental Study of the Oldest Tools and Artifacts from Traces of Manufacture and Wear*. Chatham: Barnes and Noble.

Shafer, Harry J., and Richard G. Holloway. 1979. Organic residue analysis in determining stone tool function. In *Lithic Use-Wear Analysis*, ed. Brian Hayden, 385–399. New York: Academic Press.

Shea, John J., and Joel D. Klenck. 1993. An experimental investigation of the effects of trampling on the results of lithic microwear analysis. *Journal of Archaeological Science* 20:175–194.

Sheets, Payson D. 1978. Chipped stone artifacts from the Zapotitan Basin. In *Research of the Post Classic Project in the Zapotitan Basin, El Salvador: A Preliminary Report of the 1978 Season,* ed. Payson Sheets, 83–88. Manuscript on file, Boulder: Department of Anthropology, University of Colorado.

—— 1983. Summary and Conclusions. In *Archeology and Volcanism in Central America: The Zapotitan Valley of El Salvador,* ed. Payson Sheets, 275–293. Austin: University of Texas Press.

Sheppard, Peter J. 1993. Lapita lithics: Trade/exchange and technology. A view from the reefs/Santa Cruz. *Archaeology in Oceania* 28:121–137.

—— 1996. Hard rock: Archaeological implications of chert sourcing in Near and Remote Oceania. In *Oceanic Culture History: Essays in Honour of Roger Green*, New Zealand Journal of Archaeology, ed. Janet Davidson, Geoffrey Irwin, Foss Leach, Andrew Pawley, and Dorothy Brown, 99–115. Dunedin North: Special Publication.

Sidrys, Raymond. 1977. Mass-distance measures for the Maya obsidian trade. In *Exchange Systems in Prehistory*, ed. Timothy K. Earle and Jonathon E. Ericson, 91–107. New York: Academic Press.

Siegel, Peter E. 1985. Edge angle as a functional indicator: A test. *Lithic Technology* 14(2):90–94.

Sinoto, Yosihiko H. 1982. A preliminary report on a hafted adze and some adze handles from archaeological excavations on Huahine Island, French Polynesia. *New Zealand Journal of Archaeology* 4:169–177.

Smith, Ian, and Helen Leach. 1996. Adzes from the excavation and museum collections. In *Shag River Mouth: The Archaeology of an Early Southern Maori Village*, ed. Atholl Anderson, Brian Allingham, and Ian Smith, 103–147. Canberra: The Australian National University.

Smith, P., and M. Wilson. 1992. Blood residues on ancient tool surfaces: A cautionary note. *Journal of Archaeological Science* 19:231–241.

Spaulding, Albert C. 1953. Review of "Measurements of some prehistoric design developments in the Southeastern States". *American Anthropologist* 55:588–591.

Speth, John D. 1972. Mechanical basis of percussion flaking. *American Antiquity* 37:34–60.

—— 1975. Miscellaneous studies in hard-hammer percussion flaking. *American Antiquity* 40:203–207.

—— 1981. The role of platform angle and core size in hard-hammer percussion flaking. *Lithic Technology* 10(1):16–21.

Stafford, Barbara D. 1979. A technofunctional study of lithics from Payson, Arizona. Unpublished PhD dissertation, Arizona State University.

Stanfill, Alan L. 1988. Avonlea projectile point manufacture: A testable model. In *Avonlea Yesterday and Today: Archaeology and Prehistory,* ed. Leslie B. Davis, 251–256. Saskatoon: Saskatchewan Archaeological Society.

Stanford, Dennis. 1991. Clovis origins and adaptations: An introductory perspective. In *Clovis: Origins and Adaptations*, ed. Robson Bonnichsen and Karen L. Turnmire, 1–13. Corvallis: Center for the Study of the First Americans.

Stothert, Karen E. 1974. The lithic technology of the Santa Elena Peninsula, Ecuador: A method for the analysis of technologically simple stonework. Unpublished PhD dissertation, Yale University.

Strathern, Marilyn. 1969. Stone axes and flake tools: Evaluations from two New Guinea highlands societies. *Proceedings of the Prehistoric Society* 35:311–329.

Sullivan, Alan P., and Kenneth C. Rozen. 1985. Debitage analysis and archaeological interpretation. *American Antiquity* 50:755–779.

Summerhayes, Glenn R., and M. Hotchkis. 1992. Recent advances in Melanesian obsidian sourcing: Results of the 1990 and 1991 PIXE/PIGME analysis. In *Poterie lapit et peuplement*, ed. Jean Christophe Galipaud, 127–133. Nouméa: Orstom.

Taçon, Paul S. 1992. The power of stone: Symbolic aspects of stone use and tool development in Western Arnhem Land, Australia. *Antiquity* 65:192–207.

Tankersley, Kenneth B. 1989. A close look at the big picture: Early Paleoindian lithic resource procurement in the Midwestern United States. In *Eastern Paleoindian Lithic Resource Use*, ed. Christopher J. Ellis and Jonathan C. Lothrop, 259–292. Boulder: Westview.

Taylor, R.E., C. Vance Haynes Jr., and Minze Stuiver. 1996. Clovis and Folsom age estimates: Stratigraphic context and radiocarbon calibration. *Antiquity* 70:515–525.

Thomas, David Hurst. 1986. Points on points: A reply to Flenniken and Raymond. *American Antiquity* 51:619–627.

Titmus, Gene L., and James C. Woods. 1991. Fluted points from the Snake River plain. In *Clovis: Origins and Adaptations*, ed. Robson Bonnichsen and Karen L. Turnmire, 119–131. Corvallis: Center for the Study of the First Americans.

Tomka, Steven A. 1989. Differentiating lithic reduction techniques: An experimental approach. In *Experiments in Lithic Technology*, International Series 528, ed. Daniel S. Amick and Raymond P. Mauldin, 137–161. Oxford: British Archaeological Reports.

Torrence, Robin. 1986. *Production and Exchange of Stone Tools: Prehistoric Obsidian in the Aegean*. Cambridge: Cambridge University Press.

Torrence, Robin, Jim Specht, Richard Fullagar, and Glen R. Summerhayes. 1996. Which obsidian is worth it? A view from the west New Britain sources. In *Oceanic Culture History: Essays in Honour of Roger Green*, ed. Janet Davidson, Geoffrey Irwin, Foss Leach,

Andrew Pawley, and Dorothy Brown, 211–224. Dunedin North: New Zealand Journal of Archaeology Special Publication.

Tringham, Ruth, G. Cooper, G. Odell, B. Voytek, and A. Whitman. 1974. Experimentation in the formation of edge damage: A new approach to lithic analysis. *Journal of Field Archaeology* 1:171–196.

Tsirk, Are. 1974. Mechanical basis of percussion flaking: Some comments. *American Antiquity* 39:128–130.

—— 1979. Regarding fracture initiations. In *Lithic Use-Wear Analysis*, ed. Brian Hayden, 83–96. New York: Academic Press.

Turney-High, Harry Holbert. 1974. *Ethnography of the Kutenai.* Memoirs of the American Anthropological Association 56. Millwood: Kraus Reprint Company.

Tuross, Noreen, Ian Barnes, and Richard Potts. 1996. Protein identification of blood residues on experimental stone tools. *Journal of Archaeological Science* 23:289–296.

Unger-Hamilton, Romana. 1984. The formation of use-wear polish on flint: Beyond the "deposit versus abrasion" controversy. *Journal of Archaeological Science* 11:91–98.

Vaughan, Patrick. 1981. Lithic microwear experimentation and the functional analysis of a lower Magdalenian stone tool assemblage. Unpublished PhD dissertation, Department of Anthropology, University of Pennsylvania.

—— 1985. *Use-wear analysis of flaked stone tools*. Tucson: University of Arizona Press.

Vickers, J. Roderick. 1986. *Alberta Plains prehistory: A review*. Archaeological Survey of Alberta Occasional Paper No. 27, Edmonton: Alberta Culture.

Wahlstrom, Ernest E. 1947. *Igneous Minerals and Rocks*. New York: John Wiley.

Walker, Ernest G. 1992. *The Gowan sites: Cultural responses to climatic warming on the Northern Plains (7500–5000 B.P.)*. Mercury Series Paper 145, Ottawa: Canadian Museum of Civilization Archaeological Survey of Canada.

Walker, P.L. 1978. Butchering and stone tool function. *American Antiquity* 43:710–715.

Wedel, Waldo R. 1986. *Central Plains Prehistory: Holocene Environments and Culture Change*. Lincoln: University of Nebraska Press.

Weigand, Phil C., Garman Harbottle, and Edward V. Sayre. 1977. Turquoise sources and source analysis: Mesoamerica and the Southwestern U.S.A. In *Exchange Systems in Prehistory*, ed. Timothy K. Earle and Jonathon E. Ericson, 15–34. New York: Academic Press.

White, Peter. 1967. Ethno-archaeology in New Guinea: Two examples. *Mankind* 6:409–414.

White, Peter, and D.H. Thomas. 1972. What mean these stones? Ethno-taxonomic models and archaeological interpretations in the New Guinea highlands. In *Models in Archaeology*, ed. David L. Clarke, 275–308. London: Methuen and Company.

Whittaker, John C. 1994. *Flintknapping: Making and Understanding Stone Tools*. Austin: University of Texas Press.

Wiessner, Polly. 1983. Style and social information in Kalahari San projectile points. *American Antiquity* 48:253–276.

—— 1985. Style or isochrestic variation? A reply to Sackett. *American Antiquity* 50:160–166.

Wilmsen, Edwin N. 1968. Functional analysis of flaked stone artifacts. *American Antiquity* 33:156–161.
Wilmsen, Edwin N., and Frank H.H. Roberts Jr. 1978. *Lindenmeier, 1934–1974: Concluding report on investigations*. Smithsonian Contributions to Anthropology Number 24, Washington.
Wilson, Michael C., and Leslie B. Davis. 1994. Late Quaternary stratigraphy, paleontology, and archaeology of the Sheep Rock Spring site (24JF292), Jefferson County, Montana. *Current Research in the Pleistocene* 11:100–102.
Winham, R. Peter, and F.A. Calabrese. 1998. The Middle Missouri Tradition. In *Archaeology on the Great Plains*, ed. W. Raymond Wood, 269–307. Lawrence: University Press of Kansas.
Wobst, M.H. 1978. The archaeo-ethnography of hunter-gatherers or the tyranny of the ethnographic record in archaeology. *American Antiquity* 43: 303–309.
Wormington, H. Maria, and Richard G. Forbis. 1965. *An Introduction to the Archaeology of Alberta*, Proceedings Number 11, Denver: Denver Museum of Natural History.
Wymer, John. 1982. *The Palaeolithic Age.* London: Crom Helm.
Young, David E., and Robson Bonnichsen. 1984. *Understanding stone tools: A cognitive approach*. Peopling of the Americas Process Series Volume 1. Orono: Centre for the Study of Early Man, University of Maine.
Zeitlin, Robert N. 1982. Toward a more comprehensive model of interregional commodity distribution: Political variables and prehistoric obsidian procurement in Mesoamerica. *American Antiquity* 47:260–275.

Index

C

H

I

J

K

L

M

N

Q

R

S

T